SOCIAL WELFARE AND THE LIQUOR PROBLEM

Studies in the Sources of the Problem and How They Relate to

its Solution

by

Harry S. Warner

First Fruits Press
Wilmore, Kentucky
c2015

Social welfare and the liquor problem: studies in the sources of the problem and how they relate to its solution, by Harry S. Warner.

First Fruits Press, ©2015
Previously published: Boston and Chicago: United Society of Christian Endeavor, 1914, ©1913.

ISBN: 9781621713630 (print), 9781621713647 (digital)

Digital version at http://place.asburyseminary.edu/christianendeavorbooks/35/

For all other uses, contact:

First Fruits Press
B.L. Fisher Library
Asbury Theological Seminary
204 N. Lexington Ave.
Wilmore, KY 40390
http://place.asburyseminary.edu/firstfruits

Warner, Harry S. (Harry Sheldon), 1875-
    Social welfare and the liquor problem: studies in the sources of the problem and how they relate to its solution / by Harry S. Warner.
        311 pages; 21 cm.
        Christian-Endeavor edition.
        Wilmore, Ky. : First Fruits Press, ©2015.
        Reprint. Previously published: Boston: United Society of Christian Endeavor, 1914, ©1913.
        ISBN: 9781621713630 (pbk.)
1. Drinking of alcoholic beverages -- Social aspects. 2. Social problems. 3. Temperance. I. Title.
HV5035 .W3 2015

Cover design by Jonathan Ramsay

asburyseminary.edu
800.2ASBURY
204 North Lexington Avenue
Wilmore, Kentucky 40390

First Fruits
THE ACADEMIC OPEN PRESS OF ASBURY SEMINARY

First Fruits Press
The Academic Open Press of Asbury Theological Seminary
204 N. Lexington Ave., Wilmore, KY 40390
859-858-2236
first.fruits@asburyseminary.edu
asbury.to/firstfruits

Social Welfare and the Liquor Problem

Studies in the Sources of the Problem and How
They Relate to its Solution

By HARRY S. WARNER

Revised Edition, Completely Rewritten

UNITED SOCIETY OF CHRISTIAN ENDEAVOR

BOSTON AND CHICAGO

First Edition, 1909
Second Edition, Revised and Rewritten, 1913
Reissued February, 1914
Adult Bible-Class Edition, August, 1914
Christian-Endeavor Edition, September, 1914

PREFACE.

"The so-called personal liberty argument in behalf of alcoholic drink loses more and more of its force. Consideration of the public welfare continues to grow and overshadow the rights of the individual. *The drink question must be fought out upon the ultimate foundation of morals, hygiene and social order*—in other words, *the public welfare.* If the public welfare requires the suppression of the alcoholic drink traffic it should be suppressed."
—From an editorial in the *American Brewers' Review.*

In a debate the first step necessary is to state the question—to agree on a ground on which to disagree. No social or political writer has more correctly stated the basis on which the liquor question is to be fought out, and satisfactory settlement reached, than has this editorial writer on the pro-liquor side of the controversy.

On this basis the question is before the American people "on its merits" alone.

In this volume an attempt is made to collect, in systematic order, for purposes of study and further investigation, the main facts of the actual present-day American liquor problem; to get together the materials needed by all who would understand the question broadly, and be of lasting service in bringing it to solution.

It is as necessary to understand the question as a whole, not merely its fragments, as to attempt to tell how it should be settled. It is the hope here very briefly but clearly to state the sources of the problem, the place of the liquor institution in human affairs, its grip on human nature, and its consequences under present-day living conditions. Such a broad view should suggest remedies with some degree of scientific value. Whether the purpose is here accomplished or not, it may be said that the attempt has been made honestly and conscientiously.

Whatever place drink may have served in the evolution of society in the past, its present worth to humanity depends upon present day facts and consequences. What to do about it should be determined by its broader influences in human life and living, on health, wealth, social happiness, moral ideals, and spiritual values. No theorizing about "inherent wrong," on the one hand, or "personal liberty" on the other can be of much service. The question is one of practical consequences on every-day life.

The book does not assume to discuss methods. It endeavors to bring out the broad sociological facts and principles relating to the widespread use of alcoholic liquor on which permanent methods of individual and social reform should be based.

To college and university men and women, and to others anxious to be of service to public welfare in the overthrow of drink—in that to which the book frankly leads, its complete banishment, it is respectfully dedicated.

HARRY S. WARNER.

CHICAGO, ILL., September 25, 1913.

CONTENTS

(Bibliography Classified by Chapters and Topics)

I

SOURCES OF THE LIQUOR INSTITUTION

II

THE DEMANDS OF SOCIAL WELFARE

5

IV

THE SOCIAL DEMANDS FOR COMPLETE ELIMINATION

There is a loftier ambition than merely to stand high in the world. It is to stoop down and lift mankind a little higher.
—HENRY VAN DYKE.

The alcohol question presents itself at every corner to every man and woman desirous of solving the great social problems that await solution.

It is a kind of root problem, the settlement of which would necessarily involve an adjustment of innumerable other things which have a destructive effect on every hand. As a mere matter of economy and time this is a question worthy most serious consideration.
—SIR VESEY STRONG, *Lord Mayor of London.*

CHAPTER I

LIQUOR A SOCIAL INHERITANCE

Almost as far back as written history goes there can be found traces of a struggle with strong drink. The use of alcoholic beverages dates back yet further into prehistoric times, to a period long before any suggestion of its dangers was discovered.

But the modern liquor problem, of which drinking and drunkenness are but one part, has grown up recently and in a way possible only in the highest industrial civilization. The struggle with personal intemperance is hoary with age, but the conflict against social institutions which encourage intemperance is new, peculiar to the last part of the nineteenth and the first of the twentieth centuries. Vital with controversy, it is one of the most burning social problems of the present day.

Development of the Problem.—The temperance problem of a century ago, when serious efforts toward its solution first began, was very different from that of today. A hundred years ago almost everybody "took a little something" occasionally or oftener. The use in the home generally, at social affairs, in religious conventions, in business, and among all classes, gave alcoholic indulgence an unquestioned public sanction quite in contrast with much of the present-day sentiment. The saloon as it exists today, with its politics and commercial influence, was unknown; retail sales were made at grocery stores, taverns, and public houses, and manufacturing was carried on in numerous small stills scattered everywhere and entirely independent of each other in ownership or management.

There was no "temperance problem"; no "organized liquor power"; no "saloon in politics"; no cry of "personal liberty" on the one hand, or "for the protection of the home" on the other. The trade was not united, nor separated from other trades, nor organized into a political force. The right or wrong of selling or of licensing was not discussed. The foolish actions of a man in a state of intoxication were regarded as a matter of course, or of jest, not as a sort of temporary insanity. Science had not turned its attention to the problem, while religious leadership, yet friendly to the older customs, was just beginning to speak out on some of the more obvious evils of excessive drinking.

The first important change took place when Dr. Benjamin Rush, a signer of the Declaration of Independence, as a physician began calling attention to the consequences of the use of ardent spirits. He called for men to give up the use of toddy and grog—a radical move for that day—for churches and ministers to aid in the new crusade, and for the government to limit the number of taverns, impose heavy duties on spirits, and punish drunkards. A few years later—1808—the first temperance society was formed—the first organized effort—its members pledging themselves to abstain from the use of spirits and wine except in case of sickness, at public dinners, and on special occasions. Malt liquors were not included; they were supposed to be temperance drinks. A fine of twenty-five cents was imposed for breaking the pledge and one of fifty cents for actual intoxication.

Thus was initiated publicly the effort to influence public sentiment on the personal problem of temperance. But the question did not long remain one of simple temperance. During the first half-century, while the effort to win men to moderation or total abstinence was growing out from a few small societies until it became a great national total-abstinence movement, the problem itself became more complicated than it had been previously, or than it had ever been in the history of the world. Society slowly became differentiated into two classes— drinkers and non-drinkers. This created other new factors. The opposing forces became more distinct; antagonism developed; both grew strong together. During the past half-century, political and commercial forces have entered, producing a liquor problem vastly different from that of a hundred years ago.

The development has been somewhat as follows:

1. *The simple temperance stage,* resulting in a division into drinking and non-drinking classes; into those who retained and those who discarded the long-established customs. At first the end sought in temperance effort was "moderation"; later, after experience, it became "total abstinence." The methods of winning men away from drink, man by man, were fitted to the conditions to be met in this stage.

2. *The development of the saloon* and its side attractions as a social and commercial force in the community, replacing the tavern and liquor-selling grocery. This set aside and emphasized the trade as a distinct "business," with influences different in character from other lines of business.

3. *New drinking ideals and customs* from time to time were introduced by new arrivals from foreign lands. It

should be noted that those of the first half-century, who long since have become part of the bone and sinew of the national life, were much less moderate users of intoxicants on their arrival than are those of the past few decades. But the later immigrants, falling under the worst influences of our cities, have not had the opportunity to break away from the old customs and become part of the new, as did the earlier people who settled in the purer environment of a newer country. This constant reintroduction of pro-liquor customs, whether tenaciously held or not, has offset the growing temperance sentiment here to no small degree.

4. *The steady increase in the use of beer,* from a per capita consumption of 1.38 gallons in 1840 to 20.66 gallons in 1911, is so excessive, in view of the fact that the use of other intoxicants has not correspondingly diminished, as to constitute a vital point in itself. Three factors have aided this increase: First, the early impression that beer is a temperance drink and a good substitute for those with a higher percentage of alcohol; second, its wide use by the nationalities that yielded the heavy immigration of the latter two-thirds of the nineteenth century; third, new manufacturing and shipping facilities, making it possible, as it was not a century ago, to preserve and transport malt liquors in large quantities.

5. *The political power and complications* of the traffic which began with the adoption by the government of the policy of taking from it, by revenue and license, an unusually large share of its profits and using this to relieve taxation. The Revenue Act of 1862, but slightly changed since, revolutionized the relation between the government and this traffic, and threw the question into politics more than it ever had been.

6. *The development of the trust stage* has been due partly to this political situation and partly to the monopolistic tendencies of recent years. In this stage have come the forced extension of the market, increased sales, increase in the social attractions of the saloon, the duplication of saloons, the cultivation of habits of excess among classes hitherto more moderate in their use, the uniting with "allied trades" for political purposes— results vastly different from those that follow the operation of the merely personal and social demand for liquors. This forcing process has gone so far in certain sections where the ideals of the community are not high, that the trade may well be called "the exploitation of vice"—the vice of intemperance—one of several such sorts of business appealing to human weakness and the distortion of natural human needs.

The Age-old Heritage.—Intemperance itself took its root in human experience long before men were capable of interpreting or even of recording their own experiences. Almost every nation and tribe, while yet in its savage state, had discovered the peculiar effect of substances containing alcohol and similar narcotics, and had made beverages out of them, or devised some other way to use them. The discovery of alcohol has been dated as far back as the beginning of the agricultural period, or 30,000 years.[1] Most of the tribes, when they quit the nomadic life and settled down to the cultivation of grains and fruits and the making of pottery, began also the making of various kinds of "fire-water," "water of life," or "drink of the gods." The fruits and vegetables not needed immediately for food would ferment; the pottery, newly added to the progress of the race, furnished the means. "The earliest Egyptian, Babylonian, and

Hebrew writings show drunkenness to have been common, and from this we infer that it existed long before the art of writing was known." [2] The warnings show that danger became apparent over three thousand years ago. Egyptian frescoes on temples reveal ale brewing as an industry 5,000 years ago; one city was noted for its breweries; a reformer 1,000 years later demanded a reduction in the number of places selling it to the people.[3] This drink, a crude sort of beer called "barley-wine" by Herodotus, became the national drink of Egypt. The discovery of brewing was attributed to Isis, the wife of the god Osiris, or Busiris. From this latter name a tradition suggests that the term "bouzy," or "boozy," used for a time as a name for a drink, may have been derived.[4] In Greece and Rome and among the early Hebrews and most other Oriental peoples, the fermented juice of the grape was the chief source of intoxication. The history and tradition of those days are filled with references to the social customs and to the prevalence of drinking which injured and debauched, while the poetry and fable indicate the delights of the supposed stimulation. Among the Hebrews waves of reform, with occasional reaction, swept over the nation at times. But finally the influence of their great religion prevailed and the race became the most abstemious and long-lived among all that have influenced the world's history. But the magnificent civilizations of the other ancient nations, lacking this force to throw off such social vices and dangers, suffered more severely.

In China, as early as 2187 B. C., there are indications of a period of heavy alcoholic drinking, accompanied by measures to reduce drunkenness. Later, the severe teachings of Confucianism and legal suppression made this nation one of the most temperate and free from narcotics of all kinds for many ages, and until the commercial power of Great Britain forced opium upon China at the muzzle of the cannon—the narcotic blight of the past half-century in that country. In India an ancient sage, Palesta, enumerates twelve kinds of liquors besides Soma, the drink of the gods and the most popular. They were made from honey, sugar, dates, pepper, and the palm. At annual feasts, as early as 1200 B. C., under the guise of religion, all classes gave themselves up to beastly drunkenness.[5]

Among the Teutonic peoples of Northern Europe the delights of the intoxicating cup were early discovered. Their drinks were usually less agreeable than were the wines of the South, but they were not more moderate on that account. The rigors of the climate emphasized excessive meat-eating and ale and mead drinking, while at the same time the forest life counteracted the results to a greater extent than was possible in the polite drinking feasts of Rome. This preserved the hardihood of the race in spite of occasional heavy drinking bouts. Ale was the beverage of the gods. In the Norse myths heaven was conceived of as a drunken revel after a big hunt of wild game; the drinking of blood diluted with wine was a foretaste of paradise. The Germanics were dubbed "the sons of malt" by the Emperor Julian. Tacitus describes the ancient Britons as having ravenous stomachs, filled with meat and cheese and heated with strong drink. Roman influence in early England made wine the popular intoxicant. The Saxons brought in mead, soon brewed in large quantities in monasteries. The Danes made ale the national drink.[6]

The art of distilling, or condensing, fermented liquors

for the purpose of heightening the peculiar feelings
which the use of alcohol yields is said to have been discovered in China 600 years B. C. by men seeking a
panacea for all the ills of life. They called the new
drink "the water of life."[7] But it was used very little
until the seventh century, when it was rediscovered in
Europe. Most of the earlier drinks were fermented or
brewed and comparatively mild. After this, brandy and
similar drinks with a much higher percentage of alcohol, became especially popular for a time—a new scourge
with immediately terrible results.

The history of Western Europe, from that until the
present day, is not complete without a mention of the
drinking habits prevailing so largely in all classes. Its
literature, poetry, and song show how widely prevalent
was the use of wine, gin, and ale. And the more serious
writings occasionally give pictures of the awful wretchedness, poverty, and social corruption resulting.

Lecky, writing of gin drinking in the middle of the
eighteenth century, says: "Small as is the place which
this fact occupies in English history, it was probably, if
we consider all the consequences that have flowed from it,
the most momentous in that of the eighteenth century—
incomparably more so than any event in the purely political or military annals of the country. The fatal passion
for drink was at once, and irrevocably, planted in the
nation. The average of British spirits distilled, which is
said to have been only 527,000 gallons in 1684, had risen
in 1727 to 3,601,000. Physicians declared that in excessive gin drinking a new and terrible source of mortality
had been opened for the poor. The grand jury of Mid-
dlesex declared that much the greater part of the poverty, the murders, the robberies of London might be

traced to this single cause. Retailers of gin were accustomed to hand out painted boards announcing that their customers could be made drunk for a penny, dead drunk for two pence, and have straw for nothing; and cellars strewn with straw were accordingly provided into which those who had become insensible were dragged and where they remained until they had become sufficiently recovered to renew their orgies.'' [8]

From the peoples which have not advanced so rapidly, but have remained primitive or savage well into the period of present-day history, may be obtained a cross-section view of the sort of intoxicants enjoyed by our ancestors. A few of these child races were ignorant of alcohol until civilization brought them ''the delights of intoxication,'' but most had discovered how to make inebriating drinks of their own. Some of these were quite mild, others were more dangerous. In savagery it should be noted that the use of such fiery drinks was limited to rare occasions. This was largely due to the facts that but small quantities could be made at a time and that it could not be preserved or transported in quantities. On such occasions, the inclination was to drink to utter excess and even oblivion whenever the supply permitted.

The Japs had saké, a sort of beer, from rice; the Tartars, koumiss, fermented from milk; the Mexicans, pulqué, from the juice of the agave; the Peruvians had several drinks. Both Mexicans and Peruvians had discovered the danger in drunkenness and had laws severely limiting the amount drunk. These laws seem to have been effective, for after the Spanish conquest, when this control was removed, the people abandoned themselves to reckless intemperance.[9] In the South Sea Islands and

Africa, the tribes had fermented drinks made from shrubs. Some of the American Indians made intoxicants from maize, manioc, cactus, or palm sap. But among all these the opportunities for indulgence were limited to special occasions. The long intervals made the total use very insignificant, indeed, compared with that of civilized peoples. There was no regular drinking, no systematic drunkenness. The intemperance of savagery is little different from that of a group of ten-year-old boys who, discovering some fermented apple cider in an old out-of-the-way cider mill, should drink it all and then be unable to find any more for a year.

Origin and Development of the Saloon.—From the earliest the use of alcoholic drinks was associated with all sorts of political, religious, community, tribal, and smaller group gatherings. It was usually an affair of social occasions. Solitary drinking was exceptional. From such usage by many gradations have come similar customs of the present time, and, as a by-product to this evolution, the place distinctively set aside for alcoholic sociability and alcohol sale, known as the saloon.

In the Roman Empire, during the period of the decline, wine parties and banquets with heavy wine drinking, similar to those among certain wealthy classes of the present time, were numerous. There are found, also, concrete examples of the predecessor of the modern saloon—a sort of drinking café not unlike those patronized by "high society" in the cities of today. When the buried city of Herculaneum was exhumed, there were found 900 public houses at which wine drinking was combined with dining, gambling, and the playing of chess and other games. The early Germanic peoples, as

well, had great drinking feasts at which many hours
were spent and vast quantities consumed.

When the Roman influence reached England, these
social customs were reproduced, in a rough way, in the
taverns scattered every twenty miles along the great
Roman highways. The tavern sign-boards of that period
are now the peculiar mark of the public house in England. The practice of drinking ''healths'' also came
from Rome. As early as the ninth century the ale house,
intended more as a place of sale and less for the entertainment of travelers than the tavern, a more direct
predecessor of the saloon, began to appear.

''Around the eala-hus, the win-hus, and the tavern,
there developed the Anglo-Saxon guild. The members
of these social confederations were required to bring a
certain amount of malt and honey to their meetings.
Delinquents in this respect were punished with a fine
sufficiently heavy to stimulate the memory. These guilds
have left their mark upon the public house in giving it
a certain respectability as a social club.'' [10]

From these in turn developed the public houses, taverns, and even literary clubs of early and later England,
where extensive drinking began to be associated with
sociability, literature, the discussion of public affairs,
and politics. At these places men met to hear and give
the latest news; they thus served in a meager way one
of the functions in the development of public opinion
now taken by the newspaper. The semi-private club is
a contribution of the Elizabethan period. It differed
from the guild in that its membership was received from
select classes and that it supported a well appointed
establishment of its own. ''The Mermaid was the first

of a long series of London clubs and included in its membership such well-known names as Shakespeare, Raleigh, Ben Jonson, Beaumont, and Fletcher. During the reign of the Stuarts and Hanovers, the ale-house and the tavern reached the complexion of the present public house in Great Britain and the saloon in America. It became 'the poor man's club!' It was the place where politicians met to discuss men and measures, where business men repaired to negotiate or conclude their bargains, where toilet conveniences were freely provided, and where social and political 'influences' began to take the form of treating.'' [11]

Thus the saloon has long served in a double capacity: first, as the place of sale and of most of the consumption; second, to a varying degree, as a place of social intercourse. In this capacity it came to America along with the colonists, ready made. Arriving here, it has been modified, especially in the last fifty years, by the more active life of the people, by the tenser business competition, by democratic ideals, and, more recently, by political forces and brewery control. This change has developed a distinct type—the stand-up saloon, with long bar and lines of men leaning over it.

Socially, the American saloon now offers every attraction, good, bad, or indifferent, that will produce more sales of liquor. Politically, it is as much a center of influence as in the earlier days of England, but of quite a different class of political issues and forces. Economically, it has recently become thru the growing power of the manufacturer, merely the local retail end of the big centrally controlled liquor distributing agencies.

Inherited Social Customs, in which drink is an important factor have been quite generally ingrained into the

every-day living of the various nationalities making up
the present American population. Among the colonists,
and during the first days of the republic, among the
North European peoples who came to this country in a
great wave of immigration from 1830 to 1850, and again
in another wave following the civil war, and among
those of Central and Southern Europe who have been
arriving at the rate of three-fourths of a million a year
for the past fifteen years, the social habits supporting
drink traditions have been strong and numerous.

Ancient convivial customs were especially numerous
among the ancestors of the colonists who came from
great Britain. A list of the more important heavy drinking occasions of a social sort prepared by Dr. Campbell [12] includes the following: Religious feasts, fairs
and saints' days; "church ales," given to raise money
for church purposes, at which the one who spent the
most was accounted the godliest; "bride ales" at weddings, where the bride, receiving the profits, seized the
"psychological moment" to procure a fund of ready
money for herself; "speeding the parting guest;"
"toasting," one of the most continuously prolific means
to drunkenness; "night-caps" at bed-time; drinking
contests, quite common at times, at which he who could
drain the tankard down to the mark the greatest number of times, was the best man. The habit of doing
business over drink was common at this time.

The colonists, so largely of English stock, brought
with them their love of strong drink and many of these
customs inherited from their Anglo-Saxon ancestors.
During the colonial days and down until the temperance movement began soon after the opening of the
nineteenth century, almost everybody "took a little

something" occasionally. Drinking was far more universal than at present, the total amount consumed was very much less. Strong drink was used at home, at the stores and taverns, and at work. It was employed in winter to produce warmth; in fact, in the northern colonies, the fathers thought that nothing else would enable them to withstand the rigors of the climate; in summer it was taken for the opposite effect. It was an apparent necessity to explorers and to pioneers as a "stimulant" and medicine. In the family it was the cure-all in case of sickness. Farmers furnished it to harvest hands in the fields, at barn-raisings, log-rollings, and always when a group of men worked together. Gentlemen caroused openly in the taverns. College commencements were the occasion for open drunkenness by students, members of the faculty, and visiting alumni alike. Weddings, christenings, and even funerals were incomplete without it. To permit a friend to call or depart without offering him drink repeatedly was the height of discourtesy. Towns sometimes supplied grog at public expense at the burial of paupers. *It was respectable, not merely to drink, but to get "gloriously drunk."*

These customs were sanctioned by the church. The clergy drank with their people and before entering the pulpit. Dealers were first-class members of nearly every church, and liquors were used on various religious occasions. Rev. Lyman Beecher describes an ordination at Plymouth, Conn., in 1810 as follows: "At this ordination the preparation for our creature comforts . . . besides food was a broad side-board covered with decanters and bottles and sugar and pitchers of water. There we found all kinds of liquors then in vogue. The drinking was apparently universal. This preparation was made by the society as a matter of course. When the consociation arrived they always took something to drink around, also before public services and always on their return. . . . The noise I cannot describe. It was the maximum of hilarity. They told their stories and were at the height of jocose talk." [13]

But even with these customs so universal among all classes at this period in the history of the nation, the amount of liquor consumed per capita was very much less than later; in fact, less than one-third what it is today. There were long periods of relative abstinence. The use was occasional and not steady and systematic, as in later years.

The people who arrived during the heavy immigration period of 1830 to 1859 at first tended to strengthen the customs already popular. The English were of the same bone and sinew as the colonial immigrants; the Irish, coming in large numbers, were heavy whisky drinkers; the Germans, just beginning to migrate in force, added certain features to the changing type of the saloon and were partly responsible for making beer a popular drink; the French, mostly wine users, brought a social sanction to the table and cafe use of intoxicants. The influence of this great wave of immigration during the latter part of the first half of the nineteenth century, with strongly approved drinking customs, counteracted, to some extent, the tremendous personal temperance movements that sprang up during the "thirties" and "forties" and the prohibition movement of the "fifties." On the other hand, as soon as these pioneers caught the progressive spirit of the new country and had lived some time in its open and freer environment, many became total abstainers and active in the temperance movement.

During the last twenty years the half million or more seeking new homes in America each year have not been so free to break away from the long-existing social endorsement of alcohol. They have been recruited mostly from Southeastern Europe, where the oppression of centuries has made them less easily adaptable to radical changes in ideals and habits. The Italians, Poles, Russians, Hungarians, Bohemians and Jews are much less given to heavy drinking before arrival here than were the earlier immigrants, but, unable to get past the great cities and crowded into colonies in these centers, they have missed the hardihood development of the pioneer days. They more quickly suffer from the vices accompanying heavy intoxication and the saloon. Sometimes their social drinking customs, comparatively innocent in themselves, have been taken up by other classes as something new and "Bohemian" and so have gained an influence out of all proportion to the drink habits of the people who brought them.

From the historical viewpoint it is not surprising that the social traditions approving alcohol are so great as they are. The religious endorsement has been outgrown; the ninety-five saints' days of old England, "almost ear-marked for indulgence in alcoholic merriment," are far in the past. But the influence of the inherited English, Germanic, Celtic, and other customs is yet strong. Literature, poetry and song preserve the social ideals of the past; the customs, habits, approvals and prejudices —every force of conservatism tends to interfere with any serious change in the liquor institution in the same way that it retards other changes involving the daily habits and feelings of millions of people.

References and Authorities

Development of the Problem.

Fehlandt, *A Century of Drink Reform*, 19-218.

Woolley and Johnson, *Temperance Progress in the 19th Century.* 54-86.

Dorchester, *The Liquor Problem*, 392-407, 452-471. (The Beer Invasion.)

The Age Old Heritage.

Kelynack, *The Drink Problem*, ''The Evolution of the Alcoholic,'' 22-35.

Samuelson, *The History of Drink*

Hackwood, *Inns, Ales and Drinking Customs of Old England*, 29-38.

Woolley and Johnson, *Temperance Progress in the 19th Century*, 1-31.

Gustafson, *The Foundation of Death*, 1-24.

Eddy, *Alcohol in History*, 49-59, 75-174.

Partridge, *Studies in the Psychology of Intemperance*, 22-37.

Dorchester, *The Liquor Problem in All Ages*, 11-107.

Lecky, *England in the 18th Century*, I (2nd ed.) 476-481.

[1] Kelynack, 25.

[2] Cutten, *The Psychology of Alcoholism*, 1.

[3] Hackwood, 30.

[4] Eddy, 49.

[5] Ibid, 4.

[6] Hackwood, 36.

[7] Gustafson, 27.

[8] Lecky, 479.

[9] Kelynack, 31.

Origin and Development of the Saloon.

Hackwood, *Inns, Ales, and Drinking Customs of Old England*, 59-79.

Samuelson, *History of Drink*.

Lecky, *England in the 18th Century*, I, 516-521.

Woolley and Johnson, *Temperance Progress in the 19th Century*, 20-31.

Calkins, *Substitutes for the Saloon*, 45-46.

[10] Woolley and Johnson, 23.

[11] Ibid, 26.

Inherited Social Customs.

Fehlandt, *A Century of Drink Reform*, 19-51.

Woolley and Johnson, *Temperance Progress in the 19th Century*, 32-53.

Eddy, *Alcohol in History*, 176-207.

Samuelson, *History of Drink*, 102-168.

Kraepelin, ''*The University Man and the Alcohol Question,*'' Tr. for *Scientific Temperance Journal*, Dec., 1912.

[12] Kelynack, *The Drink Problem*, 46.

[13] Woolley and Johnson, 41.

CHAPTER II

But the worst of all . . . is the systematic alcoholizing of mankind on the strength of a bad custom, which is old enough, to be sure, but which has become an acute pestilence in our modern civilizations.
—Dr. AUGUST FOREL, *University of Zurich.*

The truth is, in my opinion, that the consumption of alcohol is kept up by tradition, by the assumption that so prevalent a practice must have virtues, by the fear of individuals to break away from custom, and by the well known difficulty of emancipating one's self from drug habits.
—PROF. IRVING FISHER, *Yale University.*

CHAPTER II

The dangers of strong drink have been known and acknowledged for ages; the organized conflict with intemperance has been going on for a century. Why is it that intemperance is yet so great? Its social evils so generally known, yet unrelieved? How account for its grip on modern civilization and for its place in present-day institutions? Its presence no one denies, but the forces back of it are not always so clearly recognized or so frankly acknowledged, if known.

The Sources.—There are four sources to the liquor problem based upon primary traits in human nature and social organization. These are: First, the impulse for excitement or stimulation; second, economic gain; third, the instinct of sociability; fourth, political approval. All of these operate to make the American liquor institution what it is today. It rests upon these four supports. The relative responsibility that each bears for the problem as a whole, or for the difficulties in its solution, can not be determined. The practical fact is that each source has an important part, and that all should be considered in dealing with the liquor habit and traffic and their consequences. The four sources may be discussed as follows:

1. *The Psycho-Physical.*—There is a very natural human desire to escape from ordinary or disagreeable states of feeling into those more novel, agreeable, or

exciting. This craving is both mental and physical, but chiefly the former. It is a desire for a stirring of the emotions, for more exciting activity, for relief from monotony, oppression, or pain. It may be called a stimulation impulse. Alcohol and other narcotics seem to yield the excitement and relief desired. They make the user feel good. After experience men learn to depend upon this artificial source to produce these feelings, to depend heavily, and to use such agents in place of those conditions which furnish normal gratification to the desire-for-stimulation instinct.

The alcohol thus taken creates another condition— the craving for the liquors themselves. This new desire has a tendency to grow steadily stronger and stronger with each gratification, demanding larger and larger amounts to yield the expected results; that is, it creates the well-known liquor appetite which, when fully established, demands satisfaction at any cost and becomes complete master of its victim. Taken together, the craving for excitement gratified by artificial means thru the use of alcohol, and the peculiar appetite when once created, constitute the most persistent and universal source of the whole liquor problem.

(2) *The Economic.*—The business of supplying intoxicating liquors is run, as is any other, purely for the money there is in it. It is very profitable, giving large returns for comparatively small investments. The commodity furnished finds a ready market. The demand for it, when established, is very constant and imperative. By judicious management and appeal it can be extended to almost any limit. Alcohol habitually used by a consumer tends to compete with and drive out the consumption of other commodities; this makes it an

exceedingly valuable article of commerce. *In the fact that the men who use liquor, rich or poor, will have it if it can readily be procured lies the tremendous power of the economic source*—a demand created largely by the presence of the supply itself. Habit and trade become mutually cause and effect; a vicious circle is established that encourages excessive use and strengthens the demand for this article of trade.

Being such a source of financial gain, it is not surprising that modern financial methods have developed this "business" to the greatest possible extent; that the market is thoroly worked; that efforts to extend the sales are pushed to the extreme by legitimate and illegitimate methods; that systematic advertising and educational campaigns are conducted to extend the trade, to increase the average consumption, and to preserve and fasten upon the public the social customs favorable to drinking; that the political influence of the traffic is exceedingly powerful.

(3) *The Social.*—One powerful source of the liquor institution, too frequently overlooked or minimized by temperance workers, is its extended use as a means of social enjoyment. In every day meeting of man with man, in business, at social affairs, and yet more in the saloon after a hard day in the factory or mine, the offering of a drink is an expression of good fellowship. Often it may be the only known means of expressing friendship. To refuse this act of kindliness seems churlish, or at least cold. Social customs and usages endorsing such use of alcoholic drinks are very common among large classes. Until they have opportunity to learn something better these habits have a strong hold.

The fact remains that the social attractions are one of the prominent features of the question. The saloon is the chief representative of this sociability phase. It is a place where men come together for various reasons, among them that of meeting their fellows and being in their company. It has frequently been called "the poor man's club" and, in certain places there is good reason for this name.

(4) *The Political.*—Another vital source, emphasized by temperance leaders who have met it in actual conflict but often overlooked by other students of the subject, is the standing and political influence given the traffic by laying on it unusual revenue, tax, and license requirements. Licensing authorities are given the power to create a valuable property right and confer it on whom they please. It becomes good political policy to preserve intact this source of steady and uncomplaining financial income, political power and apparent relief to tax payers. This gives the traffic an undue influence in governmental affairs, serves as a bribe upon the public conscience, and makes better control difficult. Indirectly it adds to the force of private greed and social custom in causing intemperance. *It is the most inexcusable and morally corrupting of all the sources of the liquor evil.* It is the occasion for the political power of the traffic.

Legally, this close association of the government with the traffic is not intended to give it privileges over other lines of business, but the actual effect is to give unusual power and sanction. The legal aim is lost in the wider social principle that the interest which contributes most largely in taxation demands most in governmental protection.

The Problem Today: What Is It?—What is the liquor problem? Is it the temperance question? Is it a question of temperance at all?

Is it a matter of how much a man should drink? Or whether he should drink at all? Or whether alcohol is a food? Or a poison? Or a stimulant?

Is it a question of morals? Is it wrong to drink a glass occasionally? If not, why not?

Is it a personal question? An inherent right to drink or let it alone? Or has personal liberty anything to do with it? Has society the right to interfere with the tastes and habits of individuals? Where does the right of the individual, of society, begin and end?

Is the saloon "the poor man's club," or "the pest house of crime?" What service does it render the community? Is it usurping the place of other institutions or is it "the evolution of a neglected need?" Are its evils inherent or may they be eliminated? Is it a question of "the liquor traffic in politics?" Of seeking to control parties and councils and legislatures and congress? Or is the traffic merely asking return for the heavy share it pays toward public support?

Or is it a matter of public health? Of race vitality? Of money taken from the family income to pay the drink bill? Or of the cost of crime due to drink? Or of percentages of poverty, imbecility, vice, and misery?

Or of social customs which should be preserved and respected or that may well be spared as an obstruction to advance?

It is not a moral question. Neither is it a hygienic, social, industrial, economic, nor even a political matter. *It is all of these combined.* It is the whole, not a part, and the relation of all these parts to each other and especially to other and larger interests of human living.

In current every-day use the term "liquor problem" has two distinct meanings. The one is the temperance question including over-indulgence in alcoholic liquors, the effects of intoxicants upon the health, finances, morals and social surroundings of the drinker and his family. The other relates to the industrial and political power of the liquor trade; its influence in business, in public affairs, on justice and in politics.

No study is complete which does not include both. Public welfare is intimately connected with both intemperance and the trade that supplies and encourages it. Some of the perplexing features met in an attempt to remedy the evils can be understood only when both of these factors are taken together. Pledge signing crusades in behalf of the drunkard, regulation, the license policy, and public ownership, have each failed wholly or in part because they were thought sufficient to cure the whole evil without regard to all of its sources.

Among the big outstanding factors at the present time, are the commercializing of the vice of intemperance, the strong appeal of all narcotic habits under the high-tension of modern economic and city living conditions, the organized liquor traffic in politics, and the continuous inexhaustible supply of drink, cheap and near at hand, almost unavoidable, for all classes.

In another respect there is a marked contrast of the problem of today with that of the past—a smaller per cent of the people drink a much larger total and per capita amount of intoxicating liquors. When the temperance fight began in America almost everyone drank, at least occasionally. At present large classes absolutely abstain, and other large classes use it so rarely as to amount to little. On the other hand, there is a tremendous increase in steady daily drinking. A hundred years ago the per capita consumption was less than one-third what it is today, yet the number of users proportionately was nearly twice as great. Men went on occasional sprees and then, not having access to it so constantly, had periods in which to "sober up."

The magnitude of the question is almost beyond comprehension. It infests every source of public welfare and is intermixed with almost every question of the day. From this institution come poverty, vice, and crime; from it also come pleasure unbounded and the homely enjoyment of things long accustomed. Solution may involve the breaking of customs of ages, economic loss immeasurable, and change of ideals for vast numbers of people, but solved it must be. The antiquity of its use is neither a justification nor a discredit. Alcohol began with slavery, and the lottery, and polygamy, and gambling—also with the origin of the family, and was long associated with religious worship. Its future depends upon its value to present needs.

Only when all these conflicting facts are somehow taken together can we gain an adequate conception of the task bequeathed by the past to the Twentieth Century.

The Relation of the Trade to the Habit.—It is common opinion that the "drink traffic" is merely the economic means for supplying the demand created by "the drink habit." Rather these terms stand for two phases or different views of the same problem. They indicate forces that are acting and reacting upon each other mutually as cause and effect.

Under the ordinary operation of economic law, demand creates supply; the need for an article, its habitual use, or the customs calling for its consumption lead to the production of that article in sufficient quantities to meet the need. With every-day necessities and conveniences the operation of this law is normal. But with luxuries a tendency to create demand where none existed, and to extend it to an almost unlimited degree, begins. With narcotic drugs, such as opium, alcohol, cocaine, and even in a degree with tobacco, which tend, when used more than very rarely, to create an increasing demand for themselves, the ordinary operation of this rule is yet further distorted. There is no such thing as a normal demand for narcotics in health. It must first be created against the protest of nature. The fact that the first taste is usually disagreeable is nature's warning against the introduction of a danger. The self-increasing demand is abnormal.

There is doubtless a market for alcoholic drinks based upon the usual laws of supply and demand irrespective of this peculiar effect. Social custom calls for them; they are an accompaniment to recreation; they give relief and ease after a hard day's work, tho not in the best way. But beyond all such demands for the production and sale of liquors is the created demand, the usual law working backward, based upon the narcotic effects of the alcohol and appealing to human weakness and excess. In the early days the liquor traffic merely supplied the existing demand. In later years it has gone out after trade, duplicating saloons, adding attractive features, offering facilities for the most continuous and even excessive drinking, supporting retail dealers on salary in new neighborhoods until a market is established, and acting consciously upon the fact that alcohol tends to create an ever increasing demand for itself.

From 1860, just before the liquor trade began to be organized and united, until 1912, the consumption of intoxicants in the United States increased from 6.43 gallons per capita to 21.98 gallons, or slightly over 240 per cent. If the laws of supply and demand had operated alone during these fifty-two years, the only increase would have been from the influence of immigration. But during this period there was tremendous temperance agitation; great pledge-signing campaigns were conducted, and temperance instruction was given in the public schools thruout the nation. It is perfectly reasonable to assume that these forces were sufficient to off-set the influence of immigration. It would seem, then, that the 240 per cent increase must be due in large part to the other new forces that were active—the organized liquor traffic creating a tremendous additional demand for its goods. This is the reversal of economic law that makes the traffic itself a powerful cause of the whole problem. As Dr. Crane puts it:

"The licensed liquor traffic is here in violation of the economic law of supply and demand. It confesses this when it pays exorbitant license fees, and we are impressed by the same fact when we remember that *most of the trouble* comes from the supply and not the demand."

Or as Turner shows in a vivid description of how the process actually works in Chicago:

"The great central power in the liquor business in America is the brewery. . . . They have a distinct policy; if there are not as many saloons as there can be, supply them. This is what has been done in Chicago. Fully ninety per cent of the Chicago saloons are under some obligation to the brewery; with at least eighty per cent, this obligation is a serious one.

"The brewers employ special agents to watch continually every nook and cranny in Chicago where it may be possible to pour in a little more beer. . . . If a new colony of foreigners appears, some compatriot is set at once to selling them liquor. Greeks, Lithuanians, Poles . . . have their trade exploited to the utmost. Up to last year, no man with two hundred dollars, who was not subject to arrest on sight, need go without a saloon in Chicago; nor, for that matter, need he now. The machinery is constantly waiting for him. With that two hundred dollars as a margin, the brewery sorts out a set from its stock of fixtures, pays his rent, pays his license, and supplies him the beer. He pays for everything in an extra price on each barrel of beer. The other supplies of his saloon,—liquor and cigars,—are bought out of his two hundred dollars cash capital. Under this system of forcing, Chicago has four times as many saloons as it should have from any standpoint whatever, except, of course, the brewers' and the wholesalers'. . . . There is now one retail dealer to every two hundred and eighty-five people; . . . every man, woman and child in Chicago drank, in 1906, two and one-quarter barrels of beer—three and one-half times the average consumption in the United States. Each also drank about four gallons of spiritous liquor —two and one-third times the average. The main object of the brewing business, the thoro saturation of the city, especially the tenement districts, with alcoholic liquors, is well fulfilled."[1] The retail dealers are so bound by contract to the brewer who started them in business that they cannot quit, even should they want to do so, without incurring heavy damages. They dare not buy from another but are bound hand and foot to the firm that started their "place."

Brewery ownership and control of saloons is responsible for the starting of many in residence sections, new parts of a town, or in temperate communities where as yet there are few drinkers. A man is set up in business, he is paid a salary, furnished fixtures and beer, and goes to work to create a drinking constituency for himself. The big liquor firm can support such "missionary" effort when the private dealer could not. The rivalry among the different brewing firms accounts for the solid lines of saloons, five, six or seven long, in some of our large cities. Many a man who would resist the inducements of a single saloon has not will-power sufficient to pass a whole line of them.

The side attractions of the saloon, its reports of the ball-games, prize fights, free lunch, music, games, and free-for-all conversation, are intended to increase the sale of liquor. If it existed merely to supply some inborn instinct there would be no need for such expense. The public saloon, as it is managed today, is a vast organized system for inciting and exploiting appetite.

The Shift to Beer.—For more than sixty years there was a steady increase in the consumption of intoxicating liquors in the United States. The maximum seems to have been reached in 1907 and 1911, the amount being the same in each of these years, viz., 22.79 gallons per capita. The heaviest increase occurred during the years from 1880 to 1890, corresponding very closely with the period of largest growth in the use of malt liquors. During this sixty-year period there has been a slight reduction in the amount of spirits,—a change from 2.24 gallons per capita in 1850 to 1.42 gallons in 1910. At the same time the amount of malt liquors has tremendously increased, a shift, to some extent, from whisky, rum, and brandy, to beer.

This is an important item in the development of the liquor problem. But its greatest meaning lies in a direction not usually suspected. The change seems to indicate a substitution of the milder for the more highly alcoholic drinks and suggests a preference for the latter on the part of the people of the present time. Some believe that this substitution has been a temperance advance. Before reaching such a conclusion a more careful examination of the facts should be made.

To understand the social meaning of the change that has taken place the amount of alcohol in the different liquors must be taken into account; the consumption of actual alcohol at the present time must be compared with that of sixty years ago. Distilled spirits may be said to contain, on the average, 45 per cent alcohol; wines, 10 per cent, and malt liquors 4 per cent. In 1850, before the use of malt liquors became general, and when whiskies, brandies and wines were the most available drinks, and about the only sort that could be transported in large quantities in the absence of the transportation systems of later years, these furnished by far the largest share of all the alcohol that was consumed. Distilled spirits supplied 1.008 gallons per capita of absolute alcohol, out of the total of 1.098 gallons per capita drunk at that period.

By 1912 the situation had completely changed. The amount of absolute alcohol from all sources had increased

37 per cent; the share contributed by spirits had decreased 35 per cent, while the part supplied by beer and other malt liquors had increased more than 1,000 per cent, far more than sufficient to off-set the decrease due to the lower consumption of the stronger alcoholics. *The beer route had taken the place of the whisky thorofare* as the highway supplying humanity with alcohol, and *an increase of 37 per cent in the consumption of absolute alcohol was the result.* The alcohol consumption from all sources in 1850 was about 1.098 gallons; in 1912 it was 1.504 gallons; 37 per cent higher.[2] Beer had triumphed over whisky, and more alcohol was used than ever before.

Just what would have happened had the comparative supremacy of spirits remained undisputed by the malt-king, of course, cannot be known. One indication is suggestive—that the actual reduction of the amount of the stronger liquors used has been almost infinitesimal. Therefore, the beer invasion without doubt has created a new field for itself, instead of becoming a substitute for whisky and brandy.

On the basis of this estimate beer has not tended to stop or delay the increase in the consumption of actual alcohol. Rather, the fact is that the change from distilled spirits to "light beers" has brought an actual increase in the use of alcohol, the common injurious element of all such drinks.

Liquor a Social Institution.—The drinking of intoxicating liquors is to a large extent a personal matter. But by no means wholly so. Even the personal desire and habit in each individual owes its beginning almost always to social influences—to an invitation from a friend, to custom, to fear of appearing unlike others, to ideals held by a community in common. Even the desire for the peculiar effects of intoxication, from the savage days, has been associated with another equally strong, to have other people present.

On the other hand, the traffic that supplies the drink is almost exclusively social. It is a public institution that cannot exist apart from social influences. It is here in the heart of our modern social life, as a social inheritance to be reckoned with, whether we will have it so or not.

(1) All trade, buying, selling, transporting, manufacturing, is social. These acts involve the concerted agreement of many individuals and so cannot be purely private. Mill says, "All trade is a social act. Whoever undertakes to sell any description of goods to the public does what affects the interests of other persons and of society in general and thus his conduct in principle comes within the jurisdiction of society."

(2) It has grown out of national habits. Alcoholic excess was the chief vice of the nationalities that entered into the formation of the earlier American people, the English, Irish, German, and French. And the later additions—Slavic, Polish, Bohemian—have been only a little less addicted to such customs than were the earlier colonists and immigrants.

(3) It has acquired a place in business, commerce, custom, and politics, which must be recognized as a simple matter of fact.

(4) It has been recognized and treated for many years as a peculiar traffic, needing more attention from government than others. It has always required more regu-

lation and has been less willingly subject to control than other lines of traffic which have acknowledged dangers connected with them.

(5) Its consequences very decidedly involve the public, and can in no way be limited to the individual. It is intimately connected with vice and crime and tends to associate with other means of social dissipation and political corruption.

Continuous every-day drinking on a large scale is possible only under highly socialized conditions. The unlimited supply always at hand for frequent indulgence many times a day, the many attractions of the saloon, the heavy labor, long hours, fatigue, and unsanitary working conditions in large factories, mines, and elsewhere that large numbers of men are worked together, the crowded tenements supplied for them instead of homes—all of these re-enforcing the craving for stimulation and intensifying the cry for even temporary relief, make the social forces in the liquor question the all-important ones. Heavy drinking has become systematic. Excessive intemperance of the individual is the vice of savagery—of the ancient savage drinking himself into oblivion, or of the delayed savage of the present time who may pass long periods between debauches or rapidly drink himself to death. But the daily soaking of vast numbers of men year in and year out is the peculiar product of the past fifty years. *The systematizing, "politicalizing," commercializing of intemperance is the social crime of civilization.*

The ancient origin of the drink institution is neither a justification nor a condemnation of it. The social customs connected with intoxication, and drinking, age-old as they are, even the gratification of any instinctive craving for stimulants by this particular means, may or may not be serviceable to twentieth-century conditions. There can be no halo of "natural rights" or privilege about the custom of offering "a social glass" in itself. On its present merits or demerits alone should it be judged. The tracing to ancient sources shows the difficulty of change—not that change is not possible, or desirable.

"**The Social Demands.**" — While private individuals and public philanthropy are endeavoring to cure the personal and social evils by every known method of amelioration, what shall be the attitude of organized society, government, toward the whole liquor problem? A complete answer will depend upon the following fundamental tests:

(1) The effects of the use of liquors, and of the liquor trade, upon society as a whole; as the sociologists say, upon the ends of social welfare, public health, wealth, knowledge, sociability, beauty, and rightness; or upon what common law recognizes as the object of the police power of the state, the public health, wealth, morals and safety.

(2) Whether the evils are contingent and capable of being remedied by regulation and control, or whether they are inherent and shall require, in addition to temperance methods, that the trade shall be banished in order to free society from the burdens resulting from the habit and the political and social vice traceable to it.

References and Authorities

The Sources.

Partridge, *Studies in the Psychology of Intemperance* (1912), 71-78.

Kelynack, *The Drink Problem: Its Medico-Sociological Aspects* (1909), 5-6, 35-51.

Fehlandt, *A Century of Drink Reform*, 139-171.

Calkins, *Substitutes for the Saloon*, 1-24.

Horsley and Sturge, *Alcohol and the Human Body* (4th ed. 1911), 13-19.

Patrick, ''In Quest of the Alcohol Motive,'' *Pop. Sci. Mo.*, Sep., 1913.

Williams, *Alcohol; How It Affects the Individual, the Community, the Race*, 112-113.

The Problem Today.

Fehlandt, *A Century of Drink Reform*, 139-218.

Kelynack, *The Drink Problem*, 30-32.

Barker, *The Saloon Problem and Social Reform*, 1-3.

Committee of Fifty, *The Liquor Problem*.

Rowntree and Sherwell, *The Temperance Problem and Social Reform*, 1-78.

Relation of the Trade to the Habit.

Fehlandt, *A Century of Drink Reform*, 172-177, 299-303.

Kelynack, *The Drink Problem*, 43-46.

Turner, ''The City of Chicago; A Study of the Great Immoralities,'' *McClure*, April, 1907.

Barker, *The Saloon Problem and Social Reform*, 5-7.

Ely, *Political Economy*, 154-159.

[1] Turner.

The Shift to Beer.

Williams, *Alcohol*, 123.

Anti-Saloon League Year Book (1913).

American Prohibition Year Book (1912).

[2]See, *U. S. Statistical Abstracts* (1912) 600.

Liquor a Social Institution.

Barker, *The Saloon Problem and Social Reform*, 1-24.

Calkins, *Substitutes for the Saloon*, 1-24.

Wheeler, *Prohibition*, 11-27.

Woolley and Johnson, *Temperance Progress*, 20-31.

U. S. Brewers' Year Book (1910), 260-270.

Hopkins, *Wealth and Waste*, 124-125.

CHAPTER III

The naked Saxon serf drowned the sense of his half-year hunger and thirst in one day of gluttony and drunkenness.

—Sir Walter Scott, *Ivanhoe.*

The basis of intemperance is the effort to secure thru drugs the feelings of happiness, when happiness does not exist. Men destroy their nervous system for the tingling pleasure they feel as its structures are torn apart.

Dr. David Starr Jordan, *Stanford University.*

Any quantity of alcohol must be regarded as considerable which causes a disturbance, even if only transitory, of bodily or mental efficiency. Every drinker is in danger of becoming an habitual drinker, and every habitual drinker of becoming a criminal inebriate.

—Aschaffenburg.

CHAPTER III

THE PSYCHO-PHYSICAL ASPECTS

The Attractiveness of Alcohol.—Mankind enjoys alcoholic liquors. He has done so for thousands of years, ever since, as a savage of the forest, he discovered that partially decaying fruits and grains could be made to yield a drink that had very peculiar effects. Long before any social customs grew up about the use of such drinks, long before there was any such thing as a saloon or "poor man's club," and yet longer before there was a "liquor traffic," intoxicants were made and drunk because their effect is pleasing. Savages, of course, may be expected to take and use, without further inquiry, whatever yields a pleasing first impression.

Alcohol for centuries has served as an unnatural means of gratifying a certain impulse for excitement or stimulation. There must be an explanation for this fact, whether there is a scientific justification for its continuance under present-day conditions or not.[1]

Thruout all history mankind has hankered after excitements, after experiences that give an exalted or romantic self-feeling, after anything that shoves him outside of or beyond his usual mental states.

He seeks a means of escape from monotony and suffering; he desires to forget his aches and pains, his sorrow and trouble, and he does not hesitate to use external and artificial agents when they will serve that end. A craving for excitement seems to be inborn, instinctive,

48

tho the specific appetite for narcotics is acquired. Nature demands change and mankind has found that these agents will give the impression of change—the feeling that these wants are satisfied. Man has hit upon alcohol almost by accident, because it happened to be near at hand. In turn it has created a place for itself. And that place, established in savagery, has been inherited and accepted by civilization. It is only recently in the progress of the race that man has begun to question whether the wide custom of satisfying a universal need by means of narcotics is normal and healthy, or whether it is artificial and dangerous.

The physiological action of alcohol is such that it furnishes quick relief to mental suffering or monotony. It gives a feeling of increased power and importance; it stirs the emotions; it accentuates the ego; "it increases the intensity of consciousness."[2] As William James, the great psychologist, says,[3] "The reason for craving alcohol is that it is an anesthetic, even in moderate quantities. It obliterates a part of the field of consciousness." It fires the imagination and lessens the control of judgment. There is a feeling of elation, a state of being "a little beyond one's self," a temporary sense of self-superiority. Men use alcohol because of its effects upon the mental and emotional faculties.[4] It is intoxication which they are after and which they get. Ever since its discovery it has been used as *a short-cut to short-lived happiness.* No one can see a tipsy man without noticing his jovial freedom from care, his return to almost primitive enjoyment. He is for the time being perfectly happy.

"Clearly, then, the essential factor in the attractiveness of alcoholic drinks is their power to intoxicate and narcotize, a conclusion which is further suggested by the fact that mankind shows a disposition to indulge in a variety of intoxicant and narcotic substances (such as opium and hasheesh) which have nothing but their drug effects to recommend them.''[5]

Occasionally people drink liquors to allay thirst of a perfectly normal kind, and sometimes because of the agreeable taste. Others find sufficient motive in ill-health and many other similar reasons. But these attractions are all secondary. The agreeable taste, the normal thirst and similar motives are not essential factors. The taste of beer, the most widely used of all common alcoholics, is disagreeable to many people; as with the crude drinks of very early days it seems to attract, not because of, but in spite of, its unpalatableness. While many of the lighter brews and wines contain a relatively low per cent of alcohol and a large amount of water, no one imagines for a moment that their every-day use is for the purpose of quenching any other than the peculiar alcoholic thirst.

When first beginning, or when use is limited to rare occasions, the psychic effects are new and unique. After continued use, when the depression of the higher mental faculties has begun to leave its permanent results, the taking of a drink or two is often necessary to put one into what formerly was his normal state. The abnormal ''alcoholic haze,'' the depression of mental activity, has become the usual, the habitual. A regular drinking man cannot do his best work without his usual dram. He has learned to depend upon it. Alcohol seems necessary to overcome the depression of an habitually alcoholized brain. Thus is created a continuous follow-up system of alcoholic attraction.

The Source of Intoxication.—The variety of intoxicating drinks in common use is very great, but there is one characteristic ingredient common to them all, ethyl alcohol. It is the one factor without which none of them would be complete. It is formed by the fermentation of sugar; this sugar is obtained usually from the starch of sprouting grains, or from fruits. Barley, rye, and corn are the great commercial sources of alcohol, tho it may be produced from almost any sort of vegetable or fruit.

Alcoholic beverages may be put into four classes: (1) the malt liquors, furnishing by far the largest share of the alcohol in common use; (2) wines; (3) distilled spirits; (4) unusual preparations, many of which are sold as "medicines," "tonics," "nerve stimulants," "bitters," etc., or others with a very low per cent of alcohol, such as "near-beer," devised to be sold as a subterfuge for beer in evasion of high license or prohibitory laws.

The proportion of alcohol in the different drinks varies widely. A fair average of those in common use in America is as follows: beer and other malt liquors, 4 per cent; wines, 10 per cent; distilled spirits, 45 per cent. American lager beer varies from 1 per cent to 7 per cent alcohol; German beers are about 4.8 per cent; ale and porter are 5 per cent alcohol; hard cider, 5 per cent; American wines run from 8 per cent to 17 per cent, champagne being 10 per cent alcohol. Among the distilled spirits, whisky ranges from 35 per cent to 45 per cent; rum is 60 per cent, and gin 30 per cent alcohol.

Certain popularly advertised "patent medicines" are little else than liquors with flavoring materials and other agents added. Under the guise of medicine they are sometimes used by people who would not touch the known intoxicants. Seeming to aid for a time, they come to be taken, knowingly or unknowingly, for the same peculiar effects that attract the ordinary drinker to the saloon. Their alcoholic contents vary from 14 per cent to 45 per cent.

The more highly flavored wines contain ethers and other alcohols in addition to ethyl alcohol. The toxic effects of some of these is even greater than that of the more common alcohol. Usually these are by-products of distillation. Occasionally other substances are added to increase the narcotic influence, or appeal to the taste, or as adulterants, or they get in as impurities. These by-products and impurities have harmful effects of their own. In some of the more expensive wines the higher alcohols are even more harmful than the standard ethyl alcohol itself. Such wines more quickly and more dangerously intoxicate. But the extent of their use is necessarily very limited.

The fact that harm does come from these by-products does not reduce the charge that must be made against the always-essential ethyl alcohol. A great many people believe that if only "pure" liquors were sold and drunk the largest part of the trouble connected with intoxication would cease. Their aim is to encourage the production of pure beverages, believing that this would be a real advance. This opinion is current among some who are anxious to reduce intemperance, and it is assiduously cultivated by high-grade liquor dealers for the purpose of diverting critical public attention from their trade and directing it against that of the "disreputable" dealers who supply the demands of the "down-and-outs."

Scientific authority, on the other hand, shows that it is not so much the by-products and impurities, tho these may have dangers of their own, as it is the chief constituent of all alcoholic liquors, ethyl alcohol itself, that produces intoxication and by far most of the evils that flow from drink. In quantity it is so very much greater than that of all other poisoning constituents together that the latter amount to almost nothing in comparison. For all practical purposes the ''impurities'' and their results are of very secondary importance.

A careful investigation of the comparative toxicity and life-destroying effects of the different constituents of the ordinary alcoholic beverages was made by Dr. John J. Abel.[6] He found that one liter of ordinary rum will destroy 64.947 kilograms of animal life, dog or man. Out of this the destruction of 64.102 kilograms is due to the ethyl alcohol in the rum, and the very small remaining portion to the by-products of distillation, the higher alcohols, and non-alcoholic constituents. As he says, ''the by-products are therefore of only secondary importance as toxic agents.'' Similar results are found for whiskies, wines, etc. With but rare exceptions *it is the alcohol,* without which no intoxicating beverage is complete, that is the *really important harmful agent.*

The whole trouble is due, in short, not so much to impure liquors, as to the liquors themselves, whether ''pure'' or impure. The question of purity is a technicality. To the public its discussion merely clouds the main point or diverts attention from it. Occasionally adulterations are added which are more dangerous than ethyl alcohol, but far more frequently they are less harmful and only aid in reducing the strength of the alcohol itself. It should be noted that the chief source of intoxication, and all that results from intoxication, is at the same time the one indispensable ingredient in all ordinary liquors.

An Age-old Delusion.—Alcohol is a very curious drug. It is the traditional "stimulant" of the ages, tho its effects have always been complex and confusing. Men have seemed to get from it almost anything they wanted. They have used it to "get away from themselves" into a state of abandonment and freedom, and have found themselves, in the end, bound to a habit that could not be broken. It has been used both to stir up and enthuse, and to deaden and soothe; as a means of keeping warm in winter and of cooling off in summer; it has been supposed to stimulate muscle, and brain, and heart, and yet it seems not to be a stimulant of any of these; it is supposed to aid in passing thru an emergency, yet it actually reduces endurance; it was an accompaniment of earliest religious expression, but is an object of attack by modern religious forces; it is employed as a means of showing hospitality and friendly feeling, yet from the place where its social influences are most unlimited, the saloon, come crime and vice and anti-social impulses and acts.

The contradictory character of the social impressions made by alcohol is expressed in a sample of the philosophy of its friends: "It is a well-known fact in every part of this country that a bottle of whisky 'as a persuader' will go at least twice as far as its value in money of the realm. Nearly everybody denounces whisky more or less, and yet everybody wants whisky, and everybody prizes it as a thing of great value, because it is really looked upon, not only as a 'first aid to the injured.' but as a panacea for all ills, and as a subtle spirit capable of awakening the best that is in us, and of lifting us up into an atmosphere that is brighter and sweeter and in every way more delightful than that which we ordinarily breathe." [7]

Similar popular impressions and contradictions come from experience with opium and other narcotics when widely used. As opium is to the Chinese, so is alcohol a source of many popular delusions among the western nations, impressions inherited from the unthinking past and unquestioningly accepted today by many who have grown up under their social influence. Many of these impressions are most deceptive; alcohol promises rest and actually makes the body less fit for exertion; it promises comfort, and then increases the total misery, sickness and poverty; it promises warmth and makes men freeze more quickly; it gives momentary relief from care and "the next day after the night before" brings a new crushing burden, mental, emotional, physical, and social—earlier fatigue, susceptibility to accident and disease, and greater mental depression. [8]

Its predominating quality is its capacity to create delusions. From the first exhilaration and heightened self-appreciation of the first drink or two, on to the extreme degree of sense deception, the "snakes" that go with the mania of delirum, all is one web of false impressions,—of things as they are not, of measuring up self and the world in a false light, of taking one's self into an imaginary dream-world of slight and temporary, or of very protracted, delusion. This effect of alcohol is universal. To obtain it is perhaps the chief motive why men drink. It is found in the delightful, refined form of mild intoxication of the "moderate," in the poetic imaginings of the educated and controlled, and in the excesses of the debauchee. The difference is merely one of variation in degree and intensity. Whether the outward appearance is pleasing or revolting, the fact seems clear that alcohol satisfies human desires only by yielding false impressions of satisfaction, by paralyzing instead of stimulating the brain and nerve centers.

It has long been thought that mental power is strengthened or made more keen by alcohol. On the contrary, "the powers of conception and judgment," says Kraepelin,[9] "are from the beginning affected, altho he who takes the alcohol is quite unconscious that it has this effect. The actual facts are exactly opposite to the popular belief." "Alcohol lengthens the time taken to perform complex mental processes, while by a singular delusion the person experimented upon imagines that his psychical actions are more rapid."[10] In spite of all popular impressions to the contrary, the voice of recent scientific investigation rings clear that higher qualities of the mind are not in any helpful way influenced by even small amounts of alcohol. And Dr. Crothers, referring to the opinion that has come down from "Grecian civilization, when wine, song, and art were all regarded as synonymous," and when "spirits were supposed to liberate the highest powers of the mind from animal impulses and bring out the best thoughts," song, and literary expressions, says that "the scholastic tradition and delusion that alcohol in some form will bring out some quality of the brain not existing before, or will give strength and vitality, should pass away as unsupported and incorrect. To imagine that spirits loaded with ethers, taken at a banquet, will arouse into activity latent forces not otherwise available, is equally fallacious."[11]

In a word, the impression of stimulation, "the age-old delusion," comes chiefly from the characteristic action of the alcohol itself—from its depressing and paralyzing of a large share of the higher mental faculties while permitting a limited number of others, temporarily, to run more uncontrolled.

What Is Moderation?—It is quite a popular impression that, notwithstanding certain well-known dangers, alcoholic liquors in so-called moderation are not injurious—that in limited amounts the habitual use is safe and under the control of the user himself.

These popular impressions are so far-extending and persistent that they are a vital part of the actual question to which broader lines of temperance education need to be applied. It is not sufficient to point out the dangers of alcohol; the application needs to be made specifically to the more "moderate" drink habits and the milder drinks. Large numbers of children from the industrial and crowded centers are so accustomed to see it used daily at home that the scientific instruction in the public schools, valuable as it is, does not yield as great results as it might. It does not appeal as practical, does not enter the realm of the real in their lives. Among other more wealthy classes social custom off-sets such instruction as may have been received in the schools in childhood. Everyday suggestion is so very strong; there are so many "moderate drinkers" who do not outwardly appear intoxicated; so many who soon recover from it, who say it never hurts them, that the conviction grows up strongly among large classes that the evils they do see come really from "the abuse," from "taking too much," from excess.

Theorists holding these impressions and those who have an interest in the trade speak of moderation as a higher state of self-control than abstinence. And it is even said that a poison may accomplish good results in spite of the injuries it leaves, or that the good outweighs the evil consequences.

Prevalent as they are, these views cannot be sustained. First, it is quite impossible to determine what is meant by "moderation," what is a "safe" amount. Second, alcohol tends constantly to create a desire for repetition of its use in increasing quantities. This fact makes the theory of low average use among any considerable number of people manifestly impossible. In every community there will be many who yield to this tendency, who "go to excess," however others, with better moral forces surrounding them, may be able to keep it in check. Third, steady drinking, as recent investigations are showing, is a greater cause of degeneracy than even periodic excesses.[12] Fourth, the moderate drinker is the strongest possible example toward inducing young men and non-drinkers to begin the use. The excessive drinker, of course, has little attractive influence. These young men may not, probably will not, have the moral influences and home surroundings that will enable them "to control themselves." All heavy drinkers were first moderate drinkers. They intended, of course, never to become more and frequently have done so only by a break down of will.

To the average mind "moderation" means safety. The drinker who believes himself safe will increase his potations and not recognize the difference. Ask a group of men what amount is moderate and there will scarcely be two answers the same. It will depend upon age, physical condition, individual idiosyncrasy, moral ideals, stage of the habit, and other factors. Whatever amount one regards as "safe" for himself he will at times exceed it; he is always trying to keep just as close to this ignis-fatuus safety-danger line as he possibly can.

After going over carefully all the scientific evidence that recent years has produced regarding "moderation," Horsley conludes that "it is quite impossible to state that any given minimal amount of the drug is harmless." [13] A popular medical writer conservatively applies the new evidence to the practical every-day question when he says that "to take alcohol habitually, *in any quantity whatever,*" is to that extent a menace to the user; that whoever assumes that he is the exception, that for him there is a small "safe" amount, will undoubtedly exceed it at times.[14] The example of Dr. Chas. W. Eliot, ex-President of Harvard, who, after taking a glass of wine occasionally at social functions thruout most of his life, quit it in old age on the basis of these new scientific discoveries, and became an advocate of total abstinence, is well known.

The fact that certain men show no obvious effects "simply means that they happen to be strong and stable in health, and so able to withstand, without immediate signs of injury, the effects of doses which are disastrous to many highly strung, sensitive persons. After a military campaign there are always some men who return alive; but this does not alter the fact that a large proportion of the soldiers are killed, disabled, or overstrained by the war." [15]

The popular idea is that a man is not drunk if he does not stagger and is reasonably clear in his speech and senses. But intoxication is not a matter of mere muscle control. The average regular drinker is always drunk; disturbances not noticeable but far from normal are taking place in his physical and psychical processes. In most persons the use of even two or three drinks of beer a day or of a bottle of wine with the meals causes distinct disturbances or unreliability. The effect often extends over many hours. Capacity for work is reduced and ''the so-called moderate drinker, who consumes his bottle of wine as a matter of course each day with his dinner, and who, doubtless, would declare that he is never under the influence of liquor, is, in reality, never actually sober from one week's end to another. Neither in bodily nor in mental activity is he ever up to what should be his normal level.'' [16]

Laitinen's experiments covering seven years indicate that so small an amount of alcohol as is contained in one glass of beer a day by parents leaves a degenerating effect on offspring. The same amount lowers the resistance of the body to disease and leaves it more open to infection. Liability to these dangers does not seem to cease below any standard of moderation.

Surely, since the term ''moderation'' suggests safety where there is no safety, it ought not be used in connection with the daily indulgence in alcoholic liquors in any quantity.

Alcohol and Insanity.—Intoxication itself is a sort of temporary insanity, an abnormal state of mind. ''It begins with a slight maniacal excitation; thoughts flow lucidly, the quiet become loquacious, the modest bold; there is need of muscular action; the emotions are manifest in laughing, singing, and dancing.'' When larger amounts of alcohol are added this mental condition is intensified. ''Now the esthetical ideas and moral impulses are lost control of, the weak side of the individual is manifested, his secrets revealed; he is dogmatic, cruel, cynical, dangerous; he insists that he is not drunk, just as the insane insists on his sanity."[17] In the different stages of intoxication, from the mildest up to "the snakes," all the varying types of insanity are found. Cutten shows that "starting with one form and continuing with the course of intoxication, we see all the varieties of madness."[18]

Alcohol seems to have a sort of affinity for the brain and nerve centers. Here the first effects are felt—the apparent stirring, but actual dulling, that makes a man feel "a little beyond himself." Reason, judgment, and spiritual qualities are retarded, while emotional faculties run more freely and sense feelings are stirred, but made unreliable. The first injury also falls upon nerve and brain centers. After a time changes in the tissues occur, accompanied by corresponding changes in the mental capacity, or by mental deterioration and instability.[19] Continuous daily use is dangerous, for the continuous irritation of the brain cells may cause more permanent states of mental derangement. For all intoxication, even temporary, is "morbid irritation," resulting from the presence of the alcohol in the brain.

Insanity and alcoholism are closely related and frequently occur together. Excessive drinking sometimes is a result, or an expression, of mental weakness; at others drink is the cause. Where drink seems to be the result, it will often be found that a generation or two back there was heavy drinking in the family and that the children of such parents were not equipped with a mentally and nervously stable make-up at the beginning of their life-history. Inherited insanity and intemperance go hand in hand; where either exists the other will very probably gain a foot-hold. No difference whether alcohol is cause or consequence, or whether both are expressions of other personal or hereditary conditions, intemperance, the preventable complicating agency authorized politically and encouraged by economic forces, gets in its deadly work.

A moderate estimate seems to be that in the United States 25 per cent to 30 per cent of the insane admitted to hospitals owe their condition directly or indirectly to alcohol.[20]   The Lunacy Commission of New York reports 28 per cent of those in state hospitals as there on account of drink.   On this basis it is estimated that at least 30,000 thruout the nation owe their insanity to this cause.   ''One insane person costs a loss to the state of $400 a year.   The total loss in money to the state of New York by alcoholic insanity must, therefore, be $2,400,000, and to the United States $12,000,000 every year.''[21]   ''Heredity occupies the first rank among the causes of insanity and alcohol comes next.''[22]   Dr. Clausen of the Royal Edinburgh Asylum says it ''is the most frequent single exciting cause of mental disease, and it acts also, as a predisposing cause in very many cases.''   Thus authorities, differing slightly in the way they classify cause, agree with great force upon the main fact that alcohol is one of the most prolific of all the causes of mental weakness and insanity.

A striking contrast, showing alcohol and the saloon to be a cause of mental break-down, arises when we compare states which have banished liquor with those which retain it.   In 1910 the eight prohibition states had one insane to 875 of the population; the nation as a whole had one to every 490.[23]   In license states in that year thirteen hospitals had 26 per cent of their patients on account of drink; eight hospitals in prohibition or almost prohibition states reported 5.9 per cent of their patients on the same basis. In Georgia, following prohibition, there was an annual decrease in the insane of 16 per cent for four years.[24] And the same story comes from Sweden and Norway—a tremendous decrease in alcoholism during the past fifty years has put a stop to the increase of mental disturbances. "Mental and nervous degeneration is strongest in the communities where there is most drinking."[25]

Prof. Berkeley, of Johns Hopkins, shows that under continued indulgence "the whole organism suffers *psychological and somatic degradation* which is not confined to the transgressors themselves. As a result of the excess of the progenitors there appears in the descendants lowered vitality, stunted growth, mental and moral imbecility, deaf-mutism, sterility, with the result that within a few generations the family becomes extinct, or consists of members physically and mentally incapable of holding their own."[26]

References and Authorities

The Attractiveness of Alcohol.

Kelynack, *The Drink Problem*, 5-7, 35-43.

Partridge, *Studies in the Psychology of Intemperance*, 71-78.

Jack London, *John Barleycorn* (1913).

Patrick, "In Quest of the Alcohol Motive," *Pop. Sci. Mo.*, Sept., 1913.

Committee of Fifty, *Summary—The Drink Problem*, 31.

Patton, "Economic Basis of Prohibition," *Annals of the American Academy*, Vol. 2, 59.

Barrows, "America Sober," *Outlook*, 91, 397 (1909).

Horsley and Sturge, *Alcohol and the Human Body*, 18.

[1] Dr. Campbell in *The Drink Problem* by Kelynack, 38.

[2] Partridge, 99.

[3] Quoted in Williams, *Alcohol*, 11.

[4] See Kelynack, 36; also Partridge.

[5] Dr. Campbell in Kelynack, 36.

The Source of Intoxication.

Williams, *Alcohol*, 121-123.

Billings, *The Physiological Aspects of the Liquor Problem*, II, 4-26.

Kelynack, *The Drink Problem*, 5-6, 34-39.

Horsley and Sturge, *Alcohol and the Human Body*, 3-19.

Kerr, *The Disease of Inebriety*, Cosmop. 21, 547.

6 Billings, II, 26.

An Age-Old Delusion.

Horsley and Sturge, *Alcohol and the Human Body*, 68-94, 137-140.

Partridge, *Studies in the Psychology of Intemperance*, 82-97.

Crothers, ''Delusion of the Tonic and Stimulant Effects of Alcohol,'' at 12th Annual Meeting of American Therapeutic Society.

Jack London, *John Barleycorn*.

Connolly, ''Is Alcohol a Stimulant? *Sci. Temp. Jr.*, Sept., 1911.

7 Col. Tom Gilmore, of Model License League.

8 Horsley and Sturge, 80, 81.

9 Ibid; quoted, 64.

10 Ibid, 80.

11 Address; see above.

What Is Moderation?

Horsley and Sturge, *Alcohol and the Human Body*, 16-19, 68-72, 80.

Williams, *Alcohol*, 11-21, 47-50.

Kelynack, *The Drink Problem*, 84-96.

Prohibition Year Book (1910), 113-114, 116.

Mason, ''The Term Moderation as Applied to Use of Alcoholic Beverages,'' *Sci. Temp. Jr.*, Feb., 1912.

12 See ch. IV.

13 Horsley and Sturge, 19.

14 Williams, 49.

15 Horsley and Sturge, 18.

16 Williams, 19.

Alcohol and Insanity.

Forel, *Nervous and Mental Hygiene*, 205-215.

Horsley and Sturge, *Alcohol and the Human Body*, 111-120.

Williams, *Alcohol*, 63-68.

Anti-Saloon League Year Book (1912), 116-121.

Cutten, *The Psychology of Alcoholism*, 231-276.

Billings, *Physiological Aspects of the Liquor Problem*, I, 340-355.

Kelynack, *The Drink Problem*, 97-107, 236-237.

Henderson, *Dependents, Defectives and Delinquents*, 90-91.

Crothers, *Inebriety*.

Folks, "Prevention of Insanity," *Review of Reviews*, May, '11.

Woodbury, "Alcohol as an Active Cause of Insanity," *Jr. of Inebriety*, 32, 141.

[17] MacDonald, *Abnormal Man*, Doc. No. 195, U. S. Bureau of Ed.

[18] *The Psychology of Alcoholism.*

[19] Horsley and Sturge, 111.

[20] Williams, 64.

[21] N. Y. State Com. on Lunacy (1911), in *Bulletin of Metrop. Life Ins. Co.*

[22] Woodbury; ref. above.

[23] *Anti-Saloon League Year Book* (1912), 118.

[24] Ibid. (1913), 64.

[25] Forel, 231.

[26] *Jr. of Inebriety*, 32, 148.

If for no other reason than the prevention of tuberculosis, state prohibition would be amply justified.

—OTIS, *The Great White Plague.*

I have stated repeatedly my conviction that a person who has attained to adult age, and who requires alcohol as a food or stimulant, or who has acquired the alcohol habit, may attain to a certain degree of richness in mind, body, or estate; but so far as the evolution or stability of the race is concerned it would be far better for the world had he or she never been born into it.

—THEODORE BULKLEY HYSLOP, M. D.,
Pres. British Society for the Study of Inebriety.

CHAPTER IV

ALCOHOL AND HEALTH: THE PRACTICAL PROBLEM

First among the essentials of social well being and personal happiness is health, physical and mental. Upon it depend the present efficiency and future possibilities of the race. The degree to which alcohol and the saloon influence the conditions which make for or against public health is a first test of their value to society.

Alcohol a Cause of Sickness.—Everyone that cares for the welfare of his fellows, as neighbor, physician minister, or social worker, will agree with the ordinary observer that a vast amount of deficiency, sickness, and disease is associated with those families and communities where alcoholic drinks are most frequently used. Directly and indirectly drink is present as cause, or consequence, or complicating agency, in sickness and misery to no small extent. Even the superficial observer will be impressed with the evident fact that its influence is largely unnecessary—that alcoholic suffering is avoidable suffering and alcoholic sickness preventable sickness.

The interference of alcohol with health is manifest in a great variety of ways. Some of the most important may be broadly stated as follows: (1) The immediate action of the drug itself upon the body and mind of the user. It injuriously affects the tissues and shortens life. (2) It weakens the resistance powers of the body against the attack of disease and makes recovery more difficult.

This action of alcohol, preparing as it does a seed bed for contagion in a whole community, has far-reaching social consequences. (3) Then there are the effects due to its influence on living conditions, financial income, moral control, and other necessary social factors, all together opening up routes for a thousand other ills of almost infinite variety.

"The traditional role of alcohol," says Williams, "is that of a stimulant. It has been supposed to stimulate digestion and assimilation; to stimulate the heart's action; to stimulate muscular activity and strength; to stimulate the mind. The new evidence seems to show that, in the final analysis, alcohol stimulates none of these activities; that its final effect is everywhere depressive and inhibitory rather than stimulative; that, in short, it is properly to be classed with the anesthetics and narcotics." [1]   The popular impression that intoxicating liquors are stimulants and helpful, or at most not really injurious, is unscientific and misleading. Most recent investigators agree that the average effect is to depress, deaden, and throw out of order the regular functions of the body.[2]   These unfavorable results are so predominant, so much more lasting, and so unavoidable that they overwhelmingly negative any apparent first impression of real help or actual stimulating influence.

One necessity to good health is the condition of the cells of which the body is composed—whether they are normal and active, or depressed and not able fully to do their work. Alcohol and similar drugs injure directly the protoplasm of the cells. They interfere with the taking up of oxygen, retard the elimination of waste material, and permit the accumulation of substances and conditions favorable to disease. Alcohol is classed with the "protoplasmic poisons," because of this direct injury to the cells. Horsley, who gathers up the latest laboratory evidence on this point, says that all observers "are now impressed with the fact that animal and vegetable protoplasm is deleteriously affected by even very small quantities of alcohol which is . . . very poisonous to living tissue and cell life." [2] This influence of alcohol on the primary body tissues has both direct and indirect consequences; direct injury resulting in a great variety of alcoholic diseases; indirect by opening the way for more ready attack from infectious and other common sources of disease and death.

Modern sanitary science is directing its best attention toward these very dangerous "protoplasmic poisons," since the ills which result are so largely preventable. Some of them, such as lead and alcohol, are introduced into the system from without; others, as the toxins from diphtheria and other contagious diseases, are created by the germs after they enter the blood. The practical effort is to prevent both germs and poisons from getting into the system in the first place. In the problem of alcohol this phase is beginning to stand out no less prominently than the moral matter of "drink" or "not to drink." It is a fact of tremendous significance to public health under present-day living conditions.

(1) Its Direct Action.—Phelps, an authority on mortality statistics, shows that alcohol is responsible, directly and indirectly, for 66,000 deaths in the United States yearly, or about one in every thirteen at adult age. The part charged to alcohol in causing the disease of which they nominally died he gives as follows: tuberculosis of the lungs, 12 per cent; heart disease, 16 per cent; pneumonia, 22 per cent; paralysis, 22 per cent;

apoplexy, 22 per cent; suicide, 23 per cent; diseases of the arteries, 23 per cent; Bright's disease, 30 per cent; cirrhosis of the liver, 67 per cent; alcoholism, 100 per cent; accidents and other causes, also a large per cent.[3] These figures are of male deaths between the ages of twenty and seventy-four, and are on the basis of that part of the United States for which accurate registrations of death are obtainable. The figures are exceedingly conservative and as reliable as may be obtained. But it should be noted that in this country the reports of physicians on the causes of death are always inclined to minimize the share due to drink, because of a desire to avoid hurting the feelings of the friends of the deceased.

These figures do not take account of the loss of life due to the social consequences of drink. The immense share caused directly and indirectly in infant mortality, among others under twenty years of age, and among women, are not included. Phelps' figures relate only to the consequence of personal indulgence upon the drinker himself. The total of all deaths in any way due to liquor can scarcely be estimated. The popular estimate of 100,000 a year in all probability is conservative. Hobson has put the total in any and all ways traceable to alcohol at about ten times the estimate given by Phelps.[4]

On the basis of Phelps' conservative figures, The Scientific Temperance Federation has placed the loss graphically at one death every eight minutes due to alcohol; also, that the sinking of the Titanic steamship in 1912 carried down 1,662 persons, while alcohol takes off a Titanic load—1,662 adults—every nine days.

Government records in Switzerland, where drinking

is more general, but where the actual causes of death are more accurately reported by physicians, show that alcohol is a prominent cause of deaths of men in the prime of life as follows: liver cirrhosis, 91 per cent; digestive diseases, 43 per cent; pneumonia, 30 per cent; diseases of the circulation, 23 per cent; kidney diseases, 25 per cent.[5] Various disorders of the digestive organs have as a prominent cause the immediate action of alcohol on the stomach. Degeneration of the heart and blood vessels, resulting in apoplexy, paralysis, etc., are well-known instances of the same cause. Alcohol seems to have a special affinity for the nerve centers, leading to many disorders, physical and mental.

Drunkenness itself is more than a habit. The progressive appetite, the peculiar craving for alcohol, when once established, is an expression of a diseased condition. Alcohol repeatedly taken tends to create an abnormal condition. The peculiar appetite, which can be satisfied only by repetition of the dose, does not exist in the healthy taste. It might almost be called a chemical affinity or craving after it has reached the higher stages of intensity. Dr. Norman Kerr, a specialist on inebriety, long ago pointed out what others have since approved, that "there is a physical element in intoxication and the strong impulse thereto"; and "that the most of those who have gone under, some of them the most highly gifted and most noble-souled of men, have been subjects of a dire disease,"[6] and that treatment and prevention must be applied as to a dangerous disease.

There are certain types of men who seem not to develop open symptoms of alcoholism, who do not have "the appetite," and who seem immune to visible intoxication. "We are surrounded by thousands of men . . .

who are indeed in an early stage of subacute alcoholism, as exhibited by the quality and quantity of their mental power."[7]   The number of such is far larger than is apparent.   The evidences, loss of energy and capacity for business or work, diminished attention to details, loosened moral sensibilities, loss of idealism and ambition, are charged to a thousand causes other than the real one. "Such changes, which are due to the slow poisoning of the highest cerebral centers, are practically never attributed to the real cause."[7]   Many of those who have boasted for years of their capacity to keep steady while drinking regularly are in fact never free from alcohol from one week's end to another. Men have died from chronic alcohol poisoning or alcoholism, or, worse yet, have left upon society the burden of caring for defective children, who have never been known to be intoxicated.   To even their most intimate friends they were regarded as nothing more than "moderate drinkers."[8]

(2) Reduces the Capacity for Resistance.—Recent attention by students of public health to the prevention of sickness and misery has brought a strong new emphasis to one vital phase of the alcohol problem—its part in opening the way for attack by various forms of disease. New facts have been discovered showing that it paves the way for tuberculosis, pneumonia, and other great causes of suffering and death.   It breaks down the resistance power of the user against attack and causes physical weaknesses in his children so that they, too, more readily yield to disease.[9]

Physicians find that almost always the man who takes liquor regularly gets sick quicker, is harder to treat, is slower of recovery, and has fewer chances of getting well, than the non-drinker. The liquor-soaked man is almost helpless. He is the first victim of contagion and the most liable to die during an epidemic. In surgical cases his wounds heal more slowly and are more liable to "go wrong" or fail to heal.[10] It makes less difference than is ordinarily supposed whether liquor is taken in large, saturating quantities or in what is regarded as "moderation." In time the system loses its resisting powers and falls a ready victim to some sort of disease. Practically all specialists agree with Welch, who says "this lowered resistance is manifested both by increased liability to contract disease and by the greater severity of the disease."[11] "It is a recognized clinical fact that a drinker is less resistant than he should be to the attacks of cholera, intermittent fever, consumption, pneumonia, and blood poisoning in all its forms."[12]

This increased susceptibility is shown in a practical way by a comparison of the records of sick benefit societies where, as in Germany and Australia, those taking only total abstainers have existed side by side with others including both non-drinkers and drinkers. The contrast is marked; members of the former have only about half as much sickness as those of the latter. "The duration of the sickness was important, also, for the abstainers were away from work on an average 6.4 weeks, but members of the societies not requiring abstinence, 10.9 weeks."[13] This means a wage loss, as well as a loss of health, freedom, and social activities for an average of four weeks longer to those of drinking habits. The difference would have been even more marked had the societies which admitted drinking men been without any abstainers in their number to reduce the average sick period. Men engaged in the liquor trade—bar-keepers, brewery workers, café waiters, and saloon-keepers in general—not only have a higher death rate, but also are more susceptible to tuberculosis and similar germ diseases, as well as to alcoholism. In England it is shown from official records that liquor sellers have a mortality 64 per cent higher than the average mortality of male adults, and abstainers a rate of 44 per cent lower than the average.[14] In America the difference is not quite so great. This is why many insurance companies either charge a much higher premium rate to saloon-keepers or refuse to carry them as risks at all.

Consumption, "the great white death," was formerly thought to be retarded by alcohol. Now it is known that the very opposite is the effect. It interferes with nutrition; it causes bad living conditions; it weakens the tissues of the lungs; it destroys or deadens the white corpuscles of the blood, whose function it is to fight invading germs. It is regarded generally as one of the chief causes of this largest of all sources of death. "In view of the close connection between alcoholism and tuberculosis," reads a resolution of the International Congress on Tuberculosis, "this Congress strongly emphasizes the importance of combining the fight against tuberculosis with the struggle against alcohol."[15] Dr. Geo. W. Webster, President of the Illinois State Board of Health, said: "The alcohol problem is far more important than tuberculosis, because it costs more lives and more money."[16] Brouardel, a French authority, calls it "the most powerful factor in the propagation of tuberculosis."[17]

If a drinking man takes pneumonia, his chance of recovery is much less than that of a non-drinker. Osler shows that in 100 cases of pneumonia, among abstainers

18.5 per cent die; among "moderate" drinkers, 25.4 per cent; among steady or heavy drinkers, 52.8 per cent.[18]

It is right among these most dangerous of all afflictions, the pulmonary diseases, that alcohol gets in some of its worst work. The fight for public health these modern days is directed toward improving living conditions, popularizing scientific facts about the causes of ill health, seeking to destroy the carriers of germs, and trying to prevent toxic poisons from getting a start— all of it the most practical sort of preventive work. Right at the heart of this new movement lie the facts about the popular alcoholic liquors in making a soil bed for disease and suffering. The presence of the drug in the blood vessels of the lungs causes dilation and congestion, keeping the membranes in a state in which they are more susceptible both to changes in climate and to invading disease infection.

Alcohol also breaks down immunity against disease by its action on the white corpuscles of the blood, "the little policemen of the body." They are less vigorous and active in the presence of alcohol. Even in small amounts it "intoxicates" or paralyzes them, making them sluggish and weak. Their work is to attack and destroy microbes, dust, or chemical irritants that enter the body.[19] When they get the better of pneumonia, typhoid, tuberculosis, diphtheria, and other germs and poisons, these diseases come to an end. But alcohol, reaching the blood two minutes after being swallowed, keeps up its blighting effect on these disease eliminators as long as it is present. The action has been vividly described by Dr. G. Sims Woodhead as follows:

"The leucocytes (white corpuscles) act as a kind of sanitary police. They appear wherever dead matter is to be removed; they attempt to prevent the invasion of the body by disease-producing organisms, and once they come to grips with their opponents, they die rather than give way. Before coming to grips, however, if their opponents appear to be too strong for them, they may attempt to keep out of the way for a time until such opponents are weakened or they themselves have had time to prepare for the fight. Disease-producing organisms getting into the tissues of animals and patients during the time that alcohol is holding back the leucocytes, and meeting with no resistance from them, entrench themselves strongly, so that the leucocytes are not able to drive them out, and a severe, often fatal, attack of disease is the result.'' [20]

The milder liquors, such as beer and light wines, seem to be little less dangerous, as a predisposing cause to disease, than are the stronger alcoholics. There are two facts to be noted: first, that the beer drinker will take a much larger number of drinks, thus running the per cent of actual alcohol up toward that of the spirit drinker; and, second, that he is usually more regular in his daily drinking, thus keeping the influence of the alcohol more constantly present. This is an important matter when resistance against disease is considered. It is the regular daily drinking, whether the amounts are large or small, that keeps the alcohol constantly present and the resisting powers always below par. In this respect the heavy drinker who goes on a debauch once a month or once a week has the advantage—there are periods of days or weeks in which these powers become normal.

Laitinen's experiments, dealing with thousands of

cases, emphasize these points. He further shows that so small a quantity of alcohol as that contained in a half-pint of 3½ per cent beer per day, *taken habitually,* lowers resistance to infection.[21] Hodge's experiments were similar—that an habitual amount which always stopped short of intoxication opened the way to infectious diseases.[22]

Many physicians believe that the beer drinker is much worse off than the whisky drinker; that he has less elasticity and reserve power; that, as one says from experience, "when a beer drinker gets into trouble it seems almost as if you have to recreate the man before you can do anything for him." Pneumonia, pleurisy, and fevers seem to have a first mortgage on him which they foreclose remorselessly at the first opportunity. The deceptive effects of beer are especially noted in the case of sudden contagion or accident. The beer drinker is much more liable to succumb. He seems to be all one vital part. A social worker gives a graphic illustration after a visit to Bellevue Hospital in New York:

"As we entered the ward the first sight opposite the door was a surgeon dressing a gangrenous arm. His words to the patient, as we caught them, were, 'No, I shall not let you go out; you would get a glass of beer, and that would kill you!' A boy in another bed, motherless, friendless, a stranger in a strange land, speaking no word of ours, had received a slight wound which pure blood would have thrown off. He was a beer victim, and his hurt, with his poisoned blood, produced erysipelas. Another had scratched his finger, and his hand was in danger of amputation. And so we went through the list, receiving testimony unexpected to us, and almost unconsciously given, that systems clogged with effete matters, which beer had prevented passing off, were incapable of resisting injury and disease.

"Some, if not all, of these, no doubt had thought the beer was doing them good. Many boast of the good it does them, or of their being strong in spite of the beer. 'I have drunk a gallon of beer every day for the last thirty years,' said a brewer's drayman, 'and I was never in better health than at this moment.' Yet the very next day he died in a fit of apoplexy. The beer told him that lie and he believed it."

In case of epidemic the community as a whole must suffer because of the drinking class. Cholera and yellow fever single out drinkers at their first attack. After one great scourge in New Orleans, a physician who served through the period said, "About 5,000 of them (the regular drinkers) died before the epidemic touched a single citizen or sober man, so far as I can get at the facts." Having acquired virulence by feeding upon this material, its vicious invasion continued until thousands more of all classes fell. In many other sorts of contagion the influence of alcohol in the community, tho much less pronounced, is scarcely less certain and constant.

(3) A Contributory Cause of Disease.—The public health aspects of alcohol should include the indirect consequences of the habit as well as those most directly traceable to it. Many social conditions are affected by it, these in turn bearing upon the public health.

The use of alcohol is often one of several factors in producing public unsanitary conditions, as well as in causing individual sickness. Some of the most important are:

(a) Intemperance induces poverty and consequent neglect of health. This is especially true among laboring men.[23] Where the head of the family must pay out daily or weekly a large per cent of his income for liquors, he cannot have sufficient to spend for necessary clothes, food, shelter, and recreation. His family must be huddled together in small unventilated rooms, fuel is lacking in winter, and the thousand pathetic stories of the drunkard's family are the result. And it is often the moderate drinker who thus makes his family suffer most for his own indulgence.

(b) The weight of the drink bill upon the family compels the mother to overwork and neglect her children. The children become mentally and physically weak and a ready prey to acute disease. Boys and girls who should be in school must go to work prematurely in order to help bear the family burden. They suffer physical injury, and the community must bear the burden of their later inefficiency. These problems have become the most difficult of all social difficulties of the day, and the drink habit stands right at the base among their chief causes.

(c) Drink and immorality go hand in hand. There is a large class of diseases due directly to immorality, for which the alcohol habit is partly responsible. It is a significant fact, worthy of special study, that in Kansas under the prohibitory law there has been a distinct falling off of venereal and similar diseases. Medical men from various parts of the state testify to this. Says Dr. Wm. B. Swan, secretary Kansas State Board of Health: "It is a fact well known among medical men that a decrease in the consumption of intoxicants lessens venereal diseases."[24] Dr. Menninger of the

Kansas Homeopathic Society said: ''The strict enforcement of the prohibition law in Kansas would reduce to the minimum the social vice, if not entirely obliterate it.'' [24] If the removal of the general sale of liquors has helped to improve to this extent these social conditions, it is certainly a long step toward improving public health.

Is Alcohol or Beer a Food?—It has long been believed that there is food value in alcohol, or especially in malt liquors. To large numbers of people beer is ''a liquid food,'' apparently as necessary as bread and more to be depended upon than meat, for it is not so expensive. These people and their ancestors, here or ''in the old country,'' have been taught that beer is an every-day necessity, and their own experience seems to strengthen this opinion. It has been given them from childhood; it is seen daily at meal time; they early go for the noon pail for father; workmen are seen going for it several times a day. It would be surprising, indeed, should not many of the regular beer-drinking classes, as well as some of the dealers, honestly believe that this article, so common in every-day living, is as necessary as bread. Among some of the poorest, long periods have been passed with little that could be called food except beer and dark bread. Most of them know that whisky is bad, for it intoxicates, but ''booze,'' they believe, helps to give strength and takes the place of food, which is so hard to get.

As with every half-truth which furnishes foundation for a public misconception, there is ground for the food theory of alcohol, especially for that of malt liquors. Alcohol is partly oxidized in the body, yielding heat and energy; it retards the break-down of tissues;

it takes away the feeling of hunger—perhaps the most far-reaching cause for the wide prevalence of the opinion; it gives much feeling of relief in proportion to its cost; large numbers who use it are sure it takes the place of food. This idea is aggressively taught by the liquor dealer who plays upon a deep-lying prejudice in its favor when he advertises his wares as "health-giving," "nourishing," "liquid food,"—that "beer is to the adult what milk is to the child."

In beer there are substances of more or less nutritive value aside from the alcohol. An ordinary glass contains by weight about 4.46 per cent alcohol, 4.61 per cent extract, .47 per cent albuminoids, .26 per cent free acids.[25] The solid matter, the extract, being digestible, serves to build tissue and so in itself may be called a food, tho the alcohol may not be so classed. But beer taken for this purpose is an exceedingly costly, deceptive, and vicious "food." If cost alone is considered, the bread claims are preposterous. Five cents' worth of flour contains eighty times more proteids and sixty times more carbo-hydrates than a glass of beer, while the latter has no fats at all. A man would have to swallow daily 108 glasses of beer at a cost of $5.40 to supply the amount of proteids needed daily, or fifty-two glasses to furnish the carbo-hydrates. This twenty-seven quarts would contain twenty-nine ounces of absolute alcohol.[25]

Taking all so-called food values of beer together, the heat qualities of the alcohol, the digestible solids, etc., it is found that a nickel's worth of beer yields 94 calories of heat, while five cents' worth of flour gives 2,785 calories, the ratio in this respect between beer and bread being 1 to 29. To furnish the heat that comes from five cents' worth of flour takes nearly thirty glasses of beer,[25] costing $1.48. No one can afford to purchase food value at such tremendous cost, to say nothing of the injurious effects of the drug, which far outweigh all possible nutritious results.

These facts, that there is a minute amount of nutritive material in beer, that alcohol gives relief by deadening the sense of hunger, as shown elsewhere, are the foundations for the most vicious of popular misunderstandings—that beer is an every-day food. Such an impression suggests and encourages continuous and heavy drinking. It encourages ignorant mothers to give beer to infants or to use it themselves, and the results are most immediately damaging. It defrauds the purpose of hunger and relieves it fictitiously.

Whether alcohol ever serves a food purpose is a question long debated by chemists and physiologists. The line of distinction between a food and a poison, between that which furnishes nourishment to the body in the performance of its functions and that which hinders and destroys it, is very indefinite at best. It may well be left to these experts as a technical question. The deadliest of poisons may at times be of great food value, while every-day foods, in certain diseases, for certain individuals, or even in excess, are no better than poisons. Just when a generally recognized poison becomes of value is a question for the expert knowledge and diagnosis of the physician and his prescription; not at all one for the personal taste and choice of the ordinary layman.

The practical questions are: Is alcohol a wholesome every-day or occasional food? How do its nourishing qualities compare with its well-known detrimental qualities? Can it safely be used regularly without expert guidance? Will it take the place of known foods in health? If it does not do these things, it may be a medicine, but it can make no claims to being a food. To these there can be but one answer—a decided negative.

The fact that a part of the alcohol taken in the ordinary liquors is oxidized in the body and liberates heat has caused a great deal of not very profitable discussion. The value of such an article as food can not be determined alone by its chemical oxidation. Many other well-known poisons, such as morphia, phosphorus, ether, chloroform, and arsenic, are oxidized and give up heat and energy in the body. But this does not imply that they are foods.[26] The burning up may be for either of two purposes: to create needed heat and energy, or to break up an intruding substance so that it may more readily be eliminated from the system. It would seem that the latter is the more useful result in the case of alcohol. While there yet may be some dispute as to how far this oxidation serves a useful purpose, there is no question at all about the poisonous action of alcohol when present in more than the most minute quantities. The drug effects far outweigh any possible good that may come from its heat-producing qualities.[26] They are so uniform and constant that it must essentially be regarded as a poison, not as a food. Dr. Winfield S. Hall, one of the ablest experts on this subject, says: "If we admit alcohol to a position among the foods on the simple ground of its oxidation, we must also admit numerous other substances universally acknowledged as toxic."[27] "The human organism can acquire the ability to oxidize, or burn, daily 100 grains of morphine or cocaine, but this fact would never lead us to support either of these drugs as a food." [28]   To admit that alcohol is thus consumed in the body, that heat results, and that, under very special conditions, it may be desirable, is no more equivalent to making it a practical food for ordinary occasions than to admit that human flesh is nutritious is an argument for the practice of cannibalism.   That alcohol has poisonous effects, even those who believe in its food value for special situations agree; and, as Forel indicates, "The statement that a poison can be at the same time a food is a play on words." [29]

The following practical points definitely take alcohol out of the possible range of foods: Larger and larger quantities are required to give satisfaction; habitual use may create an uncontrollable craving. Food is oxidized slowly; alcohol rapidly. Foods are stored in the body; alcohol is eliminated. The use of food is not followed by reaction; that of alcohol is followed by reaction. The use of alcohol is followed by a decrease in brain and muscle activity; that of food increases those functions.

Alcohol smothers the sense of hunger without satisfying it. It does away with the sensation, not with the need; it supplies nothing to the tissues and nerves and muscles that are to be rebuilt. The heat it creates is but the result of the wear and tear of the extra burden thrown upon the body to get rid of it. When food is required, to allay natural hunger in such a way is merely to delude the hunger sensation and deny the real need.

Alcohol as a Medicine.—This topic would have no place in a study of this kind except for the fact that there is extensive use of alcohol under the impression that it is one drug at least which may be taken without the advice of a physician. Brandy and whisky have long been regarded as "home remedies," to be kept on hand for all sorts of occasions. Malt liquors are promoted as a home tonic. Alcohol occupies a sort of midway position in popular impression between a beverage and a medicine. This idea, therefore, becomes a sort of secondary source of the larger drink problem.

Alcohol was adopted as a remedial agent in medicine centuries ago, when the science was young. Its use is hoary with age. It was in common usage at the time that bleeding at the arm was the prevailing method of treatment for almost every disease. It is slowly being outgrown, as bleeding and similar treatments have yielded to the better scientific knowledge of the present.

At the present time a large share of the best physicians scarcely employ it at all; the number which exclude it entirely is growing rapidly. Medical sentiment has completely changed on this point within the past twenty years. In the medical schools it is not now being recommended to students as of importance as a therapeutic agent at all; it is regarded almost exclusively as a depressant. In theory its use has practically been ruled out—the victory is complete, tho, of course, many physicians, taught in the older days, continue to use it in their practice. There is quite general abandonment of it as a stimulant; and an agreement that, if used at all, it should be only on prescription.

Some important hospitals exclude it altogether. All others have reduced its use very much in the past few years. In 1897 the Massachusetts General Hospital had an expense of 46 cents per patient for alcohol, whisky, etc.; in 1906 the average per patient was 13 cents, a reduction of 70 per cent. This decreasing use is general throughout civilized nations. As Sir Victor Horsley, London's noted surgeon, says, "The medical profession as a whole has a hostile rather than a friendly feeling toward the drug we call alcohol. When I was a student, alcohol was the traditional remedy in surgery. . . . It was the traditional remedy for infectious diseases like pneumonia. What is the practice now? That in all these cases alcohol is no longer used. Forty years ago the seven great hospitals of London spent annually about $40,000 for alcoholic liquors, and about $15,000 for milk. Now alcohol and milk have changed places. In the Infirmary at Salisbury twenty-five years ago $1,500 was spent each year on alcoholic liquors. Last year the cost was $35." [30]

If alcohol were a new drug, discovered within the last half-century, as several noted authorities have pointed out, and had but recently come into use, and the frequent cases of alcoholism and social disorder following the new use had been watched and studied, as has been the case with cocaine and other newer anesthetics, it is certain that its use would have been only with the greatest care, and very much more limited than even at present. As Dr. H. W. Wiley, formerly Chief of the United States Bureau of Chemistry, states, "Both as a means of prevention of disease and as a remedy for disease, alcohol is rapidly falling into disrepute, and bids fair to become a mere memory in the Materia Medica." In Kansas, when a recent law was passed forbidding the prescribing of alcohol in any form, very few physicians protested; most announced that they did not care to use it, as there are so many better remedies to take its place.

The medicinal aim is too often sadly confused with the beverage use. As with any other powerful drug, its administration should be left entirely in the hands of reliable and conscientious physicians. They should decide in each specific case whether it should be employed at all and, if so, should regulate the amounts. Certainly, nothing is more unscientific than for each patient to determine for himself how much alcohol he ought to have; how often he ought to take it; in what form, whether as beer, ale, brandy, whisky, or by any miscellaneous combination of mixed drinks that may happen to strike his fancy.

A Cause of Degeneracy.—Among all the signs of progress in our most highly civilized nations are to be noted, with greater and greater frequency, frightful evidences of lessening physical and mental vigor in families and in whole communities. Among the many social causes, such as increasing nervous tension, the rapid pace in business and "society," over-crowded and unsanitary living conditions, and "commercialized vice," is also to be included the influence of intoxicants—the common every-day steady indulgence in alcohol. For a long time the facts of experience have been too obvious to be overlooked; now they are being corrected and strengthened by the test of scientific study and experiment, that *the children of drinkers are not quite up to par.*

The study of this topic is so difficult and the causes so complicated and inter-related that it is necessary to use as facts only those taken from the most thoro studies. The three following are especially valuable.

In Switzerland, a few years ago, Professor Demme made a careful comparison of the children of drinking and non-drinking parents. He studied for a long period the life-histories of ten very temperate families and ten intemperate families, selecting them most carefully and from exactly the same living conditions. In the former there were 61 children, of which five died in infancy, two were diseased, two were mentally slow, two deformed, and 50 normal. In the latter there were 57 children, of whom 25 died in infancy, one was diseased, six idiotic, five deformed, five dwarfed, five epileptic, and ten normal. In a word in the temperate families, 82 per cent of the children were normal and 18 per cent defective, while in the drinking families, the figures almost reversed, 82.5 per cent were defective and but 17.5 per cent normal.[31]

In striking similarity are the results of the tests made by Professor Hodge of Clark University. Professor Hodge conducted a long series of laboratory experiments on dogs to determine the influence of alcohol on the offspring. One pair of dogs was given alcohol daily in small quantities, but not sufficient to make them intoxicated. The other pair had no alcohol. With the non-alcoholic dogs, out of 45 pups, four were deformed and 41 were normal; with the alcoholic dogs, out of 23, eight were deformed, nine born dead, and four able to live; that is, 90.2 per cent of the progeny were healthy and normal when no alcohol was given the parents and but 17.4 per cent able to live when parents had alcohol.[32]

A most recent and careful study is that of Dr. Stockard of Cornell Medical College, completed in 1912.[33] His object was to determine whether alcohol exerts a marked influence on the germ cells and developing embryos of animals and, if possible, how that action takes place. His experiments were on guinea-pigs, every precaution being taken to limit the influence to alcohol alone. The amount of alcohol given was intentionally small, about what would correspond to that of a daily drinker who never becomes really drunk. The experiment was all the more valuable and practical for this reason. In the test made between an alcoholic father and a non-alcoholic mother, in 24 matings only 12 living young were born; seven of these died soon after birth and five survived; but these five were unusually small, shy, and excitable. In the test with the mother alcoholic, or both parents alcoholic, the average results were somewhat worse. But where both parents were normal all the offspring were healthy and normal. The startling fact brought out in these experiments is that the alcohol given the father alone was almost as destructive in causing deaths at birth, defective and abnormal offspring, or nervously weak and shy animals, as when it was given the mother. It is clearly evident that defective progeny may owe its condition to the father alone.[33]

Alcohol causes degeneracy in the offspring at the very beginning of the life history. Forel, who has given special study from the nerve and mental view-points, shows that alcoholic poisoning of the body and of the germ cells is one of the most potent forces of race degeneracy, and that the injuries in one generation tend to become permanent.[34] Laitinen, after studying 17,394 children, says "that the alcohol drinking by parents, even in small quantities (about a glass of beer a day), has exercised a degenerative influence upon their offspring."[35] In New York City, out of 20,147 cases of school children examined by Dr. MacNichol, 53 per cent of those that came from drinking homes were below the average in mental capacity, or dullards; 10 per cent of those from total abstinence families, being so classed.[36] Here, doubtless, home associations, deprivations, neglect, and brutal treatment all added their share to influence that might be called hereditary, complicating and making worse the tremendous distinction between the two classes. But all these conditions are more or less related to drinking and the saloon.

Just how all this degenerative influence takes place, what defects are transmitted, and how permanent they may be in an evolutionary sense, are not yet clear. There is much ground for hope that two or three generations, free from the social blight of widespread alcoholic indulgence, would largely free itself from the fearful consequences of alcohol. But the fact for the present is clear—that the regular user of alcohol is crippling his descendants, diminishing their mental and physical health, bringing into the world defectives, deformed, epileptic, and criminally inclined, making such life as they are capable of living harder and more perilous, and casting upon present society a fearful economic burden as well as laying a foundation for steady deterioration in the future. Many a man who calls himself a "moderate" drinker is in danger of leaving upon society a greater burden than if he rapidly ruined himself thru "excess" and threw himself directly upon its support. For alcohol, as Forel says, "gives a new impetus to the progressive degeneration of the species." [37]

Health the First Essential.—The importance of the hygienic aspect of the liquor problem can scarcely be overstated. Health is the very first essential to public well-being and private usefulness. All other aims in human welfare, the getting of wealth, culture, and intellectual enjoyment, social pleasure, and even spiritual development, depend upon it or are conditioned by it. The very existence of the state is threatened by that which causes mental or physical degeneracy in any considerable number of its citizens.

If personal drinking of alcoholic liquors is injurious to health—and the facts show that this is true—it strikes at what is fundamental in society. It is therefore no longer a private matter, but a burning public question. Its consequences are passed on to others both by personal association and contact, and by transmission, thus entailing a burden upon society in the future.

The craving for alcohol is not normal, but must be created. When established it becomes the most persistent, useless, and always-acting source of the whole complicated problem. While hundreds of thousands continue to drink more or less moderately, the beginnings of degeneracy are established in such communities and families. Natural selection does not seem to provide a method by which men may become accustomed to the use of this toxic stimulant. *The "fit" who survive are not those who learn to use it with impunity, but those who abstain totally.* As Dr. Henry Campbell, after a careful study of "The Evolution of the Alcoholic," says: "We arrive, then, at the conclusion that whatever adaptation to alcohol has taken place in civilized communities has essentially been by the evolution of a type of individual capable of resisting its allurements." [38]

The first instinct of the individual and the first aim of society organized into government is self-protection. No duty under the police power of the state is more sacred than the preservation of public health. It is one of the duties which always belong to government. "Whatever refinements speculative philosophy may have taught as to the sphere of the state in regard to public morals," said Judge Pitman, "but few have ever been audacious enough to question its duty to care for the public health.'' In order to make even political and economic reforms possible when the American troops took charge of Havana in 1898, the cleaning of the streets and opening of sewers had to be attended to first. To drain the canal zone in order to get rid of the mosquitoes that cause fevers was the first engineering problem to be taken up by the Panama Canal Commission when the work was undertaken on a modern scientific basis. How much more businesslike and scientific that government should take a hand in removing the source of so vast and preventable an amount of disease and death, physical and mental, as comes annually from intoxicating liquors. Getting down to first principles in government, ''the question of high or low license, local option, and the vast machinery of moral forces that seek relief by the church, the pledge, the prayer, and the temperance society, will be forgotten, and *the evil will be dealt with in the summary way in which enlightened communities deal with other ascertained causes of dangerous diseases.*''

The organized power of government is necessary to supplement and make successful the work of education and the change of social custom to that of temperance, which must constantly go on. A craving or habit for alcoholic liquors means neither more nor less than that an artificial state has been set up, which can only be changed by a stoppage of the supply of material which feeds the conditions.

Society must prevent its own degradation at any cost of private liberty to drink intoxicants. It should protect itself from the burdens of ruinous private indulgences and must defend the innocent members of society.

The inherent nature of the evils coming from liquor, with the toxic qualities of alcohol always present in larger or smaller quantities, makes *even the moderate use a danger, actual or threatening, to society.* There is no way to cure the physical source of intemperance but by making its gratification impossible—limiting the inducements to indulge by prohibiting the manufacture and sale.

References and Authorities.

Alcohol a Cause of Sickness.

Horsley and Sturge, *Alcohol and the Human Body* (4th ed., 1911), entire work; see especially 230-231, 39-45.

Billings, *Physiological Aspects of the Liquor Problem*, II, 362-372.

Kelynack, *The Drink Problem*, 52-82, 122-151.

Williams, *Alcohol, How It Affects the Individual, the Community, the Race*, 28-31.

Hutchinson, *Preventable Diseases.*

Webster, ''Alcohol and Its Influence on Public Health,'' *Senate Doc. No. 48.*, 61st Congress.

[1] Alcohol, 4.

[2] Horsley and Sturge, 45.

Its Direct Action

Horsley and Sturge, *Alcohol and the Human Body*, 39-45.

Kelynack, *The Drink Problem*, 52-82.

Williams, *Alcohol*, 28-33.

Hall, ''Physiologic Effects of Alcohol,'' *Report of Am. Medical Assn.* (1906).

Crothers, *Inebriety.*

Phelps, *The Mortality of Alcohol* (1911).

Stoddard, ''Drink's Toll from American Life,'' *Sci. Temp. Jr.*, March, 1912.

Van Cise, *Effect of Total Abstinence on the Death Rate.*

Whittaker, ''Alcoholic Beverages and Longevity,'' *Contemporary Rev.*, March, 1904.

Sci. Conclusions Concerning Alcohol Problem and Its Practical Relations to Life, Senate Doc. 48, 61st Cong

Statement of Prof. Irving Fisher, Pres. of Committee of 100
on National Health, March, 1912.

3 *The Mortality of Alcohol.*

4 Hobson, ''The Great Destroyer,'' *Speech in U. S. House of Rep.*, Feb. 2, 1911.

5 Statistics of Basle, 1892-1906; *Scientific Temperance Jr.*

6 Kerr, ''The Disease of Inebriety,'' *Cosmopolitan*, XXI, 547.

7 Horsley and Sturge, 66.

8 Williams, 19.

Reduces the Capacity for Resistance.

Horsley and Sturge, *Alcohol and the Human Body*, 192-197, 222-230.

Williams, *Alcohol*, 32-38.

Crothers, *Inebriety.*

Kelynack, *The Drink Problem*, 70-83, 122-151.

Billings, *Physiological Aspects of the Liquor Problem*, II, 372.

Wills, ''How the Life Saving Service is Endangered,'' *Scientific Temperance Journal*, June, 1912.

Barker, *The Saloon Problem and Social Reform*, 40.

Scientific Conclusions Concerning the Alcohol Problem, Senate Doc. 48, 61st Cong. (1909).

Otis, *The Great White Plague*, 186.

9 Horsley and Sturge, 224.

10 Ibid, 229.

11 Billings, 372.

12 Horsley and Sturge, 222.

13 Dillon Gouge, *Report of Public Actuary*, S. Australia; Compiled by Sci. Temp. Federation, Boston.

14 Horsley and Sturge, 272.

15 Paris (1905), Horsley and Sturge, 224.

16 *Scientific Conclusions*, etc. (above), 48.

17 Quoted in *Great White Plague*, 84.

18 Wills (above) or *Sci. Temp. Jr.*, June, 1912.

19 Horsley and Sturge, 192.

20 Kelynack, 78.

21 Williams, 34.

22 *Physiol. Aspects of the Liquor Problem.*

A Contributory Cause of Disease.

Warner, A. G., *American Charities*, 63-66.

Kelynack, *The Drink Problem*, 122-151.

Barker, *The Saloon Problem and Social Reform*, 37-47.

Horsley and Sturge, *Alcohol and the Human Body*, 269-272.

[23] Warner, 61.

[24] Stephens, *Prohibition in Kansas*, 101.

Is Alcohol or Beer a Food?

Horsley and Sturge, *Alcohol and the Human Body*, 169-174.

Forel, *Nervous and Mental Hygiene*, 191-193.

Atwater, "Nutritive Value of Alcohol," *Physiological Aspects of the Liquor Problem*, II, 316-343.

Committee of Fifty, *The Liquor Problem*, 21-23.

Kelynack, *The Drink Problem*, 87-89.

Martin, *The Human Body*, 304-305.

Barker, *The Saloon Problem and Social Reform*, 38-39.

Hall, "Relation of Alcohol to Nutrition," *Jr. Am. Medical Assn.*, **XXXV**, 65.

Madden, "Food Value of Alcohol," *Humanitarian*, XVII, 29-33.

Holitscher, "Is Beer a Food?" *Sci. Temp. Jr.*, May, 1911.

[25] Prof. Higley, in *American Issue*.

[26] Horsley and Sturge, Ch. IX.

[27] *Jr. Am. Medical Assn.*, July 14, 1900.

[28] Boos, Biol. Chemist, Mass. Gen. Hospital, Sci. Temp. Jr., Jan., 1912.

[29] *Nervous and Mental Hygiene*, 192.

Alcohol as a Medicine.

Horsley and Sturge, *Alcohol and the Human Body*, 3-12.

Gustafson, *The Foundation of Death*, 181-225.

[30] Address at Annual Meeting of British Medical Assn., Toronto (1906).

A Cause of Degeneracy.

Forel, *Nervous and Mental Hygiene*, 205-215.

Stockard, "An Experimental Study of Racial Degeneracy in Animals Treated with Alcohol," *Archives of Internal Medicine*, Oct., 1912.

Ibid, Abstract in *Scientific Temperance Journal*, Dec., 1912.

Horsley and Sturge, *Alcohol and the Human Body*, 243-265.

Kelynack, *The Drink Problem*, 229-239.

Warner, *American Charities*, 62-66.

Booth, *Pauperism*, 140.

Williams, *Alcohol*, 44-47.

Crothers, *The Sanitary Side of the Drink Problem.*

Barker, *The Saloon Problem and Social Reform*, 42-53.

Billings, *Physiological Aspects of the Liquor Problem*, I, 372-375.

Laitinen, ''A Contribution to the Study of the Influence of Alcohol on the Degeneration of Human Offspring,'' *Proceedings 12th Internatl. Congress on Alcoholism* (1909), 263.

[31] Sci. Temp. Jr., Feb., 1912.

[32] See Billings, *Phys. Aspects*, I, 373.

[33] See two refs above.

[34] *Nervous and Mental Hygiene*, 210.

[35] See ref. above.

[36] Horsley and Sturge, 255.

[37] *Nervous and Mental Hygiene*, 33.

[38] See Kelynack, 42.

CHAPTER V

Waste: And Sampson went and caught three hundred foxes, and took fire-brands, and turned tail to tail, and put a fire-brand in the midst between two tails.

And when he had set the brands on fire, he let them go into the standing corn of the Philistines, and burnt up both the shocks and also the standing corn, with the vineyards and olives.

—Judges, XV:4, 5.

To use liquor is to the nervous system like placing sand in a watch; it wears it out rapidly, making it a worthless, useless thing.

—Luther Burbank.

CHAPTER V

THE PUBLIC COST OF LIQUOR

In this age, when money stands so high as a measure of national welfare, it is particularly desirable to estimate, so far as may be possible, the cost of the liquor institution to society in dollars and cents. Any possible settlement of the question, or any extensive control over the saloon, other than yielding completely to the growing force of the commercialized alcohol habit, means somewhere an economic conflict. In this struggle will be arrayed two elements—large existing wealth and financial interests, on one side, and a purpose to avoid social waste immense in size, on the other.

How shall we measure, in terms of economic value, the waste due to alcohol? What is the cost of the drink custom to society? What the financial weight of the social burden coming from it? What of the wealth, labor, capital, and human energy, diverted from other lines of production into the trade in this socially dangerous commodity? What value does society get in return? And the ever practical question, *"Does it pay under present-day conditions?"*

The American Drink Bill.—For more than twenty-five years the American people have paid over a thousand million dollars annually at retail for liquors which intoxicate. The annual cost is now more than one billion seven hundred million dollars, or something like a direct head tax of $18.00 on every man, woman, and child in the country. It costs each family, on the average, $90.00. For more than half a century this gigantic drink bill has been steadily mounting up, with the exception that since 1907 it has been about stationary. The amount consumed has increased to correspond with the rise of the drink bill. In 1912 the total amount of intoxicants of all kinds used for beverage purposes was 2,123,-400,000 gallons,[1] or 21.98 gallons per capita. In Chicago, as an example of our great liquor-consuming centers, during hot periods in mid-summer, a million gallons of beer are sometimes drunk daily, an average of six drinks for every inhabitant of that city.

In England, Germany, Austria, and most other European nations, the people, on the average, drink more heavily than in the United States; but in all those countries, for some years past, there has been a marked decrease in the consumption. Here, owing chiefly to the greater commercial exploitation of the liquor market by the organized traffic, the steady growth of years has scarcely more than come to a standstill. Up until 1907 the increase in liquor consumption was at the rate of about 67,000,000 gallons per year. The use of beer increased 1300 per cent from 1840 to 1912.

For a hundred years a differentiation in drinking habits has been going on. Where formerly almost everybody took a drink occasionally or oftener, now only a minority of adults use intoxicants regularly or at all. In 1887 an estimate was made by the United States Bureau of Statistics[2] that the alcohol-consuming population constituted about 25¼ per cent of the total. With the heavier restrictions against drinking men in various industries and the tremendous temperance agitation of the past twenty-five years, it is reasonable to

assume that at present it does not much exceed 20 per
cent, or, in round numbers, 20,000,000 habitual and
irregular drinkers. This would place in the drinking
class two-thirds of adult men and one-tenth of adult
women, a fair estimate for the country as a whole.
Among the drinking classes every indication is that
the regular users are much more steady and systematic
in their daily use than formerly. The supply is much
more regular and accessible; usually prices are lower and
wages higher. The largest part of the increase in past
years, doubtless, is due to this growing systematic daily
dependence upon liquors, encouraged by the commercial
enterprise and competition of saloons and brewers, as
compared with the irregular opportunities of earlier
days. The drink habit is less popular but more steady
each year. A growing per cent of people are becoming
abstainers, but at the same time, the consumption by
non-abstainers, especially regular drinkers, is becoming
greater. The differentiation into two great classes is progressing more rapidly, and is becoming more absolute.

The tremendous growth of the national burden from
drink is shown vividly when the figures are brought
together by ten-year periods. In 1850 the consumption
of all intoxicants was 4.08 gallons per capita; in 1860,
6.40 gallons; 1870, 7.7 gallons; 1880, 8.79 gallons;
1890, 13.21 gallons; 1900, 17.76 gallons; 1910, 21.86
gallons; 1911, the maximum, 22.79 gallons; and in
1912, a slight reduction from the previous year, 21.98
gallons.[1]

It is difficult to obtain a thoro estimate of the
national drink bill, that is, of the cost of intoxicating
drinks to the people, as they are ordinarily bought by
the glass, bottle, pail, or keg. There are so many factors

to take into account, such as dilutions and adulterations in the saloons, variation in the number of drinks obtained from a gallon or barrel, prices, and illicit sales. The most conservative is that made annually by *The American Grocer,* a national trade journal. Its compilation is purely for business purposes, and seems free from prejudice. According to this estimate, the total drink bill for 1912 was $1,630,000,000, a cost *per user* of $67, or *per family among users* of $335.[2]

But *The Grocer* does not fully take into account the adulterations and dilutions in the saloons; nor does it allow for extra small drinks, nor for the fancy prices obtained in high-grade cafés and resorts, nor for certain other means by which the amounts sold for the usual price are reduced or higher prices than ordinary, obtained. It has been said by a pure-food expert that 85 per cent of whisky is sold adulterated. All such factors mean additional cost to the public, who must pay for the air pumped into the beer and the adulterants in other liquors. It is not surprising to find other estimates, apparently as reliable, much higher than the above. The Anti-Saloon League gives the drink bill at $1,750,000,000. The Prohibition Year Book makes it $2,000,000,000. An able prohibition authority,[3] who has computed it carefully for a long period of years, places the 1912 bill at $2,336,000,000; this estimate seems to take into account more carefully than others the adulterants and other methods by which the cost to the consumer is increased.

For all practical purposes nothing will be lost in taking the most conservative estimate given above, in round figures, for 1912, $1,700,000,000. This is the estimate employed in this book. Certainly the direct annual cost of intoxicants to the consumer can not be less than this; it is almost certainly several millions more. The figures are so nearly incomprehensible in any case that nothing is lost in being a little more conservative than necessary.

The money thus spent in a single year would dig four parallel Panama Canals, one every three months, for a year. It is almost equal to the total gross receipts of all the railroads; it is nearly six times as great as the tariff, and would pay the national debt every seven months. The public cost of the consequences of drink, loss of efficiency in production, health, time, life, care of weakened humanity, and crime, is, of course, an amount infinitely larger yet.

The Distribution of the Drink Bill.—What becomes of the billion seven hundred million dollars annually spent directly for intoxicating drinks? There must be entries on the other side of the ledger; what are they, and what do they indicate?

This immense amount of money paid out by the consumer is distributed into four chief channels: (1) to the producer of the materials used in the making of liquors; (2) to wage-earners employed by the traffic in manufacture and sale; (3) to the traffic itself as profits, salaries of dealers, manufacturers, salesmen, saloon-keepers, and others definitely responsible for the management, and for incidental expenses of the trade; (4) the share for the government, such as special taxes, internal revenue, license fees and fines. This is a very large share, peculiar to liquor and a very few other industries. Its assessment is an implication that this traffic is, in some far-reaching way, abnormal or unusual among great industries.

(1) The Share for Materials.—The first part of the money coming from the drink bill, a very small part, goes to the farmer and other producers of materials used in the making of liquors. According to the last census, $139,199,000 was paid by liquor manufacturers for materials, almost entirely farm, garden, and orchard products.[1] By far the largest part was for the three staple grains, barley, corn, rye, used most extensively in making beer and whisky. All other agricultural products used in comparison with these were very small in amount. The extent of the wine industry is small in comparison with that of malt and distilled liquors. Of corn, now the chief source of distilled spirits, the traffic purchased of the farmer 23,000,000 bushels, or 1.1 per cent of the crop raised; of rye it used 5,600,000 bushels, or 10 per cent of the crop; of barley, supposed to be raised almost entirely for the making of malt and beer, the traffic used but 44.2 per cent, all the rest going for other purposes. In addition, the brewers and distillers took of the farmer .003 per cent of the wheat crop, and .0001 per cent of the oats raised. Hops, a small agricultural industry, turns over its yield almost entirely to the making of beer. Small amounts of many kinds of fruits, including waste materials from canning factories, and "molasses" and waste materials from sugar factories, are used for making wines, brandies, and other liquors. The proportionate amount of waste from sugar and canning factories, and of inferior grades of fruit is increasing, while that of good fruits employed is decreasing.

The whole industry, which stands as one of the greatest of the nation when capital invested is considered, and which uses as its raw material the farmer's output almost exclusively, furnished a market for only 2 per cent of the grains, or 2.5 per cent of all farm crops in the last census year.* Relatively small as this seems, it would be a very appreciable source of wealth to the farmer and fruit raiser, if it were not for other and far more powerful counteracting influences by the liquor traffic against the farmer.

The most important of these is that the sale of liquors seriously cripples the purchasing power of the consumer, upon whom finally the farmer must depend for the market for all his produce. The use of alcohol inter- feres with and reduces the demand for many other articles. It weakens energy and ambition—great sources of advancing demands. It lowers the standard of liv- ing, making the consumer willing to get along with less—or, by reducing his earning efficiency, *compels him and his family to get along with less*. Alcohol, by insisting on the satisfaction of its own demand, crowds out or deadens a healthy demand for more food, greater varieties of food, clothing, and home comforts; from this deadened market no one suffers more than the farmer. This fact is far-reaching and may be shown by this simple example: It takes much more of the farm- er's produce to furnish $1.00 worth of food or clothing than it does to produce $1.00 worth of beer.

What would be the effect upon the farmer if the money now spent for liquor should be used for other purposes? Would he lose the $139,000,000 now paid him annually by the brewers and distillers? These are practical questions that demand concrete answer.

First, as shown above, the purchasing power of the consumer would be greatly strengthened; the number of his wants would increase. The increase in the number and intensity of healthful wants is the one greatest source of increased prosperity.

Second, the money spent by the consumer would go in larger measure to the producer of materials, of which the farmer is chief, than it now does when spent for "booze." The following table, based upon 1910 census reports,[5] gives a decided answer that the money spent for liquor means a loss to the farmer, rather than an income. It shows that where, as now, the producer of materials receives $23.49 out of every dollar spent for liquors, he would receive $58.73 if the same money was spent for a variety of needed articles, including food, clothing, furniture, and woolen goods. Figures are based on manufacturers' prices:

$100 Spent by Consumer

For Boots and Shoes, gives producer of materials.$62.93
For Clothing, Men's, gives producer of materials. 52.37
For Cotton Goods, gives producer of materials... 59.04
For Furniture, gives producer of materials...... 45.34
For Bread, gives producer of materials.......... 59.97
For Woolen Goods, gives producer of materials.. 64.86
For *average all industries,* gives producer of
    materials 58.73
For *Liquors,* gives producer of materials....... 23.49

The money which goes for liquor, creating a market worth $23.49 for the farmer, would, if spent for bread, call for $59.97 worth of his produce; if for woolen goods, $64.86 of what he alone produces; if for cotton goods, which he furnishes almost exclusively, it would demand $59.00 worth instead of less than one-half which he now receives. If spent for an average of all products, as it certainly would be spent, it would yield the farmer and other producers of raw materials $58.73, or two and one-half times as much. Clearly the using up of farm material by making it into liquors means a direct loss in market value to the farmer, to say nothing of the injury to health, morals and happiness that it causes—all, forces which make people able to purchase more than when these are dulled by drink.

"Those farmers," says Richard T. Ely, "who think the liquor traffic creates a demand for their commodities, and those brewers and distillers who endeavor to instill this belief, are both deceived and deceivers."

A man who drinks two glasses of beer per day for a year spends $36.50; to make it requires three and three-fourths bushels of barley worth fifty cents per bushel. This amount of money, $36.50, spent for butter, cheese, meat and woolen goods, so often needed in the drinker's family, would have raised prices for the farmer, made trade brisk for all other retail dealers except the saloon-keeper, would have left the ex-beer drinker in better health, so he could have more regular and better work, and would have left something in the home after the wages had been spent.

From a bushel of corn the distiller gets four gallons of whisky which retails at $16.80. It is divided up as follows, the actual producers of wealth, the farmer and the laborer, getting very meager shares indeed.

The farmer gets...............................$ .45
The United States Government gets............. 4.40
The railroad company gets.....................   .80
The distiller gets............................ 3.83
The laborer's share is........................   .17
The drayman gets..............................   .15
The retailer and his employees get............ 7.00

Total $16.80

(2) The Share to Wage-Earners.—The second item in the distribution of the drink income, in some measure a return to society, for the heavy burden of the drink bill, is the part that goes to labor, to the men engaged by the liquor traffic, but who have no voice in the management of the business end. Because of the interconnection of trades it is easy to grossly exaggerate the relative importance of the employment furnished wage-earners, as the publicity agents of the liquor interests are in the habit of doing, or to minimize it, as unthinking opponents of the traffic at times may have done. The exact amount of this share of the drink bill cannot be determined, but its meaning may be known by a study of such facts as cannot be disputed.

There are employed annually about 63,000 men as wage earners, not counting salaried officials or employees, in the manufacture of liquors, malt, distilled, and vinous. The exact number in the latest census report being 62,-920, or nine-tenths of one per cent of those classed as wage earners thruout the country. They were paid $45,252,000 in wages. As an employer of labor the brewing industry stood twenty-fifth in rank, and the distilling forty-third among the manufacturing industries of the nation.[5]

The number of men that find employment in these industries seems large but, when compared with other industries with similar capital investment and general size in the business world, it is found to be remarkably small. The liquor traffic does not use its share of labor, in proportion to capital invested or the worth of the product turned out, by any means. It stands far below the average, in this respect. Someone else, not the workman, gets the profits—the investor, the big capitalist, the high-salaried manager, the politician, the government—but not, in due proportion, the wage-earner.

For example, in 1910 the capital invested in the manufacture of malt, distilled, and vinous liquors was $771,-516,000.[5] This gave to labor an average of 5.8 per cent for its share in the work of production. On the same basis the leather products industries paid in wages 23.5 per cent; paper and printing paid 21.3 per cent; lumber and its products, 27 per cent; iron and steel, 17.6 per cent; textiles and finished products, 23.9 per cent. The materials used in manufacture are unusually low in their percentage of cost, so that an unusually large share is left for profits, high salaries and revenue to the government. Looking back for a period of ten years it is found that the number of wage earners employed, in proportion to capital, is steadily decreasing—that the workingman's share is diminishing year by year.

Take it from another viewpoint. The distillery and brewery purchase raw materials from the farm at market prices, using a large amount of inferior grain. From these they get a product that sells from the factory at an immensely increased price. The value of this product is an excellent basis of comparison, for it is more nearly related to the cost to the public—to what the laboring man gets out of the amount spent by the public in proportion to what he would get out of a similar amount spent for other and more healthful articles. Here liquor again shows up to very great disadvantage. Only 1.5 per cent of the value of distilled liquors, and 11 per cent of malt liquors, or an average of 7.6 per cent of all, goes to wages. In marked contrast are the figures from other prominent industries as follows: Boots and shoes, 19 per cent; clothing, 18 per cent; cotton goods, 21 per cent; furniture, 27 per cent; bread and bakery products, 14.95 per cent; an average of all industries pays for labor 16.57 per cent of the value of the product, while the liquor industries fall below one-half of this rate.

What would be the effect upon the men employed by the distillers and brewers should the money now being paid them as wages come to them thru wages in other industries more vital to human need? What would happen to this 63,000 men should this traffic go out of business? The following table [5] gives very definite answer.

$100 Spent by Consumer

For Boots and Shoes, gives wage earner in manu-
facturing $19.20
For Clothing, men's......................... 18.78
For Cotton Goods............................ 21.14
For Furniture 27.35
For Iron, Steel, etc........................ 13.98
For Bread and bakery products............... 14.95
For Electrical Machines..................... 22.31
For Woolen Goods............................ 16.61
For *All Industries—Average*................ *16.57*
For *Liquor* *7.63*

This table shows the amounts that wage earners receive out of $100 spent, at manufacturers' prices, for each of the eight specified products. Where liquor pays $7.63 to labor, an average of all the manufacturing industries of the nation pays more than twice as much,—$16.57; or would employ more than twice as many men. If the money spent for liquor should go for woolen clothing, bread, iron and steel articles for the home or house building, the share that labor would receive would be twice as much; if for cotton clothing, boots and shoes, and electrical equipment for the home, the working man who helps to make these articles would get three times as much; if the liquor money went for furniture, where the pinch of poverty comes hard in the family of the drinking man, workmen would receive a yet greater return, or nearly four times as much as does the workman in the distillery and brewery.[5] In a word, the money spent for liquor, if spent for other manufactured articles, would create a demand for them two to three times as many wage earners merely in manufacture alone.

Charles Stelzle shows that should the money spent for intoxicants at retail be used entirely for clothing and food, where the pinch of need is hard and most destructive, "it would give employment to nearly eight times as many workers who would collectively receive five and one-half times as much wages, or nearly $200,-000,000 more, and that the cost of raw material would be over $600,000,000 more than the liquor industry now uses." Further, that the clothing and food industries, now employing 493,000 for manufacturing purposes, would require at least one-third more men, or 164,000. This would transfer the whole 63,000 now used in liquor manufacture into clothing and food manufacture, and leave an unfilled demand for 101,000 more such employees.[6]

From the above table it will be further evident that, while more than 75 per cent of the value of all manufactured articles in the United States is returned to the producer of materials and to the wage earner, the share which liquor gives to these two factors together is less than one-third of the value of the product. Should the money spent for liquor go to boots and shoes, clothing, furniture, bread, and a wide share of other articles, it would return in wages from two to three times as much, and would create, thereby, a demand for two to three times as much labor. At the same time it would more than double the demand for materials for the factories, for the products of the farm, ranch, forest, and mine, and increase the call for men in all the industries that supply these demands.

The following table taken from official sources[5] merely proves from another viewpoint the conclusions made above. Here is shown what $1,000,000 capital invested in liquor will do in the way of employing men as compared with the same amount invested in other great industries.

Comparative Employment of Wage Earners

Industry.	Total wage earner.	Wage earners per $1,000,000 capital.
Textiles, all branches...........	881,128	478
Iron and steel, seven branches...	309,201	195
Lumber and Timber products....	695,019	591
Leather Goods, Boots and Shoes..	295,406	472
Paper and Printing............	334,412	335
Average—above industries		414
Liquors, all kinds................	*62,920*	*81*

In proportion to capital invested an average of the above industries employs 500 per cent more men than do the liquor industries. Liquor is far from being a friend to labor.

(3) The Share to the Trade.—The part of the $1,700,-000,000 that is retained by the liquor traffic itself is doubtless the largest of all the four parts into which it is distributed. The total of this share cannot be known. It includes returns on capital invested, profits, salaries of dealers, manufacturers, wholesalers, retailers, commercial and advertising agents, and all other salaried employees more or less closely interested in the traffic and its policies. To this also may be added the cost of creating and extending the demand for intoxication, money paid legitimately and illegitimately for "protection" from political and governmental interference, and "defense funds" set aside in all branches of the industry against public opinion. Such items of expense in the case of liquor are always large and much greater than those of other industries not so mixed up in politics.

The principles illustrated in the manufacturing end of the industry, that money spent for liquor calls for fewer men and less material than when employed in more healthful industries, applies even to a greater degree in the distribution end. The great army of liquor dealers, office employees, traveling salesmen, bar-keepers, saloon-keepers, and others less directly connected with the traffic, would all be required—the whole distributing and selling force from top to bottom—to sell whatever manufactured articles are bought by the public in place of liquors. It is all a matter of consumption —of capacity for consumption which is never limited, except by lack of money or such blighting and disease-producing habits as alcoholic narcotization. It is not a matter of distribution. The whole liquor distributing machine could be handed over, used to supply the other needs, and yet the call for salesmen would be greater. It takes many more men to sell $1,700,000,000 worth of clothing, food, etc., than to sell $1,700,000,000 worth of liquor. "Men will go for beer, but milk must be brought to them." "This is one of the principle reasons why the item of wages is so much larger in the bread and clothing business." "If the money now spent for liquor should be spent for bread and clothing, not only would all the salesmen, saloon-keepers and bartenders find work in legitimate business enterprises, but the men who make glass bottles, furniture, harness, delivery wagons, and every other thing used in connection with the liquor business would be more steadily employed, for there would be a still greater demand for their products." [6]

"One of the pathetic arguments used by the bakery workers in favor of the saloon," says Stelzle, "is that as the saloon serves 'free lunch' it would prove disastrous to all bakers were the saloon to be closed. As if this were the only way of disposing of an equal amount of bread!"

Human need for manufactured articles for personal and home comfort, for clothing, house-furnishings, home-building, for recreations and amusements, from the barest necessities up to pianos and automobiles, has never been known to reach a limit. To assume that money saved from beer would not be so used is to assume that it would be destroyed, or thrown away, or hoarded, contrary to human nature.

"If a brewery is closed down, in its place springs up a factory. *If a saloon is closed, in its place comes a store.* It is simply a process well known to union men, the same process as follows the introduction of machinery," says John Mitchell, Vice President of the American Federation of Labor.[7] The retail sellers and their employees, the traveling salesmen, the clerical force in the big breweries, distilleries and wholesale establishments,—as well as the machinists, engineers, chemists, wagon drivers, would all be required, in increased numbers, in any new adjustment that would eliminate liquor as a commodity of commerce. And capital, too, would find a similar field in supplying the new demand for healthful commodities that necessarily would take the place of alcoholic liquors.

(4) **The Share to the Government.**—This fourth share in the division of the liquor bill is a very peculiar one. Among other great industries there is nothing to correspond with it. No other business pays so large a share of its income to the government or boasts so much of its "contribution." That the government should ask for and receive so large a share, and that it should be paid with such little protest, implies that there is some far-reaching reason in public affairs why this condition should exist.

The federal government receives from this one source 31 per cent of its entire ordinary income. In 1912 there was paid into the national treasury from internal revenue taxes on liquor and dealers and from duties on imported liquors $236,827,520.[8] The tax rates are as follows: malt liquors, $1.00 per barrel; distilled, $1.10 per gallon; wholesalers, $100 per year; rectifiers, $100 to $200 per year; retailers, $25 per year. except those who sell only malt liquors, for which it is $20. Retailers include druggists, as well as regular saloon-keepers; also illegal dealers seeking to evade license or prohibition laws. There has been a steady increase in revenue from this source since it was established in 1862.

On the basis of the twelfth census reports[9] estimated down to 1912 the income of states, cities, and counties from the liquor traffic, in the form of license fees and its equivalent, was something like $82,600,000. This makes the traffic, in such states, cities, and counties as have saloons, an important source of local revenue. Tho there has been a steady reduction in the number of saloons for several years, the total of license money collected has been increasing; the tendency of city councils and state legislatures is to raise the fees as sentiment against the saloon increases.

Combining the national liquor revenue, $236,800,000, with the $82,600,000 coming to local and state treasuries, it will be found that the total government income from the traffic, $319,400,000, is to the drink bill, $1,700,000,-000 as 1 to 5; that is, that of every $5.00 paid for drinks at the saloon, $1.00 goes to the support of the government. This is almost equivalent to a direct tax upon the drinker. Aside from the few well-to-do who spend money for drink, it is, in very large part, a tax upon the man with little or no property, and low wages, the class that can least bear it. The heavier the drinker the heavier the tax. The more abnormal and gripping the liquor "crave" the higher the per cent of meager earnings that the sheltering power of government receives. Intended as a tax upon luxury it has become, in fact, a tax upon a vice. Best authorities say a vice is a source from which tax should never be accepted.

The Consequential Cost.—The injury to human economic efficiency is by far the greatest and most vital loss that in any degree can be traced to the use of alcohol or the liquor traffic. In return for the first cost, the loss of material and time in production used by the liquor traffic, there is some return to society in wages, payment for material, support of the government, profits to the traffic itself, and social pleasure. It might be conceded that this is some just return to society for the $1,700,000,000 drink bill paid by the consumer, tho such a balancing of the account gives far more credit to the liquor institution than the facts will warrant.

But for the second series of losses there is absolutely no return. There is a great group of financial burdens cast upon society by lowered efficiency, shortening of life, and care for depleted humanity that must be charged to the liquor custom and traffic. It is a dead loss, giving no "value received" whatever. The second series of individual and social losses results from the consumption of liquor; the first occurs in connection with the production.

The direct social welfare burden is about as follows:

(1) Loss of time and efficiency.

(2) Loss of life.

(3) Deterioration of producing capacity; relation to poverty.

(4) Expense in care and support of the dependent and criminal product.

(1) Loss of Efficiency.—The muscular energy, nerve force, and mental control of millions of so-called moderate drinkers is seriously lowered by their regular use of intoxicants. Numerous scientific tests show that the loss in muscular efficiency is from 8 to 10 per cent. Aschaffenburg proved that in type-setting there is a loss in efficiency of 9 per cent when even so small an amount of alcohol as is contained in from two to three glasses of beer per day is taken.[10] In work requiring greater mental exertion the loss is usually higher; the judgment is impaired, the memory defective, and the will weakened. The irregularity and loss of time among drinking men, employers and employees, is an item of vast and unknown extent. It has been estimated by Prof. Hopkins at 10 per cent of the time of a million men, or the equivalent of full time for 100,000.[11] At $600 per year wages or salary, an extremely low wage scale, the time loss alone foots up to $60,000,000. There are also several million hard drinkers who lose practically full time. Phelps shows that from 7 per cent to 43 per cent of all accidents are due to the use of alcohol[12] All of this means loss of time and wages, temporary or permanent, to a great extent.

This loss of efficiency and time is a concrete waste of immense proportions. It is being taken into account more each year by employers of labor, and it is becoming increasingly hard for regular drinkers to obtain employment. The number of industries discriminating against intemperate applicants is steadily growing at the imperative demands of the ledger. Years ago the United States Department of Labor[13] reported that 96 per cent of railroads, 79 per cent of manufacturers, 88 per cent of trades, 72 per cent of agriculturalists, and 77 per cent of all establishments investigated, discriminated against applicants for work who use liquors, and many of them refused to employ drinkers at all.

(2) The Number of Lives Sacrificed yearly to Bacchus cannot be given positively. The most scientific estimate is that of Phelps,[14] made for life insurance purposes; he gives 66,000 yearly in the United States as owing their death to easily traced influence of drink. This is one out of every thirteen deaths of adults, or 7.7 per cent. Add those due to the social consequences of alcohol and the saloon and 100,000 lives per year is not too large for a safe estimate. The loss in any event is immense, costly, and *useless*.

The cost of a man to society at twenty-one years of age, if fairly well educated, has been set at $2,000.[15] The value of such an investment, economically, is determined by the ability of each young man to add to the wealth of society. If that is but $300 per year, or $1.00 per day, he is worth $5,000, the interest on which will amount to his yearly earnings.

A man with an earning capacity of $600 is worth $10,000; one who earns $1,200 is worth $20,000. The 100,000 who lose their lives thru drink each year are worth, at the very minimum, $10,000 each to the community and to themselves before drink begins its depreciating work in their lives—a loss of $1,000,000,000. To injure or destroy the wealth-producing capacity of a nation to such a degree as this, especially at a time when people are crying out for more wealth with which to meet "the high cost of living" is a crime against the economic need of that nation.

But the death of a drunkard is a social benefit, rather than a loss. Adding this negative "value" to his positive value as a producing citizen, as we must, how great then must have been the actual loss to society when, thru drink, he became not merely a non-producer, but also an actual burden upon the earnings of others?

The social fact is that the impairment of a man is the destruction of wealth. No man or trade has a right to destroy the economic worth of a community merely to gratify a questionable social custom or gain his own livelihood in a certain way.

The average of life is a little under forty years. The drinking man dies younger than the average. Whether this shortening is one, three, five or ten years. it has special meaning to the prosperity of the nation, because

practically all liquor deaths are at or near the prime
of life. They occur at the age when experience has
been added to training and when maximum earnings are
to be expected. Each year of service at this age means
more to the community than at any other period.

The facts of the English life insurance companies,
which for years have given special attention to this point,
are very telling. The Scepter Life Association reported
in 1911 that in its general section the mortality rate was
77 per cent of the expected deaths; in its total abstinence section it was 51 per cent of the expected. For
twenty-eight years the percentage of actual to expected
deaths has been, in the general section, 79.7 per cent;
in the temperance section 52.45 per cent. The social
status of the policy holders and their occupations are
the same in both classes. It is noted that as time goes
on there will be a more and more marked difference in
the longevity of drinkers and abstainers. The sons of
abstainers will fare better than their fathers, many of
whom were the children of drinkers, inheriting lessened
vitality. In other words, the increased vitality of the
children of the third and fourth generation will show
itself in yet longer life, other conditions being equal.

The same story comes from the records of The United
Kingdom Temperance and General Provident Institution
of London. Its records extend back for sixty years and
embrace all classes of people that are usually accepted
as insurance risks. During a period of forty years the
percentage of actual to expected deaths in the temperance section was 71.52; in the general section, including
both moderate drinkers and non-drinkers, 94 per cent
of the expected deaths actually occurred.[16] This tremendous difference in favor of the abstainers would have

been much greater had all in the general section been users of intoxicants. The difference is especially marked in the active working years between the ages of 25 and 60 years. This total abstinence section was founded at a time when people who refrained were thought to be dangerous risks since they were so very exceptional.

William Farr, in Vital Statistics, an authority on the subject, shows that the saloon-keeper has the most unhealthful of all trades. There may be minor branches of work of extraordinary character, such as file making or deep-sea diving, which are more destructive of life, but as a regular trade employing vast numbers of men, that of liquor selling stands lowest. Of 1,000 each of the following classes, there died within a fixed length of time: farmers, 363; grocers, 383; laborers, 442, and saloon-keepers and their assistants, 605. Oliver, in his Dangerous Trades,[17] calls them "notoriously a short-lived class." Long days without open-air exercise, in an atmosphere reeking with the "odor of spirits, tobacco smoke, and emanations from men who lounge at the bar; and this, coupled with the numerous temptations to drink, and his irregular meals, sooner or later, induces structural alterations in the liver, lungs, and heart, that bring life to a premature close."

(3) **Relation of Liquor to Poverty.** — Intemperance has long been regarded as a chief cause of poverty and pauperism. The poverty of the drunkard, the money lost in the saloon's till, and the immediate consequence upon the family have been so obtrusive that but one conclusion seemed possible. Drink took the money— drink is the cause.

But deeper study indicates that back of the drinker's poverty are often sad stories of deficiency, inherited weakness, sickness, and bad homes. All of these are causes, direct or remote, in the same class with drink. But all of them are aggravated—and in the past may have been caused, largely by alcohol and the social life of the saloon. Liquor is ever a fearful, complicating cause of poverty, disease, and misery, tho its direct percentage may not easily be figured out from the force of a half-dozen causes operating together. Intemperance and poverty are mutually cause and effect; men take to drink to drown sorrow and suffering and monotony, or to gain a temporary respite from a poverty that may have been life-long. On the other hand, the persistent demand for drink, when the peculiar alcohol habit has once been created, has an economic force of its own; one that demands gratification at the expense of earning efficiency, of use of wages for home needs or comforts, of family, personal respect, clothing, even food, as time goes on. The old-fashioned "temperance" tales of the drunkard's hovel and the baby's shoes sold for drink may be harrowing, and unwise as arguments in the present stage of progress, but there lies back of them the hard economic fact that, for certain classes of drinkers the insistency of the craving does crowd out and make impossible the satisfaction of real human wants. Even when drink is a result, rather than cause of poverty and misery, it is an aggravating cause of further deterioration in the family or community—the living conditions, lack of ambition, carelessness, neglect of children, loss of moral ideals, due to it, are in turn cause of inefficiency, crime, and poverty in children. At best it is a vicious circle of action and reaction; drink is one active first cause of poverty; poverty finds relief in drink. Stop the drink and one source will be removed; remove all poverty and intemperance will yet flourish, since there is more drinking during a period of prosperity than during hard times.

Much of the suffering and other poverty coming from drink may better be charged to the false belief that alcohol relieves fatigue, depression, and unhappiness, or that it takes the place of food. Back of these stand personal ignorance; but these social delusions are kept alive, not only by lack of education, but also by the positive mis-education of those whose financial interests are involved.

In New York City 60 per cent of 18,606 cases relieved at one of the municipal lodging houses was charged to drink. The Committee of Fifty has made one of the most careful and extensive investigations; it gives drink as producing 25 per cent of poverty, 37 per cent of the pauperism within almshouses, and 45 per cent of the destitution of children as due directly to the personal use of liquors or to their use by someone else. But the committee is very conservative, not attributing any case to drink "unless it was obviously the principle and determining cause."[18]   Prof. A. G. Warner attributes 28.1 per cent as due to it directly and as a contributory cause. In London Charles Booth found 25 per cent out of 1,447 cases chargeable to drink.[19]   The Massachusetts Bureau of Statistics investigations are very reliable and cover a large number of cases and conditions fairly average in America; this report shows 39.44 per cent of poverty due to personal use of alcoholics and 5 per cent more to its use by others, a total of 44.44 per cent.[20]

In Kansas, in marked contrast with saloon states, thirty years of prohibition have almost done away with poverty. The poor farms of fifty counties, having no inmates, have been turned into branch agricultural experiment stations and are called "prosperity farms." [21]

But it is not among paupers that alcohol gets in its worst work. A vast host of people, just on the verge of becoming dependents, who support themselves but never lay aside a cent for the future, were brought there and are held there because of the margin of wages that goes to the saloon. They might have been financially successful and even been able to buy a little home if it were not for the excessive drink burden they bear. "The ravages of intemperance are most plainly to be traced in classes distinctly above the pauper class. It is among artisans and those capable of earning good wages that the most energy is spent for alcohol and the most vitality burned out.[22] Booth well summarizes the needless share that drink had in poverty as follows: "Of drink in all its combinations, adding to every trouble, undermining every effort for good, destroying the home, and cursing the young lives of children, the stories tell enough. It does not stand as apparent chief cause in as many cases as sickness and old age; but if it were not for drink, sickness and old age could be better met." [19]

It is often the earner of good wages that suffers most and who, saving nothing, is ready when overtaken by a slight misfortune or sickness, to drop below. This burden on the individual, on the family, and on society must certainly be greater than the more direct one caused by actual poverty and pauperism. Being paid thru the ordinary channels of business, in reduced earning and consuming capacity, it is not noticed as are the more direct burdens paid thru taxation and philanthropy.

Just exactly how much poverty drink causes need not

and cannot be stated in figures. Poverty and alcoholism are partly results of depleted stock and bad social conditions. But if so, the burden of responsibility shifts heavier than ever to the community and the state. If men are poor on account of drink it may be largely their own fault; but if because of inherited deficiency and weakness it is nothing less than a social crime to permit deficient stock steadily to alcoholize itself. However complicated the causal connection, the liquor influence in poverty is a very great social burden.

(4) The Burden in Care and Support of that part of the product of the saloon that shows itself in crime, dependency, and defectives—the building, equipping, and maintaining of the necessary storage granaries, such as jails, penitentiaries, asylums, hospitals for the inebriates, epileptics, and other defectives—constitutes a decisive answer to the self-centered plea that "if you let drink alone it will let you alone."

(a) It has long been a social duty to create institutions and homes to care for those who have no means or capacity or friends to do it for them. It is the first crude and most necessary form of government philanthropy. The public expense is borne by taxation on citizens in sympathy with the liquor institution, a source of much of the burden, and those unfriendly to it alike. Then there is the additional expense carried by private, religious, and other philanthropic organizations—all a part of the larger social burden. An estimate of the share that may justly be charged to alcohol has been made by Prof. Collins as follows:

Hospitals, 40 per cent...................$ 4,000,000
Insane Asylums, 35 per cent.............. 5,500,000
Feeble Minded, 45 per cent..............   5,400,000

Alms Houses, 37 per cent.................. 3,200,000
Public Orphan Homes, 46 per cent........ 4,100,000
Outdoor Relief, 30.5 per cent.............. 12,000,000
Private Charity, 30.5 per cent............ 30,500,000

The total actual cost of this portion of the drink product alone is $64,700,000. Besides this there is the immense private burden borne by the families and children of drunkards, amounting to not less than $220,000,000.

The hunting down and prosecution of prisoners is a gigantic task and a proportionate cost. To provide for public safety is the first purpose of government. On the average, at least 50 per cent of crime, large and petty, is due to liquor and its sale. The testimonies of judges, police officials, keepers of penitentiaries, reformatories and bridewells place it at from 60 to 90 per cent, the average being about 75 per cent. It varies with localities and with the character of criminals sent to the respective institutions. The Committee of Fifty puts liquor as "first cause" in 31 per cent of the cases; as "sole cause" in 16 per cent, or a total of 49.95 per cent, as due to liquor in various forms and combinations. The Massachusetts Labor Bureau investigation gets almost an identical result, 50.88 per cent. The actual share so chargeable in our large cities is undoubtedly even larger.

Taking, then, one-half of the cost of police and constables necessary to catch criminals, of courts to try them, of jails and penitentiaries in which to confine them, and of other precautions necessary to guard against crime we have, as cost of crime resulting from drink, a bill of more than $40,000,000 yearly. It is noted that in prohibition states and counties that have been free from saloons for some years, the amount of crime is very decidedly reduced.

126   *Social Welfare and the Liquor Problem*

References and Authorities

The American Drink Bill.

"The Nation's Drink Bill," *American Grocer*, July 4, 1913.

American Prohibition Year Book (1912), 34-37.

Anti-Saloon League Year Book (1913), 17.

Bagnell, *Economic and Moral Aspects of the Liquor Business*, 65-74.

Williams, *Alcohol*, 105-108.

[1] *U. S. Statistical Abstract* (1912).

[2] *American Grocer*, see above.

[3] Ferguson in *The Vindicator*, March 14, 1913.

Distribution: the Farmer and Wage Earner.

Stelzle, *American Social and Religious Conditions* (1912), 71-83.

Ely, *Political Economy*, 156.

Bagnell, *Economic and Moral Aspects of the Liquor Business*, 66-70.

Waldron, "Economics of the Drink Traffic," *Chautauquan*, June, 1908.

Fehlandt, *A Century of Drink Reform*, 207-218.

Hopkins, *Wealth and Waste*, 57-61, 81-97.

Patton, "The Economic Basis of Prohibition," *Annals Am. Academy*, II, 59.

Barker, *The Saloon Problem and Social Reform*, 4-10.

American Prohibition Year Book (1911), 113.

[4] *Reports of 13th Census and Am. Pro. Year Book compilations.*

[5] *Abstract of 13th Census.*

[6] See Stelzle above, 79.

Distribution: the Traffic and the Government.

Fehlandt, *A Century of Drink Reform.*

Hopkins, *Wealth and Waste.*

"Drink and Revenue," *The Vindicator*, May 16, 1913.

American Prohibition Year Book, 1911 and 1912.

[7] See *Am. Pro. Year Book* (1912), 83.

[8] Report, *Commissioner of Internal Revenue* (1912).

[9] Report, *12th Census; Wealth, Debt, and Taxation*, 987.

Consequential Cost: Efficiency, Life.

Kelynack, *The Drink Problem*, 152-160.

Fehlandt, *A Century of Drink Reform*, 214-216.

Barker, *The Saloon Problem and Social Reform*, 12-14, 51-53.

Hopkins, *Wealth and Waste*, 98-105.

Koren, *Economic Aspects of the Liquor Problem*, 229-239.

Whittaker, "Alcoholic Beverages and Longevity," *Contemporary*, March, 1904.

Patton, "The Economic Basis of Prohibition," *Annals Am. Academy*, II, 59.

Stelzle, *The Workingman and Social Problems*, ch. 3.

Am. Prohibition Year Book (1911), 104.

[10] Horsley and Sturge, 72.

[11] Wealth and Waste, 98.

[12] *Mortality of Alcohol.*

[13] *12th Annual Report*, 71.

[14] *Mortality of Alcohol.*

[15] Hopkins, 102.

[16] Kelynack, 153.

[17] Oliver, *Dangerous Trades*, 800.

Consequential Cost: Poverty and Pauperism.

Williams, *Alcohol*, 85-98.

Kelynack, *The Drink Problem*, 199-208.

Koren, *Economic Aspects of the Liquor Problem*, 96-98, 120-125.

Warner, *American Charities*, 60-63.

Committee of Fifty, *The Liquor Problem; Summary*, 89-104, 108-121.

Mass. Comm. on Cost of Living, "Wastage from Drink as a Factor in Increased Cost of Living," *Sci. Temperance Jr.*, Oct., 1912.

American Prohibition Year Book (1911), 104-105.

[18] Koren, 96, 120, 130.

[19] Booth, *Pauperism and the Endowment of Old Age.*

[20] *26th Annual Report of Statistics of Labor*, 507.

[21] *American Prohibition Year Book* (1911), 214.

[22] Warner, 61.

Consequential Cost: Relief and Crime.

Williams, *Alcohol*, 72-84.

Koren, *Economic Aspects of the Liquor Problem.*

Barker, *The Saloon Problem and Social Reform*, 14-16.

Fehlandt, *A Century of Drink Reform*, 214-216.

Hopkins, *Wealth and Waste*, 106-114.

American Prohibition Year Book (1911), 104-105.

If a brewery is closed down, in its place springs up a factory. If a saloon is closed, in its place comes a store. It is simply a process well known to union men, the same process as follows the introduction of machinery.
—JOHN MITCHELL,
Vice President American Federation of Labor.

Because the liquor traffic tends to enslave the people, to make them satisfied with improper conditions, and keeps them ignorant, the leaders of the trades-union movement are called on to fight the saloon.
—TOM L. LEWIS,
President United Mine Workers' Union.

CHAPTER VI

INDUSTRIAL WELFARE AND THE LIQUOR PROBLEM

National Wealth and Social Welfare.—Reasonable financial prosperity is an essential to individual and national welfare. It is one of the chief conditions of success. In importance it may be secondary to health, social enjoyment, intellectual culture, and morality; but as a direct object of endeavor, as a purpose for which men and society exist in this "money age," it stands ahead of any of these. The desire for wealth seems to be the strongest driving force in society today. More than ever before each individual must have a minimum amount to be able to do and be his best. The liquor habit in the individual and the liquor traffic in the nation strike at the very foundation of economic welfare by causing waste of wealth-producing capacity, as well as of wealth itself.

(1) The wealth-producing capacity of the community. Every industry should produce, add to the sum total of the possessions of society, or contribute to the distribution of those possessions. It should take the raw product and make it into something that will be worth more to the consumer than that raw product itself. The liquor factory takes grains and fruits, valuable for food, which, by their consumption would yield work-power and make men capable of producing more, and gives, in turn, an article which has the very opposite effects. Not only is the health-giving value of the food lost when

alcohol is formed, but the wealth creating power of the consumer is reduced in proportion to the frequency and amount he takes. The distillery and brewery waste public wealth instead of adding to it. This traffic causes improper distribution. It takes legitimate wealth out of the hands of the producer, the working man, and puts it into the hands of the brewer, the producer of false wealth. The liquor traffic wastes natural resources; as Professor Patton, of the University of Pennsylvania, shows, "Two temperance people can be supported on the land needed to satisfy the coarse tastes of one regular frequenter of the saloon." [1]

(2) Intelligent and self-respecting labor, both mental and muscular, is an essential to an increase in public wealth. It is labor that produces. The value of its intelligence, reliability and soberness as factors in production cannot be overestimated. The use of liquor injures every one of those qualities of manhood which belong to every wealth-producing citizen. "An economic millennium would be an epoch in which there was no waste . . . above all, no waste of health, substance and self-respect, in drunkenness and its attending vices." The temperate laborer, as well as the intemperate workman, himself, and the general public, must suffer because of drunken labor.

(3) A healthful interrelation of all industries. No one business should thrive at the expense of others, or feed on the evil tendencies or vices of the public as does the liquor traffic. The oversupply of the market and consequent inability to effect sales is a very frequent complaint of manufacturers. There is no such thing as over-supply so long as there is such crying poverty, distress, and need on every hand. There cannot be an

over-supply of boots and shoes while tens of thousands of drinking men and their families go with ragged shoes or none at all. A period of prosperity is a farce to thousands of suffering people. It is a case of under-consumption coupled with improper distribution, largely chargeable to such destructive habits as drink. "From the standpoint of the community," says the economist, Hobson, "nothing else than a rise in the average standard of current consumption can stimulate industry." [2] That business which injures and destroys those who use its product is an obstruction to the prosperity and success of every other business.

(4) The persistency of the demand. The human need of change, variety, excitement, or stimulation, when deadened and deceived by the narcotic influence of alcohol, teaches the user to depend upon this artificial means and makes him believe he must have it whether other needs are satisfied or not. *The intense insistency of the liquor demand is a most important economic factor.* It is called "inelastic"—the demand for it varies but little with price alterations. In this respect it cannot be classed with luxuries, and when the "appetite" is once developed, it even persists against the call for necessities, reducing the amount and quality of food, clothing, and home furnishings. This "narcotic demand" for drink competes with the demand for necessities. Unless purchasers have unlimited wealth, the saloon flourishes at the expense of the grocery, the clothing store, and others which furnish necessities and comforts to the surrounding community.

(5) Drink lowers the standard of living. It makes men, and families and whole communities willing to get along with poorer grades of food, less clothing, and with

far fewer furnishings, books, musical instruments, and other means to recreation and culture in the home. When a drinking man becomes sober he wants more things; he is able to purchase more things; these, in turn, cause him to want yet more. So with the living standard of a whole community.

The Burden on Labor.—Upon no other section of society does the burden of intemperance rest so heavily as it does upon the laboring classes. It is among those who, aside from the farmer, must earn their subsistence by daily and regular physical work, that drink causes the most harm and in the greatest number and variety of ways.

In the prominent industrial and mining states, where the masses of population are centered, almost all of the men engaged in unskilled, and many of those in the more skilled, trades are frequent or constant users of malt liquors. It is this steady average use of beer, extending from very moderate to constant soaking, that makes laboring people the greatest of all sufferers from drink. Some men in factory, shop, and mine would vote to banish the saloon, if given an opportunity. But while it remains they are its constant patrons. Without property to fall back upon in case of sickness, accident, or loss of work, dependent for daily living upon steady employment, this constant narcotizing of the mental faculties prevents advancement, leads to accidents, causes unsteadiness in work, and opens the way for attack by tuberculosis, pneumonia and other acute diseases to which the drinker is peculiarly liable. The steady expense makes it impossible to save; when work is stopped suffering quickly follows. Liquor is the wage earner's heaviest handicap in his noble struggle for advancement and an important complicating source of his industrial dependence.

"The average workingman," says John Mitchell, Vice President of the American Federation of Labor, "does not yet earn enough to give his family all the comforts they deserve. He has no money to spend on drink without robbing his family."[3]

The English labor leader, John Burns, in a lecture at Manchester, October 31, 1904, said: "There is no class in ancient, nor any section of modern, society, in which the evil of drink or the scourge of drunkenness has so mischievously impressed its destructive effects and sterilizing influences as on the class who can least resist it—the industrious poor, the working classes, on whom the lot of manual labor falls."

The burdens of sickness and reduced mental and physical vitality are distributed almost evenly among all classes that use liquor. The social burdens of crime, poverty and degeneracy, are borne by the whole community, rich and poor, those who indulge and those who do not, alike. But the weight of the individual or family drink bill, with the money that it takes and the income that it prevents, falls first and always upon the laboring man and those dependent upon him. He must share with other citizens the public expense while carrying as his own burden the heaviest of them all. If alcohol were simply a harmless luxury, it would not be so bad. It would be merely a loss without adequate return.

But the workingman's liquor bill is not mere useless luxury. The waste of the money spent directly is the smaller loss. The greater is the direct injury to efficiency. His ability to work is his only resource. It is the only commodity he has for sale. Alcohol slowly or more swiftly lowers his value in the labor market; it unsteadies his nerves, makes his brain unreliable, his muscles weak, and slowly reduces him in the scale of producing capacity. Thus the loss of the money spent on liquor, reacts to cause a second and more serious loss —his own personal economic value to himself, to his employer and to the community.

It is the better classes of labor that must suffer most in this respect simply because they have the better qualifications and therefore the most to lose. ''The ravages of intemperance are most plainly to be traced in classes distinctly above the pauper class. It is among artisans and those capable of earning good wages that the most energy is spent for alcohol and the most vitality burned out by it.''

A third way in which liquor increases the burden of the wage-earner is by forcing cheap labor into the labor market. The scaling down of family necessities on account of the father's drink bill too frequently compels the mother, or children, or both to help earn the living. Driven by the cry for bread, such laborers are willing to work for any price. Wherever there is a heavy drinking community, there will be a plentiful supply of this pathetic sort of labor. Wages are reduced in response to this sort of competition, men are sometimes thrown out of employment, and the temperate workman and his family, innocent of any personal cause in the matter, share in the general consequences.

A false idea of sociability has developed the treating custom. On the night after payday many a man spends far more for drink, to be a ''good fellow'' with the boys, than he would for himself alone, and so adds to his own excessive drinking as well as to his expense. This custom is common to nearly all drinking classes, but it has an important bearing to the laboring man, since his liquor bill takes already so large and steady a part of his income.

Wages and the Standard of Living.—Intemperance is a secondary but very vital factor in that most discussed of all economic problems of the day, the wage question.

The wage standard in general is determined by such economic forces as the supply of labor, its degree of organization or capacity to co-operate, and the standard of living among the competing workers. The general use of intoxicating liquors seriously interferes with the operation of all these laws, and, without variation, to the disadvantage of the working man. Its bearing, often overlooked, is exceedingly vital, and especially critical in the present struggle of wage earners for a larger share in the general returns of production. It touches and demoralizes the labor market at the following points:

(1) The efficiency of labor as a producer in adding to the general wealth of the community, and in winning for itself its legitimate share of the profits of production.

(2) The number and insistency of the competing unemployed. This is an acute factor in fixing the wage scale at any particular time.

(3) The standard of living and the consequent demand for new production and labor.

That drink reduces earning capacity among the more highly skilled and responsible classes of labor, where keen perception, quick judgment and technical skill are required, is too evident to need discussion. Certain trades are more and more requiring total abstinence. A generation ago railroad employees were among the heavy drinking classes. At the present time such men, better paid than formerly, are total abstainers while on duty, and very moderate drinkers, if not abstainers, while off duty. It has been proven by a very careful experiment that in typesetting, the use of one ounce of alcohol, the amount contained in about three glasses of beer, even when taken only on alternate days, leaving one day for the effect to pass off, reduces working ability 9 per cent.[5] Drinking men always experience greater difficulty in getting the usual amount of work done on Monday following the heavier drinking on Saturday night and Sunday.

Thus drink acts as a rough means of classifying labor according to efficiency. And this is a fundamental fact in the fixing of wages where competition exists.

This sifting process among the various grades, from the highly skilled to the most desultory of day workmen, leaves the upper classes with fewer competitors and adds to the second and lower grades. So on to the purely muscular work where brain action, judgment, and care are superseded by mere brute strength. Here the already overcrowded labor market becomes glutted by the constant addition to it of those sent down from above— men driven by the necessity of a bare existence and the craving of an abnormal appetite who are willing to work for the lowest of wages.

Temporarily, the temperate skilled may profit by this reduction in their ranks thru intemperance or any similar vice that takes off the edge of skill. They gain the advantage of a sort of monopoly. This is true so long as competition is the only operating force. But other powerful factors enter. The lowest classes are degraded by this influx of liquor-benumbed labor. They are compelled to adopt the lowest possible standard of living, and consumption, the prime source of production, and so of the demand for labor, reacts finally upon all laboring classes.

It is a primary economic fact that ministering to present wants creates new ones. The man who buys a home immediately needs a great variety of articles with which to furnish it. In a poor family free from such self-destroying vices as drink, a new want created by a cheap musical instrument gives successive calls for more music, for the services of a teacher and finally for a piano, in the manufacture and transportation of which a very large share of labor, skilled and unskilled, is required. Gratified desire creates in multiplied form new wants; leave desire unsatisfied and it dies down to the most servile standard of subsistence. Here overbearing capital steps in, takes advantage of the oversupply of this cheap, unprotesting class, and all labor is robbed of its rightful share in the fruits of production.

The desire for alcohol tends to create a further demand for itself. In its manufacture fewer laborers are required than in the production of any of the ordinary necessities, conveniences, or even luxuries, of everyday average living.[6] Money spent for liquor does less, therefore, in creating a demand for new labor than when spent for any one of a thousand legitimate needs. The use of intoxicants, instead of producing new wants, merely monopolizes more healthful ones; slowly but surely it drives out of existence many of the normal demands of home life. The greater the gratification of a normal demand the greater other industries are benefited. The more the liquor demand is satisfied the more other industries suffer. The higher the per cent that goes to the capitalist—the brewer and distiller—and to the government, and the less other wants of the drinker's family are satisfied. The standard of living sinks lower until even drink itself can scarcely be purchased.

The drunkard cheapens the labor market in the same way that the dealer who sells books below cost cheapens and demoralizes the book market. The drunkard is ready to sell, not only his own labor, but that of his wife and children, at less than the real market value.

"Who can deny," says John B. Lennon, of the American Federation of Labor, "that the liquor traffic is driving women to work in factories, in workshops, and at washtubs who ought not to be there? The trades-union movement is opposed to child labor, yet who can deny that the liquor traffic is driving into industrial life boys and girls who should be in the schools or on the playground?" [7]

The place where drink hurts labor most is where it cuts down the standard of living in the family and prevents the enjoyment of an all-round normal life. The great army of consumers in this country are the producers themselves, not the extravagant rich. Therefore, anything that lowers, or keeps down their ability to buy, or blights hope and courage, injures production and wages more than any other force can possibly do. The radical defect is not over-production but under consumption and uneven distribution. Liquor blights consumption, as above shown, and is one powerful factor in enabling the wealthy to retain so unjust a share of the wealth produced by the joint operation of labor and capital.

"It is the man with many wants, not luxurious fancies, but real legitimate wants, who works hard to satisfy his aspirations." [8]

The economic value of moral qualities, sobriety, thrift, strength of purpose, etc., is to create a whole new series of wants and to give the mental strength and power of co-operation necessary to see that these wants are gratified. To deny this would be to say that the lowest laboring classes are hopeless. It is said that abstinence from liquors would make the workingman willing to labor for as much less per day as is the price of his beer,—that the capitalist alone would get the profits from his abstinence. But this view assumes that moral qualities have no economic value to their possessor—that a temperate man is no more able to assert himself, to unite with other workmen in protracted efforts against aggressive capital,—that he is less a man than the deep drinker. All science and experience deny such an assumption and prove the opposite. A man who has ''sworn off'' does not work for less than before. As a result of his increased self-respect (a) his standard of living is raised and he will not work for as little as before; (b) his soberness makes him able to enforce, to a larger degree, his demands; (c) his wife and children, needed in the home and at school, have a better chance of being withdrawn from the overcrowded ranks of the unemployed.

The Struggle Between Capital and Labor.—Labor is demanding more and more strenuously every day a larger share in the value it has done so much to create, higher wages, shorter hours and better treatment,— demands in themselves most just and reasonable. Entering into this struggle, intensifying its differences and hindering solution, is this intruding factor, the drink habit. Liquor may not be classed among the causes, but it is an active factor in keeping the dispute open, and one of the fundamental reasons why labor is so hampered in its efforts to defend itself or gain its full rights.

The wealthy man may be able to carry the weight of excessive alcoholic indulgence and suffer little financially on account of it. He has money to pay for it; his family need not suffer and his position in the community may be maintained by the use of money. Not so with the poor man. *The drink burden strikes his welfare at more vital places.* Indeed, liquor seems to be an ally to the oppressor of labor.

An investigator of the early sources of the liquor problem, Dr. Lees, of London, cites manuscripts of the Elizabethan reign to show that *the saloon, as such, was early devised by the ruling classes as a means of restraining the growing independence and wealth of the common people.* It was recommended to Secretary of State Cecil that this "must be cured by the providing, as it were, of some sewers or channels to draw or suck from them their money by subtle and indirect means, to be handled insensibly." Accordingly, licenses to sell ale and wine were lavishly dispensed and the business encouraged by the government.

It is certain that the wide-spread saturation of workingmen by beer at the present time is accomplishing this very result. The brain, not brute force, must be the weapon of warfare against overbearing capital. Against the alcoholization of his keenest mental powers the out-to-win worker must be relentlessly alert.

Dr. Fröhlich, a Socialist labor leader of Vienna, states a foundation fact in the following words: "Alcohol deceives the man with the promise of a happy present, and hinders his appreciation of the weight of misery that is upon him. There is no easier way possible to make the unfortunate man content with his misfortunes than a couple of glasses of beer. Every disagreeable thought vanishes then, because the cortex of the brain is deadened and the man is lulled into a soporific state. We need men who are awake. The alcohol which puts men to sleep is an enemy to labor and a bitter enemy to the laborer, though it come under the deceitful mask of a friend.'' [9]

It is for the reason that liquor ''tends to enslave the people, to make them satisfied with improper conditions, and keep them ignorant,'' that Tom L. Lewis, former president of the United Mine Workers, believes in fighting the saloon as an enemy to trades-unions.

The workman, sodden with drink, is willing to put up with anything; his wages will be low to correspond with his low standard of life, and he will become more and more unable to hold his own in the struggle with capital.

The use of liquor leads to outbreaks, riots, destruction of property and lives in the event of strikes. It is the liquor-excited subleaders who incite to riot, the liquor-excited mob that destroys property and endangers lives, not the honest strikers themselves. It is this, more than anything else that has disgraced organized labor and its undoubted right to strike. This phase of the liquor-labor question has become so serious that if the righteousness of the power to strike is to remain, drunken labor must go.

The ''scabs'' who break up strikes come from the reckless, heavy-drinking classes. Drink is an enemy to union organization in that it interferes with the self restraint necessary to carry out steady co-operative effort for more distant ends. The influence of the unions is now against the saloon. President Gompers of the

American Federation of Labor said, "Fifteen or twenty years ago the common meeting place of union labor would be a saloon or the room adjoining a saloon, but we have changed all that. It was not good for the men. It was not good for the unions. There was more likelihood of violent talk and unwise measures. It hurt the standing of the unions in the community. Hence that is practically done away."

At present the strike is one of the most effectual means by which just demands against capital may in the end be enforced. When saloon viciousness and drink corrupt it, the strike becomes a public menace which society has no right to permit.

It is not a defense of low wages to say that there are men who, if they had more money coming in weekly, would only spend the more for liquor, hasten their own destruction, and be a greater burden upon society. Cesare Lamorosi, the noted Italian criminologist, concludes that an increase of wages alone means an increase of drunkenness and its accompanying crimes. Labor, we may say decisively, ought to receive more from its large share in production, but it can never win its just rights in its struggle against aggressive capital, nor, if it should, would it be permanently better off afterward, while bearing its awful burden of drink.

Burns, an English leader, shows the weight of this burden by comparing it with the cost of strikes. "In 1901," he says, "the much abused trade unions, with all their 648 strikes and lockouts, 68 per cent of which were wholly or partially successful, inflicted a loss of half a day per annum on all the working classes at work. This involved a loss of less than £1,000,000, for which they secured £24,000,000 in higher wages and a net gain of over 11,000,000 reduced hours of work, beyond other important conditions; yet on drink, betting, and gambling, and the loss entailed in time and money, from thirty to fifty days per annum were lost, with no adequate advantage at all.''

There is no security against tyranny, capitalistic or political, except in the power and disposition to resist tyranny. Drink must be banished as a step toward what appears to workingmen as the greater end—a more just distribution of the product of labor.

Industrial "Prohibition."—Perhaps the most effective of all temperance forces in America is the growing demand among various industries that employees shall not drink. Great establishments, in response to the demands of the ledger and the efficiency expert, are passing rules more and more strenuous each year. There can be but one object—to prevent loss of time, to keep machinery busy, to avoid accident, to forestall carelessness and poor work, to insure dependence in men under responsibility, to keep employees healthy and capable of advancement, means less expense and more profits. The ledger and the laboratory are telling the same story— drink destroys economic capacity.

The railroads have been most effective in preventing alcoholic indulgence among employees. Their example has suggested the great advantage of sobriety to other industries. The railroad companies of the United States, operating 246,000 miles of road, employed in 1911 more than 1,600,000 men. The American Railway Association, which includes most of the companies, absolutely forbids, as its minimum requirement, the use of liquors of any kind while on duty, or the habitual use at other times, or the frequenting of places where liquors are sold. The breaking of this rule is cause for dismissal. Most of the larger companies in the association have gone far beyond this requirement, absolutely forbidding the use of intoxicants at any time. The influence of the alcohol is seen to hang over for several days. A Fourth of July accident in 1912 in New York, costing the lives of forty people and injuring seventy-five more, was caused by the failure of the engineer to see the signals on account of drinking the previous day. The company, compelled to pay damages and sustain the loss of property, then raised its rule to that of the most advanced roads, that "trainmen must not drink or enter saloons even when off duty."

Most automobile accidents are caused by drinking chauffeurs. Factory hands, working with machinery, endanger their own lives and those of other workmen, and waste property, after drinking. Life and casualty insurance companies are warning employers not to have men about their factories who drink. Scientific tests, made with the greatest care, indicate the loss of 9 per cent in efficiency in such work as typesetting[11] when even two or three glasses of such "light" liquors as wine or beer are taken. In mental work of certain kinds the loss runs from 7 per cent to 40 per cent. Errors, petty accidents, lack of coördination, result even the day following. The closing of saloons in certain cities and counties is beginning to bring the meaning of all this with greater force to many industries. As an example, in one Ohio county there is one shoe factory employing 1,700 men.[12] For three years the saloons were banished; then they were returned. The managers made detailed investigations for both periods and found a loss of 5 per cent from the pay roll during the "wet" period on account of absences while drunk; the loss of efficiency in the men recovering or not actually drunk could not be measured.

Such large firms as Marshall Field & Co., of Chicago, will not permit their thousands of employees to drink in public and private, to frequent places where liquors are sold, or even to associate with those who do drink.

Nations whose laboring classes are relatively sober are progressing; those where they drink are falling behind. Great Britain is becoming aroused to the fact that the United States is getting ahead of her commercially. One London paper, searching for causes, finds a chief one in drunken labor. One shipyard suffered in one year an injury of 25 per cent in its output due to drunkenness. The writer concludes: "If we are not able to produce better, faster, and cheaper than other countries, our rivals will come and capture our trade." One important factor in the relative advancement of American industries is the widespread system of temperance instruction in our public schools.

"The United States Department of Labor found that 90 per cent of railways, 79 per cent of manufacturers, 88 per cent of trades, and 72 per cent of agriculturists discriminate against employees addicted to the beverage use of intoxicants. The great barrier to wage-earners in general and to the elevation of young men in business in particular is the drink habit." [13]

This movement means nothing less than industrial prohibition. The command is decisive and absolute. There must be no drinking, or business relations cease. It is more severe and far-reaching than legal prohibition; the latter applies only to the manufacturer and the seller, the social acts; industrial prohibition applies directly to the use, the individual and personal acts.

The purpose is, of course, purely economic. It is because higher moral qualities pay, that morality is encouraged or required. This reason may be analyzed into three points: (a) The total abstainer is worth more to the company than the man who drinks; (b) he will take better care of the property placed in his hands; (c) in the case of transportation he will take better care of the lives of passengers. It is the suits for damages that railroads fear as a result of accidents that make them value so much the lives of the public.

The Demands of Economic Welfare. — Ordinarily, "the first purpose" of government that, in America, is most sacredly fulfilled is the guarding of wealth. People are interested in the regulation of property, and require that such laws shall be enforced, even while those relating to morals, or even to public health, are permitted to become dead letters. Most liquor regulations have been passed in the interests of morality and safety, aiming to compromise between the apparent need of protecting liquor property and the obvious duty of restricting the evils of intemperance. In passing regulation laws government has failed to recognize the source of the difficulty; it needs to know that public wealth, no less than public morality and health, calls for severe action in regard to this social evil. Prohibition is necessary economically no less than morally.

The first cost is the burden cast upon society by intemperance and the wasteful trade that supplies the necessary means to intemperance. In addition is the burden of caring for the product in crime, poverty, and defective humanity. The great total cannot be given accurately, but certainly it is not less than twice the cost of the $1,700,000,000 annual drink bill.

In return, the trade furnishes social and personal enjoyment to its users, but often of a personally corrupting and dangerous-to-the-public sort, pays the farmer for a small share of his crop, and furnishes employment to a few men in manufacture and to a large force in its distribution and sale, and pays nearly one-third of the entire running expenses of the national government as well as a large amount to local and state governments.

Considering the fact that intemperance is so destructive of life and happiness, as well as of money and capacity that should be used to increase wealth in the community, the trade that caters to it is little less than a wholesale public robber. In taking from the nation the earning capacity of its sober every-day citizens, it is striking deep at future progress. Other trades produce more wealth than they consume; the liquor business is a parasite, consuming what they store up and returning practically nothing. Its overthrow by governmental action is necessary:

(1) To remove the worse than useless burden in care and support of one-half or more of all crime, 37 per cent of pauperism, 40 per cent of the insane and feeble-minded, and an equally large share of others thrown upon the public for support; to get at the sources of delinquency and dependency and save the victims as men and women rather than to permit them to be cared for or punished at public expense.

(2) To supplement other agencies for social relief and education; the social settlement, the school and church cannot do their work successfully while competition by the legalized saloon is so unrestricted. The license sys-

tem now followed throws the burden entirely on the relief organizations, while it gives an undue prestige and protection to the liquor trade and the saloon.

(3) It is a primary function of government to protect public wealth.

(4) Because it interferes with normal consumption, thus injuring markets for other trades and labor. "Under-consumption is the economic cause of unemployment. The only remedy, therefore, which goes to the root of the evil is a raising of the standard of consumption to the point which shall fully utilize the producing power." [14]

(5) The safety and progress of the nation depend upon the quality of its citizens. The amount of money now being spent, especially among the poorer classes, is depriving the children of necessary home comforts, food, clothing, a proper share of play and recreation, and is preparing them to be heavy burdens both to themselves and to society.

It is Dr. E. R. L. Gould who says: *"The danger resident in these huge national drink bills reaches beyond misery and moral degradation. Civilization itself is menaced by this growing economic waste.* If it be true —and there seems to be a general opinion to that effect— that excesses are less frequent now than formerly among the upper classes, the burden must be falling chiefly upon those who are relatively least able to support it. Certainly the family budget of the wage-earner is not so flexible that liberal expenditures for drink may be made with impunity. So delicately adjusted is the balance that the status of a new generation is largely determined by the quantity of alcohol the fathers consume." [15]

Since the liquor traffic and the resulting drink habit

strike so vitally at the very source and necessary conditions of public wealth, nothing less than the total destruction of that traffic, and with it the removal of the chief source of intemperance, can adequately solve the problem from an economic point of view.

References and Authorities.

National Wealth and Social Welfare.

Patten, ''The Economic Basis of Prohibition,'' *Annals American Academy*, II, 59.
Hopkins, *Wealth and Waste*, 46-53, 63-65, 83-89.
Barker, *The Saloon Problem and Social Reform*, 9-11.
Rowntree and Sherwell, *The Temperance Problem and Social Reform*, 21-58.
[1] Patten, 66.
[2] *The Evolution of Modern Capitalism,* 283.

The Burden on Labor.

Stelzle, *The Workingman and Social Problems*, 37-40.
Stelzle, *American Social and Religious Conditions* (1912), 67-85.
John B. Lennon, (Am. Fed. of Labor) Talks to Men, *Am. Pro. Year Book* (1913), 173-174.
Hopkins, *Wealth and Waste*, 62-70.
Horsley and Sturge, *Alcohol and the Human Body*, 72-75.
Roberts, *The Anthracite Coal Communities*, 222-243.
Rowntree and Sherwell, *The Temperance Problem and Social Reform*, 21-34.
Warner, *American Charities*, 60-62.
[3] Stelzle, *Am. Soc'l and Relig. Conditions*, 84.
[4] Warner, 61.

Wages, and the Standard of Living.

Rowntree and Sherwell, *The Temperance Problem and Social Reform*, 26-29, 55.
Hobson, *Problems of Poverty*, 178-181.
Streightoff, *Standard of Living Among Industrial People.*
Horsley and Sturge, *Alcohol and the Human Body*, 72-75.
Stelzle, *American Social and Religious Conditions*, 80-85.
Hopkins, *Wealth and Waste*, 62-70.

Ely, *Political Economy*, 156.

Thierry, ''A Wonderful Town of Prosperous Toilers,'' *Leslies'
Weekly*, Aug. 1, 1912.

[5] Horsley and Sturge, 73.

[6] See ch. V.

[7] Stelzle, 84.

[8] Gould, *Social Condition of Labor*, 31.

Struggle Between Capital and Labor.

Calkins, *Substitutes for the Saloon*, 303-313.

Rowntree and Sherwell, *Temperance Problem,* 44-58.

Woolley and Johnson, *Temperance Progress in 19th Century.*
396-405.

Wheeler, *Prohibition*, 68-70.

Frölich, ''Alcohol, the Workingman's Antagonist,'' *Sch. Phys.
Jr.,* Nov., 1908.

[9] See ref. above.

[10] Quoted in *Am. Prohibition Year Book* (1912), 84.

Industrial Prohibition.

Barker, *The Saloon Problem and Social Reform*, 11-12.

Johnson, ''Railroad Temperance Regulations,'' *Chautauquan,*
June, 1904.

Wheeler, *Prohibition*, 90-92.

Committee of Fifty, *The Liquor Problem*, 127-133.

[11] Horsley and Sturge, 73.

[12] *Anti-Saloon League Year Book*, 1913, 253.

[13] Barker, 11.

The Demands of Economic Welfare.

Patton, ''The Economic Basis of Prohibition,'' *Annals Am.
Academy*, 11, 59-68.

Hopkins, *Wealth and Waste*, 52, 131-142, 207-216.

Wheeler, *Prohibition*, 7-20, 49-56, 67-76.

Gould, *The Social Conditions of Labor.*

[14] Hobson, *Problems of the Unemployed*, 98.

[15] See ref. above.

CHAPTER VII

John Barleycorn is with me because in all the unwitting days of my youth John Barley-corn was accessible, calling to me and inviting me on every corner, and on every street be-tween the corners. The pseudo-civilization into which I was born permitted everywhere licensed shops for the sale of soul-poison. The system of life was so organized that I—and millions like me—was lured and drawn and driven to the poison shops.

—JACK LONDON, John Barleycorn.

CHAPTER VII

Perhaps no other enterprise of an industrial character, save only the newspaper and publishing, has a more direct influence on public sentiment than has the liquor traffic. Its power for good or bad, in this respect, is far beyond that of any purely commercial enterprise. It educates public ideals and personal character thru its grip in social life, its competition with educational institutions, its active propaganda, and by means of the suggestive presence of the saloon, always open and ever active in the neighborhood. In the extent and persistence of its educational activity it may even be classified with the newspaper, the school, the church, the political campaign, and the suggestive force of "the latest styles." Education is a primary purpose of social well-being; how about the educational influence of the liquor institution under present-day conditions?

The Saloon and the Public School.—The saloon is not merely a place of retail sales. It is a great public educational institution. It influences the thoughts, morals, politics, social customs, and ideals of its patrons as its fellow retail stores, the grocery and shoe store, never do. It has an atmosphere of its own very much unlike that of any ordinary business, in addition to its function of supplying intoxicating drinks to those who call for them.

The saloon is a day school, a night school, a vacation school, a Sunday school, a kindergarten, a college, and a

university, all in one. It runs without term-ends, vaca-
tions, or holidays. Its enrollment is among all classes
and its attendants are of all ages and from many grades
of society. Unlike other schools, its largest support
comes from the poor and the rich, rather than from the
middle economic classes.

But the saloon is only the representative of the larger
field of liquor interests back of it. The "superintend-
ents" and "boards of education" who hire the "teachers" and control the methods and policies of instruction
in this gigantic pro-liquor educational system are the
promoters of the trade, the brewers who start the saloon-
keeper in business, the publicity bureaus which plan the
advertising that will create new forces of drinkers,
youths and foreigners, and, beyond all these, the public
policy of license and special taxation making the saloon
an apparent necessity to pay the expenses of its rival
educational institution, the public school.

In our great cities and many other communities the
saloon, in certain vital respects, is an open competitor
with the school.

(1) It counteracts directly the kind of instruction
and character development given by the school. Social
conditions in the home where drink is frequent, the neglect, quarreling, selfish indulgence, reduced income, or
poverty due to much indulgence, give no opportunity
for normal childhood. Weakened nervous and mental
capacity, due to drinking by parents, make learning
difficult. The effect of much taught at school, respect
for law, for the rights of others, patriotism, obedience,
are weakened or offset by the example of the sort of
thing seen about many saloons every day in the week.

(2) It mis-educates the new arrivals to our population

from foreign shores, teaching many wrong ideals of liberty and government, and encouraging them to cling to habits and anti-social ideas unfitted to this country.

(3) It is a vast university for large numbers of adults who, after having left the public school at an early age, have *no other public or social institution that plays so large a part in their lives.*

In its competition with the school, the saloon is constantly in operation. Morning, noon, and night, thousands of children, going to and from school, pass its doors, open from 18 to 20 hours each day, often seven days a week and 365 days each year. The school opens at 9 a. m. and closes at 4 p. m., running five days a week and nine months a year. Imitation is a primary social fact especially strong in children. Whatever they see going on about them comes, sooner or later, to be a part of their own habits, customs, and views. It is true that the right sort of home influence will largely counteract the repeated suggestions from the saloon, and its evils will even make children hate it, but such vast numbers do not have the right home training, due also, in part, to alcohol and its use. Besides, what a useless burden of care, solicitude, and painstaking instruction is thus thrown upon temperate parents to counteract the unhealthy suggestions constantly thrown out by the saloon upon their growing children. Any effort to protect the children is met by counter effort to place a halo of "personal liberty" about this community institution.

The saloon has been called "a school of crime," because of its defiance of legal restraint and its social atmosphere which attracts the criminally inclined. Some are; some are not. The fact that so many crimes are committed in saloons or by men intoxicated gives some foundation for this charge. Yet many saloons, apparently obedient to law, which do not encourage excess, are greater sources of evil on account of the sort of ideals they suggest into the lives of growing children than are the low-down groggeries which turn out the Czolgoszs, Guiteaus, Schranks, and Booths that strike at the lives of men high in public authority.

School Attendance and the Saloon.—The competition of the saloon with the school is keenest in the upper grades and the high school. It shortens the period of attendance at school usually of those who need it most.

The force of this competition is best shown by specific instances; the fact itself is so well known. Connecticut is a state where a high educational system is found side by side with an unusually strong industrial demand for young people in the factories. It affords a good field for comparison. In 46 cities and towns having saloons, the attendance in the high schools in 1912 was 123 to 10,000 population; in the 22 no-license towns and cities, it was 158 to 10,000 population.[1] More than one in five of those denied high school attendance in the "wet" towns of a whole state apparently would be in school if they had lived in a "dry" town. In Nebraska, an average western state, the "wet" county seats together show a high school enrollment of 29 per 1,000 inhabitants; in "dry" county seats, the ratio is 65 to 1,000 population.[2]

In Massachusetts, in 1910, the ratio of attendance in high schools of no-license places exceeded that of license places by 37 per cent.[3] In Indiana, the same year, the attendance in the high schools of the seventy "dry" counties was 40,687, or 9 per cent of the enumeration; in the "wet" counties it was 18,000, or 5.9 per cent of the enumeration. Thus the various social conditions usually found in saloon towns, together with the influence of drink itself, were responsible for keeping 9,500 out of the high schools of this one state.[4] The great reason why students quit in the midst of a high school course is "to go to work." The saloon need not be charged with all that the figures here suggest; there are many other causes. But that the necessity for quitting school should be, in many parts of the country, so much greater in saloon communities than in no-saloon communities is intensely significant.

Where prohibition has become a settled policy on sufficiently wide a scale to affect more thoroly the social conditions, the difference is yet more marked. The State Superintendent of Education of Kansas says that attendance at school is much more regular in the interior towns than on the border near liquor states. "Of the one-half million boys and girls in Kansas, only the smallest fraction have ever even seen an open saloon."[5]

A tremendous revolution in school attendance, especially in the older grades, follows the expulsion of the saloon on a large scale. Assistant Attorney General Trickett, of Kansas, shows that when the saloons were closed in Kansas City, Kan., July 3, 1906, by September an additional force of eighteen new teachers was needed. Says Mr. Trickett:

"I went to the teachers and said, 'From whence comes this large demand for admission to our public schools?' The result was a list of 600 boys and girls from 12 to 18 years of age who attended the public schools last year for the first time. And they gave as a reason why they had not attended in former years that they had to assist a drinking father to earn a living for the family."

Delinquency and Disability in School Children.—
Harmful as is the educational effect of the saloon upon
normal children, the part that drink plays in the life-
history of those not quite up to par and those who need
special moral restraint is yet more varied and powerful.
Its influences during the school period are hereditary,
environmental, and personal.

The schools are full of dull children made so thro
inhuman treatment or neglect by drinking parents, or
who inherited deficiency because of alcohol used by parents or grandparents. The records of the juvenile courts
are crowded with impulsive crimes by children. "Within
a brief period in New York City six boys aged seven,
nine, ten, eleven, twelve and fourteen, respectively, were
convicted for burglary, three of them having developed
a shrewd plan to rob sixty houses. Two boys, fifteen and
seventeen years old, were found guilty of assault and
highway robbery. Three boys, ten, fourteen and sixteen
years of age, were convicted of murder. In each of these
instances alcohol bore a conspicuous part in the family
history. Hardly a day passes without its record of
juvenile crime." [6]

Dr. T. Alexander MacNicholl of New York, after a
very extensive investigation, shows how the children of
drinkers often inherit a susceptible nervous tempera-
ment which is easily developed into a passionate fond-
ness for drink. "Alcohol, by destroying the integrity of
nerve structure, launches hereditary influences and im-
plants tendencies which a good environment may not
hold in check." As an example among the "better"
class of families, he gives the following: "Two little
girls, four and six years of age, had the desire for drink
aroused by a medicinal dose of whisky, and for months

greedily drank iced whisky which an indulgent mother provided in response to their strenuous appeals.'' He shows its relation to deficiency in mental capacity in the following summaries: ''From 15 to 25 per cent of drinkers, free from hereditary alcoholic taint, are dullards. From 53 per cent to 77 per cent of the descendants of a drinking ancestry are dullards. From 4 to 10 per cent of the descendants of a total abstaining ancestry are dullards.'' [6]

Of 12,919 children classed as dullards, coming to school from prosperous families, 75 per cent had drinking parents, while but 32 per cent of all children from well-to-do homes had parents who drank. From poor families there came 3,193 dullards, 85 per cent of whom had parents who used liquors.

Alcoholic environment in the home and on the streets is very unfavorable to good, or even average, school work. It accentuates evil proclivities and offers a field for the unfolding of physical weakness and moral depravity. Ignorance, especially among recent immigrants, causes many children to be taught to use beer with their meals. While a few adults may drink this way occasionally and appear none the worse for it, children can not do so under any conditions. The free lunch, the specially prepared drinks, the occasional free drinks of beer, the ''doctored'' soft drinks, the games and amusements, and the desire to imitate older men, attract boys and ''create the appetite'' or develop that already started. Largely in proportion to the number and attractiveness of the saloons in a neighborhood does the moral and physical strength among children, and especially among boys, decline.

The Committee of Fifty show that 45.8 per cent of the

neglect and destitution of children is caused directly by drinking parents or guardians.[7] So far as the child and its education is concerned, the evil is partly remedied by the public in taking charge of such children and placing them in institutions. But this is only a substitution for home, at best. The greatest cause of child labor in factories and shops is support of mother and brothers and sisters neglected, or worse, by a drinking father; or by one confined in a workhouse or prison on account of crimes committed under the influence of drink.

The extent to which children are taught to use liquor in our great centers of foreign population would be astounding to the average rural American. It is laying a large foundation for future diseased and inefficient citizens. Notwithstanding the fact that scientific instruction in health and the effect of narcotics in the schools has largely increased the number of total abstainers, the "vast immigration of inferior peoples, . . . bringing with them their vices as well as their virtues, augmenting our drinking classes, furnishing additional soil from which to propagate criminals, . . . renders more imperative the necessity for these movements which will alleviate and enlighten."[6] But it is not the foreign children of school age alone that drink; nor is it confined to the poorer classes. Dr. MacNicholl found that in 34,000 cases of children attending school from prosperous homes there were 27 per cent who drank, 4 per cent using spirits, and 23 per cent beer, leaving only 73 per cent that were total abstainers. In 6,879 cases of poor children, the abstainers were 50 per cent, beer drinkers 43 per cent, and drinkers of spirits, including wines, 7 per cent. But 40 per cent of the drinking half used both spirits and beer. These latter, classed by nationalities, bring out the fact that 36 per cent of the Americans and 50 per cent of the foreigners, including children of foreign-born parents, drink. Ninety per cent of the drinking Americans have foreign-born grandparents.

Certainly, not much in the way of respect for order and decency in the neighborhood can be expected from children and youths who drink. In the Illinois State Reformatory, at Pontiac, 59 per cent of the boys there confined were found to have used liquor before being committed.[8] Of those under 14 years of age, 56 out of 86 drank. *The larger part of the whole number had fathers who drank to excess.*

Mis-education of the Foreigner.—The saloon is one of the great welcoming agencies to the foreigner on his arrival in this country. He is brought into immediate and close contact with it in a way and to an extent he has never known in the old country. Here he finds a welcoming hand, someone who speaks his language, someone to explain the new conditions here, and someone to help him into his new political rights. The American saloon is a different institution from the one he has known heretofore. It is a center of politics; it has greater tendencies to encourage excess, social vice, and gambling, and offers to the new arrival much of the worst, instead of the best, that he has come here seeking. It misinterprets America to him.

The worst enemies of the immigrant on arrival in this country are those of his own race who, being here some time, have learned the language and the vices of our commerce and politics. Most of the sweatshop manipulators, who take advantage of the poverty, ignorance, and confiding trust of the new arrival in a fellow country-

man, are comparatively recent immigrants; their victims
are of their own nationality. The padrone system, which
exploits ignorance, contracts laborers, at a very small
price, puts them under obligations by supplying transportation and food, and manages them closely while employed in construction gangs, is always managed by foreigners. American greed supplies the incentive, but
English-speaking foreign men do the work. The city and
ward politicians who prey upon the public treasury find
these new arrivals the easiest recruits to their army of
voters. Their sub-agents herd these would-be citizens
by nationalities, secure their naturalization papers in
groups, and vote them in the interests of any vicious
proposition that may be up. The saloon-keeper, usually
himself foreign-born, is the intermediate agent; his place
is not only headquarters, it also furnishes the necessary
"medium of exchange."

The new arrival gets much of his first impression of
how the newly obtained liberty actually works from his
association at the saloon. Here is found a spirit of indif-
ference to authority such as he has never before experienced. After a while he learns that there are laws
regulating the sale of liquors to children, the hours of
closing, and against selling on Sunday. He may see no
wrong in buying or using beer or wine at any time, and
may have no objection to giving it to his children. But
that the law should be so openly ignored is a new experience. That the policemen are indifferent and the aldermen even aid the law-breaker to escape justice are startling in their contrast with his former conditions. Coming
from a country, doubtless, where he was subject to "too
much government," and where obedience was strictly
enforced, the natural tendency is to drift to the opposite

extreme; to disrespect government, to follow the example set by the saloon into other affairs. He gains the impression that liberty means license to do as you choose, and refuses to be governed by the regulations under which liberty is possible.

"More than any other one factor, the saloon has broken down the American Sabbath and ushered in the Continental Sunday, disdaining even to change the law, but accomplishing its work in spite of the law. It is in the saloon that Anarchism finds a rendezvous and an inspiration, and the red flag has never floated to the American breeze except from an American saloon." [9] Under cover of loyalty to the customs of the fatherland, and in accordance with this distorted idea of liberty, organized defiance to law and its enforcement is made in our great cities, and candidates are elected to office on this issue. The so-called "United Societies for Local Self-Government" in Chicago, composed of beer-loving Germans, Polish, and Bohemians, has for its one purpose political activity against all laws, state or local, that in any way restrict the saloon. They claim to represent the German element; they do not; they stand only for that part that is determined to have "booze" at any cost of public decency. The best elements of these nationalities in the city are strictly opposed to such "liberal" principles.

The children of foreigners, born in this country, show a much higher rate of crime than do the foreign-born children of these same families.[10] Under the environment furnished by the saloon, its vices, its political power and defiance of law, and associated evils, the first native-born generation of foreign parentage is the most crime-hardened of all classes in this country—much worse than the new arrivals themselves.

"But above and beyond all, the saloon has organized, and in a large part created, a purchaseable vote whose proportions have alarmed even American optimism." . . . "It is this above all that makes the drink question one that lies, as Cobden said, 'at the foundation of all social and political reform.'" [9] Sought after at once, on account of his prospective vote, assisted to get fraudulent naturalization papers, shown how he may send these back home as a means of admitting other undesirables, selling his vote from year to year for a few drinks or a dollar or two, "in every way the alien is put on the wrong track and his American experiences are such as would naturally make him lawless and criminal rather than a good citizen. He needs nothing more than protection against corruption and venal agencies which find their origin in politics and the saloon." [11] "'Where God builds a church, the devil builds next door a saloon,' is an old saying that has lost its point in New York," says Jacob Riis. "Either the devil was on the ground first, or he has been doing a good deal more in the way of building. I tried once to find out how the account stood, and counted to 111 Protestant churches, chapels, and places of worship of every kind below Fourteenth street, 4,065 saloons. The worst half of the tenement population lives down there, and it has to this day the worst half of the saloons. Up town the account stands a little better, but there are easily ten saloons to every church today." [12]

Its Mis-education of the Public.—The American spirit of fair play grants to every industry the privilege of creating and maintaining for itself a place in the public mind. Publicity means not only attention, but also favorable attention. It is the life of trade under twentieth-century methods. The opportunity to educate sentiment in a business way is an outgrowth of the fundamental right of free speech.

But publicity getting, that is, education of public attention for private financial ends, is a right that must be strictly regulated. The most monstrous hoaxes and frauds have been perpetrated upon the public with every semblance of scientific truth and logic to support them. "Patent medicine" "cure-alls," first viciously suggesting disease where none exists, breaking down self-respect and then supplying useless and dangerous nostrums, are a common but mild form of abuse of this right. Government finds it wise to regulate strictly such sales under pure food and drug acts.

Vicious, mendacious, and obscene literature is forbidden the use of the mails and is subject to police confiscation to prevent wholesale blighting of the public ideals of morality.

Few would think of denying to the liquor trade the privilege of holding and enlarging its place in public opinion by reasonable and honest methods. As it now stands, it has years of public approval back of it. If questioned, it has a right to show cause, at the bar of public opinion, why it should continue unrestricted. It may cite the millions of dollars it pays each year as license, tax, and revenue, to the support of the government, local and national, as proof of its loyalty and reason for its continuance; it may point to the saloon as a place of democratic sociability, where men may have recreation after a hard day's labor; to the pleasure it furnishes those who drink, and to its importance as a business industry in the community.

But the liquor trade sadly abuses the American spirit of fair play. Being engaged in supplying an article of merchandise which tends to produce the vice of intemperance, the reaction of such a trade upon the men engaged in it seems to cause them to lose all regard for the truth. Apparently they are afraid to trust their wares to be judged on merit alone, and must make their appeal for favorable attention on deception.

There has long been a regular and systematic attempt to defraud the public as to certain qualities of alcohol. Long extended series of newspaper and magazine advertising with false claims and spurious testimonials are constantly appearing. The use of certain brands of whisky are said to produce long life and health; but the arguments used to substantiate the claim are misrepresentations, and gross fraud. A favorite testimonial is the picture of a very old man, or woman, with a letter, apparently from him, stating or suggesting that his health and long life are due to the constant use of that brand of whisky. When traced down, these cases are found, almost invariably, to have been people who were temperate all their lives, and who were induced to take a sample of the ''medicine'' as a gift in return for signing a testimonial already written. Sometimes these testimonials are pure fabrications made up in the advertising section of the liquor firm.

There is a widespread mis-instruction of the public as to the sociability features of the saloon. Retail dealers and their organizations constantly proclaim the saloon to be ''the poor man's club,'' whereas, in fact, it is patronized by rich as well as poor.

The saloon cultivates, by direct instruction and suggestion, the same false ideas of liberty in American-born children and older people as it teaches to the newly arrived foreigner. Under the constitution there is no such thing as "personal liberty." It is "civil liberty" or "liberty of conscience," not "personal." This idea, which carries with it so much implication of unrestricted opportunity to do as one pleases, without regard to the rights of others, is of more recent growth. Liberty without law is not the original American conception that has gained the praise of the whole world.

The public is constantly being deceived as to the extent and power of the liquor trade. The number of votes it controls, the amount of money invested, its influence over other lines of business, more or less related, and the unity and strength of its organizations, local and national, are constantly exaggerated for the purpose of fixing deep the belief that it is useless to attack so powerful an enemy. It indicates shrewd understanding of social psychology on the part of the trade's press agents.

The liquor trade purchases and controls newspapers and their editorial policy. Large payments for advertising space are made to prevent publication of news reflecting upon the saloon. The opportunity thus furnished of dictating editorial policy on the liquor problem has meant more, doubtless, to the liquor traffic than the direct publicity gained for the particular brands of beer or liquors advertised. It has been one of the powerful means of keeping in check so long the present rising tide of local and general prohibition. But there is now a distinct revolt among the best and most independent papers against this policy of dictation by a community-corrupting trade. Many magazines and dailies refuse to carry liquor advertisements at all on the same grounds that they throw out thinly veiled frauds in the form of patent medicines, ''get-rich-quick'' schemes, and holes in the ground, called gold mines. Others are becoming more free, and, while receiving advertisements, are yet editorially attacking the evils of the saloon and giving freedom to anti-liquor news. The business control of liquor over the ''people's university,'' the newspaper, is being loosened gradually but surely, and more rapid progress toward the settlement of the whole problem may now be expected.

Looking beneath the current methods of gaining publicity employed by the liquor traffic and the devices it uses for retaining a good trade and favor with the public, we find the following:

(1) Intense fear of a straight-out contest on the merits of the question itself.

(2) That the real strength of the pro-liquor propaganda and of the whole liquor traffic is the brewer and the distiller, not the individual saloon-keeper or even the united saloons of a town or county. Ordinarily a few saloons alone are too small to withstand public sentiment. Besides, from one-third to one-half are owned or controlled by the brewers. The real liquor problem, so far as organized opposition to temperance is concerned, is the larger ''trade'' back of the retailer.

Education and the Liquor Problem. — The saloon comes into direct conflict with the school and what it stands for in a thousand ways. It makes it necessary for vast numbers to remain out of school on account of drinking parents; it counteracts by suggestion and example the teachings of the school. Education by personal contact, suggestion, and observation, is stronger than direct instruction—and these forces are always acting, in youth and older age alike. In its mis-education of the three-fourths of a million arrivals from foreign shores each year it is positively criminal.

The saloon exists as a public social fact. That gives it standing. Anything that law permits, legalizes, and secures revenue from is, in the eyes of most people, legitimate and right. For many, no higher code of morals, public or private, exists than that which law recognizes. The saloon is educating public sentiment towards its own standards.

Liquor leaders for a long time have endeavored to connect the public revenues from liquor license, taxes, and fines with the cause of public education. It is one of their standard claims that the community cannot get along without these fees: that popular education will suffer. On the one hand, it seems like a sort of rude justice; make the saloons pay the expense of education, the trend of which is away from the cultivation of such habits as intemperance. Also, from this point of view, the taxpayer seems to have his assessments lowered by the application of the license income to such close-at-hand public expenses as to the support of the schools. On the other hand, the broader social view, are two incontrovertible facts: first, the payment of these fees into the school, or any other local fund, intrenches the saloon behind short-sighted cupidity and insures its perpetuation; second, the saloon, running continuously day after day, is able to counteract, to a large extent, much of the work of the school in the cultivation of morals, and always to secure a full quota of new recruits for itself.

Notwithstanding the immense amount of money that this trade pays into the public treasuries each year, to be used for school purposes, the saloon is in competition with our public schools. The government has no right to accept money from the one to apply to the other.

References and Authorities.

The School and the Saloon.

> *Anti-Saloon League Year Book* (1912), 129-132; Ibid (1913), 93-94, 134, 158-159, 103.
>
> 1 *American Issue.*
> 2 *Anti-Saloon League Year Book* (1913), 158.
> 3 Ibid, 134.
> 4 Ibid, 93.
> 5 Ibid, 103.

Delinquency and Disability in School Children.

> Koren, *Economic Aspects of the Liquor Problem*, 126-132.
> Benedict, *Waifs of the Slums.*
> MacNicholl, "Alcohol and the Disabilities of School Children," Address at 57th Annual Session, American Medical Assn., Boston, 1908.
>
> 6 See ref. above.
> 7 Koren.
> 8 *Report of Ill. State Reformatory* at Pontiac, for 1903-4.

Mis-Education of the Immigrant.

> Roberts, *The New Immigration*, 117-119, 171-180.
> Hall, *Immigration*, 183-189.
> Turner, "The City of Chicago," *McClure's*, Apr., 1907.
> Riis, *How the Other Half Lives.*
> Barker, *The Saloon Problem and Social Reform*, 49-50.
> Wheeler, *Prohibition*, 81-88.
>
> 9 Wheeler, 84.
> 10 Hall, 150-151.
> 11 Grose, *Aliens and Americans*, 216.
> 12 *How the Other Half Lives*, ch. 18.

Mis-Education of the Public.

> Fehlandt, *A Century of Drink Reform*, 187-191.

*Even a slight exhilaration from alcohol re-
laxes the moral sense, throws a glamour over
an aspect of life from which a decent young
man would ordinarily recoil.*

—JANE ADDAMS.

*Every interest of my developing life had
drawn me to it. A newsboy on the streets, a
sailor, a miner, a wanderer in far lands, always
where men came together to exchange ideas,
to laugh and boast and dare, to relax, to forget the dull toil of tiresome nights and days,
always they came together over alcohol. The
saloon was the place of congregation. Men
gathered to it as primitive men gathered about
the fire of the squatting-place or the fire at the
mouth of the cave.*

—JACK LONDON, *John Barleycorn.*

CHAPTER VIII

THE SOCIABILITY PHASE OF THE LIQUOR PROBLEM

The Sociability Source of Intemperance.—As a means to sociability, it is well to state frankly the use of alcoholic liquors has been common among both savage and civilized nations for ages. It is quite thoroly mixed up with the customs and traditions of large classes in our most advanced nations. From the days of savagery, our ancestors have used some sort of intoxicating drink at social, religious, political, and other occasions where people come together to enjoy the presence of each other. In the past, solitary drinking was exceptional. Steady daily drinking for the sake of the drink alone is a by-product of civilization.

It was early discovered that alcohol gives a sort of good feeling, removes restraint and hesitancy, makes men loquacious, and increases self-importance and the desire to express one's self. These all imply the presence of other persons, if full satisfaction is to be obtained. These emotional qualities, along with the desire that others shall experience them, too, bring sociability into close connection with the peculiar sensations of intoxication. Alcoholic sociability is toxic, out-of-the-usual-state-of-feeling sociability.

These qualities have something to do with the growth of the sociability features of the saloon. Of recent years the saloon has taken advantage, more and more, of some of these tendencies, and so, notwithstanding its dangerous influences, has obtained strong hold on the social life of many communities. Drinking has been largely transferred to the saloon, heavy drinking has increased, the family neglected, and questionable amusements or temptations to vice have **grown** up about the life of this social institution.

Without regard to whether the consequences are good or bad, or whether a better means to sociability might not be procured, alcoholic liquors, both in the saloon and elsewhere, do serve as a popular and convenient method of gaining the friendship of companions, or of expressing feelings of good fellowship already existing. Sociability, with large numbers, has got into a habit of showing itself chiefly in this manner.

In this sense the saloon appeals to a fundamental social instinct—sociability. It supplies something really necessary in human life, it is true, but in quality a very shoddy article at an excessively high cost in morals and money. The appetite for alcohol, the most relentless source of the liquor evil, is a perverted taste, a diseased appetite. The desire to gain wealth, which prompts the dealer to push his sales so vigorously, while all right so far as the honest earning of money is concerned, has gone so far that it is nothing less than money-making out of the vices and excesses of other people—the worst of economics. The government sanction of the traffic by taxation and license affords a fine revenue, but puts a fearful moral blight on the public conscience. So, perhaps, the only point that may be made in favor of the saloon is that it does furnish a certain amount and kind of social pleasure. It is no respecter of persons, but purely as a business matter it is open to everybody, rich and poor, at all times and without regard to social or moral stand-

ing. The saloon-keeper never asks embarrassing questions or places restrictions upon the conduct of his
patrons so long as they do not become too boisterous.
The saloon has thus seized upon social want and proceeds
to supply it in its own way. ''The public house problem
is largely—by no means wholly—a question of forgotten
needs,'' that is, of sociability needs. *This ground the
saloon has filled, or usurped, and these needs are there
satisfied, not by, but in spite of, alcohol and intoxication.*

Methods for the solution of the saloon problem as a
part of the larger liquor problem, social and political,
as we have it, must take the sociability feature into consideration. If there is a certain amount of usefulness
in the saloon, it should be known. There is no use going
at the work blindly. If, on the other hand, the saloon
is a powerful competitor with better means of sociability,
and a source of social vice to the community, the good
which it may do can be no excuse for the greater evils.
Palliative measures will be found to be both insufficient
and wrong.

The welfare of society as a whole, and the effects of
the saloon upon it, must be the only final test of its social
worth.

The Saloon as a Social Center.—The seeking of pleasure of the right kind is one of the legitimate aims of
every individual in society, as well as a chief aim of
social organization. It is as important to health and all-
round manhood to be able to relax after hard labor as
it is to work. ''The destruction of a legitimate pleasure
is a positive moral loss to the world, and no nature can
be anything but dwarfed in which the faculty of enjoyment has not been developed.'' [1]

The strongest plea that can be made for alcohol is that

it seems to increase social pleasure. This it does, first, by means of the "social glass" to the two or three or more taking it together, and, second, by means of the saloon serving as a meeting place or social center for certain classes of people who either prefer the kind of society to be found there or who have, or can find, no other place open to them.

It is only among certain classes of people that the saloon acts in this capacity. There are many users of intoxicants who get all their recreation and amusement elsewhere. They are largely the more able classes financially, who can pay for a better quality of entertainment. There are large numbers in all grades of society who patronize the saloon exclusively, or chiefly, for the liquors. After all that may be said in its favor as a social center, the saloon is first, last, and all the time, the place for the sale of intoxicants; and the primary purpose of the saloon patron is to obtain alcohol and alcoholic drinks. The saloon-keeper makes his place free and hospitable to all for the one purpose of selling more liquors.

The people who respond in any important degree to the sociability features of the saloon are:

(1) The more well-to-do or wealthy classes who distinctly prefer the sort of sociability that accompanies or follows alcoholic intoxication; those with blunted moral tastes and distorted social ambitions, the degenerate rich. They make the saloon a sort of club or transform their club into a saloon. They might get excellent society elsewhere, but they are not satisfied with it. They can offer no valid objection against any interference that may be made with this sort of personal liberty in the interests of public welfare.

(2) The outcast and degenerate of other classes who

seek their associates among the ex-criminals, embryonic criminals, loafers, and professional beggars of the low-down groggery. Saloons of this type are found in all our large cities. They are the rendezvous for all kinds of evilly inclined men who are a burden upon society. Among both of these classes, the rich and the very poor, the sort of sociability offered caters directly to social viciousness of many sorts.

(3) There is a relatively small, but important, class of business men who use the saloon as a place for business appointments. Customers are more readily won and better bargains made, as they believe, over a glass of beer or champagne. This sort of business sociability is decreasing among most successful houses. It is no longer an important factor in the liquor problem.

(4) There yet remain the working classes who regard the saloon as a place for social intercourse. Here the real problem is found. First, this class is the largest in the total and per capita consumption of liquors. Second, their opportunities for social enjoyment, separate from the saloon, are more limited, and so they are compelled to depend more upon it. In a word, it is the laboring man, and he alone, who may claim the saloon as in any sense a real "social center."

Here he finds relaxation after a long day in the dust and roar of the factory such as the crowded and slouchy rooms he calls home will not furnish; here he can escape the crying children and get the companionship of men interested in the same things he is; there are games, cards, pool, reports from the baseball games, races, and prize fights, sometimes music, and a warm place in which to enjoy them. There is no feeling of constraint; on the contrary, the manager is glad to have him remain so long as he is spending money. All these enjoyments may be purchased for an evening at the exceedingly small price of a few beers or even of a single glass, with a free lunch thrown in. The saloon is a democratic institution, open freely to everyone and criticizing no one.

"The Poor Man's Club."—The tendency toward club life is growing in this twentieth century. Never before were people so anxious to unite into associations with more or less organization and frequent meetings and with social, or social and economic aims combined, as at present. Everything from a "street arabs'" gang and a college fraternity to a labor union and a mutual benefit association emphasizes this fact.

The average unskilled workman takes out his club life almost exclusively in the saloon. It is the social center for hundreds of thousands of the dwellers in our cities, chiefly the poorer classes of people. Those who are not patrons of the saloon find their social enjoyment elsewhere. They usually have fair or good homes and take a part in self-supporting club or church or other organized social life. The workingman does not enter these. The saloon is where he meets his associates, plays his games, and relaxes after the day's labor. Here he gets his free lunch as well as his drink. It has therefore come to be called "the poor man's club." Efforts to do away with it are resented as an attack upon the poor man by the more well-to-do. There is a strong and not altogether unreasonable opposition, often amounting to hatred, among laboring men, especially the more unskilled, against temperance and prohibition workers for this very reason. It is needless to say that this is fostered by the liquor dealers themselves and class antagonism is appealed to in support of the traffic. The unreasonableness of the claim that the saloon is the poor man's club is shown when the large number of saloons, sometimes of the worst kind, supported exclusively by the wealthy, is pointed out. The so-called "upper classes" are found to maintain clubs in which drinking is one of the very chief purposes. *The saloon is not so much the poor man's club as it is the drinking man's club.*

On one hand, it may be conceded that the saloon is the place in which vast numbers of laboring men find their only enjoyment. On the other, it is no less evident that it is the presence of the saloon that makes better social life impossible. It is here, ready established, easy to adopt by every young man or boy. It is able to compete, in the sense of drawing men to it, both by means of its liquors and by its less harmful attractions, with any and every "substitute" that has yet been placed in the field. With the brewers' millions of wealth behind the saloon-keeper, if occasion demands, it can hold its own in furnishing entertainment to an almost unlimited extent. Many saloons offer evil inducements, the satisfaction of evil appetites, questionable amusements, and gambling. This is not the kind of social club workingmen or any other men need.

The low cost at which the saloon furnishes its numerous attractions is one of the strong features in making it popular. One reason why laboring men do not form clubs of their own is because they cannot afford the membership dues that would be required to pay for well-furnished quarters and equipment. Yet no one doubts for a minute that the saloon-keeper does all this purely as a business venture, often furnishing to lodges, labor unions, social clubs, and athletic societies, rooms, heated and lighted, near to the saloon, free of cost. It is inconceivable that the money which pays for the drinks, plus the ''attractions'' provided by the saloon would not pay for the attractions alone if the drinks were absent.

How can we help concluding that while the saloon now acts as a sort of poor man's club, it is the club which, taking advantage of his poverty and of his desire for intoxicants, makes him pay more for his recreation and social life than any other class of people with moderate or low earnings?

Counter Attractions.—''The negative and destructive methods employed in social reform movements should be accompanied or followed by positive and constructive ones.'' The application of this sociological principle to the saloon question calls for ''some broad, rational, and practical method of counterbalancing the various motives that lead men to patronize the saloon.'' [2] The idea of a ''substitute,'' however, should not be limited to a rival business in competition with the saloon—a social institution run next door or across the street to draw men away from it, but to satisfying the motives, so far as they are worthy ones, or indicate any real need, in other and more natural ways.

There are many organizations and clubs both philanthropic and self-supporting, which provide healthful amusement and recreation. These, intentionally or unintentionally, serve as counter attractions for the saloon to some extent. But the great need of our large cities is for more, many more and better ones, in which there will be more inducements, as well as more of a feeling of freedom on the part of those for whom they are established. The most successful of these institutions at present are moving-picture shows, coffee houses, lunch rooms, reading rooms, bowling alleys, and other athletic games not in connection with saloons, recreation centers, social settlements, the better grade of theaters, and parks, especially the small parks in dense residence neighborhoods. These all supply means to sociability of a pure kind away from the temptations of the saloon. But their number is all too meager and the hours of closing often too early. The Young Men's Christian Associations to some extent serve in this capacity, but their field is largely limited to clerical and railroad men and strange young men of the better classes coming from the country and small towns. They do not, to any marked extent, counteract the attractions of the saloon to those whose need is greatest.

The essential principle of this movement must be the supplying of healthful relaxation free from the sale of intoxicating liquors. There can be no temporary surrender of this principle in favor of the lighter alcoholics, or increased temptation to the young is sure to follow. If the lightest beer should be served in connection with the best of amusements, it might be a good means of weaning off the old toper, but it would be the fatal attracting influence that would start thousands of young men and boys to acquiring the alcohol habit under respectable surroundings. Anything that does this is sure to increase later the number of regular saloon patrons who go there for the liquors alone. The absence of liquor must be complete or the attraction will be toward, instead of away from, the saloon.

The man who takes his recreation and social pleasure at the saloon feels that he is paying for what he gets. And he certainly is paying full price. The saloon is not run for charity, but for business. The independent wage-earner, even if he is quite poor, knows this and appreciates it. If he is at all self-respecting, he resents having things done for him by outsiders with an air of charity about them. The rightly organized counter attraction will take note of this principle by requiring that the accommodations which it gives shall be good, and that payment, at least in part, shall be insisted upon. But the saloon patron himself must remember that a self-respecting man cannot secure the social enjoyments he so much needs while so large a share of his earnings go for beer.

The question of providing counter attractions rightly belongs to the school, the church, the popular lecture, the night and trade schools, the trade unions, the private clubs and organizations, the park boards, the moving-picture shows, good theaters, and the thousand and one forms of social enjoyment open to healthful society. *It is the saloon that, for economic ends, has usurped this ground and that tends to run sociability into vice.*

Voluntary organizations of this kind should be supplemented by more radical restrictive or prohibitory measures. Organized social force, government, has an indisputable part to play. In the new profession, or mission of social service a force of our best college trained men and women is needed in our large cities as workers.

With substitution measures alone the power of the saloon to corrupt society will remain practically unbroken. Its power to offer attractions is unlimited. "All too frequently the saloons that attract most men are those that harbor gambling and shelter prostitutes. The saloons with concert halls, where so many men and women are lured to drink and dance, have their walls decorated with suggestive and indecent pictures, and one hears songs of the most revolting character. The whole atmosphere reveals a total lack of modesty and common decency.''[3]   No philanthropic or semi-philanthropic, or even legitimate business enterprise, can counteract the fascination of the average saloon, with such ''attractions,'' combined with the appetite for liquors, as it offers to vast numbers of people in all grades of society.   The saloon is not the ''poor man's club.''   It is primarily the drink-loving man's club, whether poor or rich.   *So long as alcohol is one of the forces in the saloon there is and can be no substitute for it;* furthermore, *social welfare demands that there shall be no such substitute.*

''Reform the Saloon''—The Subway Experiment.— Frequently efforts to reform the saloon, to make it more respectable and free it from some of its most open objections, or to eliminate private profits in the retail sale, are proposed as temperance measures.   These suggestions originate sometimes from liquor men who wish to keep the trade in better opinion before the public by eliminating the most apparent evils and shutting down the low groggeries.   Such efforts are only in a restricted sense of the nature of substitutes, and have none of the advantages of true counter attractions.   They do have all their objections, however, and many others besides.

(1) Saloon reform fails to take into account the appetite for intoxicants and the opportunity to cultivate it, that all kinds of drink, and especially the most ''pure,'' afford.

(2) That the quality of sociability that comes with intoxication is abnormal, and that it soon tends to become unhealthful, vicious, and a danger to all-round welfare.

(3) That even the well-regulated saloon, with or without its private profits eliminated, will bring into existence

some sort of groggery where the appetite it has formed may continue to be satisfied after the respectability of the drinker has been lost.

(4) The attractions about a saloon will increase the amount of liquor sold, but the liquor will not increase, but will rather diminish, the trade in ''soft drinks'' and other features designed to take the place of alcoholics.

The noted Subway Tavern of New York, opened in August, 1904, was intended as a model reform saloon. It was incorporated by a company of men especially interested in social movements. Their honest purpose was to free it from all the evils of the ordinary saloon, except alcohol. The drinks were to be pure and of the best quality, but sold at usual rates. The element of private profits was eliminated almost entirely, the manager being paid a salary, and the profits, after a certain fixed per cent to stockholders, were to go toward establishing similar places. A restaurant and lunch counter, a room right in the front where only temperance drinks were sold, and opportunities for reading, recreation and amusement, were to make it a ''poor man's club,'' where men could drink alcoholic or non-alcoholic drinks without getting drunk, and could enjoy themselves under good moral surroundings.

The place was opened with much publicity and an immense amount of newspaper advertising. The opening service, in which Bishop Potter, one of the incorporators, said, ''This is the greatest social movement New York has ever known,'' closed with the doxology and the bishop's prayer of consecration upon the new social enterprise.

Although it received more free advertising than any reform institution ever started in that city, it did not succeed. The beer-drinker went back to the ordinary bar-room, where he could have more freedom and get as much beer at the same price. The sightseers and curiosity crowds that made it run smoothly the first few months ceased to be attracted by the novelty. In thirteen months the place was sold out and is being run now as a regular saloon. A new bar has taken the place of the soda fountain and men may now walk boldly in at the front door to get their beer instead of going furtively through the side entrance.

In the words of the new owner, "You can't follow the Lord and chase the devil at the same time." "The biggest patron of the saloon is the man with the biggest thirst."

A typical near-by tenement dweller, who has lived in the neighborhood twenty years, seemed to catch the social principles underlying counter attractions for the saloon better than did the sociological gentlemen who promoted the Tavern when he said: "When I see how them rich people spend money to do something for our wives and children, I take my hat off to them, but when they get 'bit' for a thing like that, when they let every Tom, Dick and Harry come along and get them to put up money for that kind of a thing and *think we want it, then I know they don't or don't want to understand us*—and I get discouraged."

Substitution as a Temperance Measure.—The modern effort to find a satisfactory substitute for the saloon is a recognition of the part that the sociability source has to play in the whole vast liquor problem. It is well for the temperance cause that this is being better known, so that constructive efforts by social service workers may accompany and follow the repressive and restrictive measures made necessary by the three other sources.

Substitution aims directly at one of the foundations of the evil, and at *but one* of them. But it is intimately connected with the problem of better homes for the poor of our great cities, with home and public sanitation, instruction in the values of food and cooking, the question of wages and hours of labor, and other industrial and metropolitan problems. Much can be done in these respects to keep men from ever going to the saloon. Far more can be accomplished when the saloon, as the unjust competitor with these righteous efforts, is driven out by organized force. To the extent that substitution is or can be successful it is a decided temperance meas-ure and worthy of the greatest support.

But it takes into consideration only one of the four sources of the actual liquor problem.

(1) The most persistent source of the liquor evil, the desire for the liquor itself and the feelings it yields, is only indirectly influenced by substitute measures. The improvement of the workingman's home life, better cooking, better sanitation, reduced hours of work, will to some extent reduce the popular dependence upon alcohol. But only to a degree. It is a well-known fact that many in the well-to-do and middle classes, people with the best of home life, every opportunity for good cooking, etc., yet fall back upon the frequent use of intoxicants.

(2) The economic source, the profits of the dealer, cannot be touched by this method. In fact, it but accentuates this source. It makes the saloon-keeper, backed by the brewer, more intense to secure new trade, en-

courages him to offer more temptations to the young and out-attract the most successful counter attractions. Sidney Webb has applied Gresham's law of currency, that bad money will drive out good money when both are in circulation, to all forms of competition. Counterfeit money must be ''prohibited'' before good money will circulate. The sale of liquors must be removed before homes, social clubs, settlements, reading rooms, healthful athletic associations and Y. M. C. A.'s can do their best work. *It is the saloon which is the counterfeit social center; the others are the normal fields for the expression of the social self.*

(3) The legal sanction of the government is upon the saloon rather than upon the ''substitute,'' as matters now stand. It takes from the saloon a $500 or $1,000 license fee to pay city expenses, provide a strong police force to take care of the crime product of the saloon, and relieve private taxation. In doing so it gives the dealer an excuse to demand protection from irritating enforcement of restrictive laws. The license policy gives the saloon an undue social prominence, while the ''substitute'' must struggle for a precarious public support. Further, what law pronounces as right most people accept at once as right and permissible for them in conduct. Every effort to win people away from the saloon has to meet this attitude.

Notwithstanding its limitations, work which amounts to substitution is a most valuable temperance measure; first, as a means of co-operating with and supplementing legal destruction of the saloon and its evils, and, second, as a part in the broad general cause of social advancement just where it is most needed. But for the ordinary American stand-up saloon, where men go to drink as their chief purpose, there is, and should be, no substitute.

The following bit of direct testimony is exceedingly valuable as showing the attitude of that class of men most dependent of all upon the saloon for their social enjoyment if they are to have any at all. C. M. Stocking, of Minneapolis, superintendent of the Union City Mission, on December 4, 1905, conducted a meeting of 150 men, most of whom lived in lodging houses, and all of whom were regular drinkers. The object was a free-for-all discussion of the saloon and substitutes for it. Specific questions, after abundant discussion, were voted upon as follows: "Do men first go to the saloon to enjoy a social hour or do they go there to take a drink?" The vote was, drink 50, social hour 15.

"If all saloons in this city ceased to sell liquor, but kept every other attraction they now have, could they retain one-tenth of their customers?" Only eight voted affirmatively.

"How many of the men here tonight go to the saloon for the sake of the liquor sold there?" One hundred and five hands were raised.

"Can you suggest any substitute for the saloon?" The vote stood, Yes 30, No 50. On further discussion a clean-kept lodging house with opportunity for amusements at a reasonable rate seemed to be most desired. A few wanted places where pure liquors could be sold. But all agreed upon one thing—that nothing furnishing the accommodations and attractions and comforts of the saloon, with intoxicating drinks left out, would be of any special interest to them. The other things were good, but they would not take the place of the drink.

References and Authorities

The Sociability Source of Intemperance.

Calkins, *Substitutes for the Saloon*, 1-7.
Peabody, ''Substitutes for the Saloon,'' *Forum*, 21, 595.
Kraepelin, ''The University Man and the Alcohol Question,'' *Sci. Temp. Jr.*, Dec. 1912.
Barker, *The Saloon Problem and Social Reform*, 184-188.
Stelzle, *The Workingman and Social Problems*, 40-46.
Koren, *Economic Aspects of the Liquor Problem*, 210-240.

The Saloon as a Social Center.

Calkins, *Substitutes for the Saloon*, 1-24.
Wheeler, *Prohibition*, 90-92.
Peabody, ''Substitutes for the Saloon,'' *Forum*, 21, 595.
Barker, *The Saloon Problem and Social Reform*, 184-188.
Turner, ''The City of Chicago,'' *McClure's Magazine* (Apr., 1907), 28, 575.
Koren, *Economic Aspects of the Liquor Problem*, 210-240.
1 Wheeler, 90.

''The Poor Man's Club.''

Calkins, *Substitutes for the Saloon*, 45-53.
Stelzle, *The Workingman and Social Problems*, 37-50.
Rowntree and Sherwell, *The Temperance Problem*, 364-367.
Turner, ''The City of Chicago,'' *McClure's*, 28, 575.
Barker, *The Saloon Problem*, 184-185.

Counter Attractions.

Barker, *The Saloon Problem and Social Reform*, 179-195.
Calkins, *Substitutes for the Saloon*, 25-44, 196-207, 216-242.
Peabody, ''Substitutes for the Saloon,'' *Forum*, 21, 595.
Smith, ''Liquor and Labor,'' *Catholic World*, 47, 539.
Stelzle, *The Workingman and Social Problems*, 48-50.
2 Barker, 180.
3 Ibid, 186.

''Reform the Saloon.''

''The Temperance Problem and the Subway Tavern,'' *International Magazine*, Jan., 1905.
''Collapse of the Subway Tavern,'' *National Temperance Advocate*, Oct., 1905.
Independent, June 22, 1905.

Substitution as a Temperance Measure.

Barker, *The Saloon Problem and Social Reform*, 179-195.

Calkins, *Substitutes for the Saloon*, 25-30, 216-242.

Stelzle, *The Workingman and Social Problems*, 48-50.

Wheeler, *Prohibition*, 90-92.

Smith, ''Liquor and Labor,'' *Catholic World*, 47, 539.

Rowntree and Sherwell, *The Temperance Problem*, 393-407.

CHAPTER IX

The Decalogue and the Golden Rule have precisely the same place in public and private life.

—THEODORE ROOSEVELT.

That liquor should be sold is bad enough, but that for the sake of a paltry revenue, the state should become the partner of the liquor seller—that is a bargain worse than that of Eve or Judas.

—HORACE GREELEY.

CHAPTER IX

THE ETHICAL PHASE

Everyone acknowledges that there are serious evils connected with the general use of intoxicating liquors and the traffic which supplies the demand. It is frankly accepted, even by those who believe most fully in the unlimited right of every man to drink and of the traffic to flourish. To understand the question broadly and honestly, as well as to be able to see clearly the principles involved in any lasting solution, the moral consequences of the liquor institution must be considered no less than the economic, the public health, and the social. What sort of ideals does it cultivate? How is it related to ethical and religious institutions? What is the place for alcohol and intoxication in a developing standard for a better and nobler type of every-day living?

The Social Ethics of the Saloon.—The saloon stands for both the habit and the "trade." It is where the former is created and gratified by the ordinary business sagacity of the latter. It affords a concrete example of the whole problem, ethically, although by no means is it a complete representative of the power of the liquor trade, economically or politically. We should judge the saloon by an ethical standard that will permit the greatest possible degree of individual freedom, to would-be user and dealer, conformable to public welfare as a whole. This standard is *whether its acts and its product bring the greatest happiness to the greatest number.*

The saloon is good or bad, relatively, as it leads toward or from this standard. The self-benefit or injury to the immediate maker or user is not a sufficiently broad unit with which to measure an institution so fixed in social life. It would not be right to deny to a majority a healthful, or merely a relatively non-injurious, pleasure on account of the intemperance and excesses of a few. It is the great average run of normal, inevitable consequences upon the family, the dependent friends, and the community, that condemns the saloon and the drinking habit as socially bad.

One of the greatest authorities on social ethics says that conduct in relation to our fellows is "good or bad according to its assumed effects upon the largest range of associations that we can take into account."[1] John Stuart Mill says: "The standard of morality is the rules and precepts of conduct which procure the greatest happiness in quantity and quality for all mankind."[2] Certainly the saloon takes into account only a very small range of human needs and associations. For the sake of furnishing a choice of livelihood to a few thousand men, and for the purpose of satisfying a normal desire, sociability, in a questionable way, it injures millions of non-indulging women, children, and even men, as well as those who actually become victims to the habit, physically, financially, morally, blighting them for this world and for eternity. It throws upon society a burden in the care of paupers, criminals, and defective humanity greater than that caused by any other one source. It degrades the public conscience by permitting the government to take a share of its profits as a small compensation for the immeasurable burdens it entails upon present and future generations. Balancing by the number and quality of associations to be taken into account we get a result which condemns ethically both the saloon and the drinking custom.

Freedom to the dealer in the choice of a trade is offset by the dangers and losses which that trade brings the community. It is not a difficult matter to enter another business. The sum total of public wealth would be greater without this parasite upon economic welfare; therefore, each man's share, including the ex-saloonkeepers', would be greater. Increased consumption of legitimate articles would call for labor in production and sale that will far more than take up that spent in the production of liquors.

The financial profit to the dealer is now offset by the moral and financial losses to the community, and by the fact that no trade has a right to exist that makes its profits out of individual or community vices.

The happiness of the drinker in his freedom to drink is balanced by that of his wife and children, an average of four to one in quantity, and equal in quality, to say nothing of that of the public which must share in the results of his conduct.

It is only in its sociability features that the saloon gets any real ethical support. Here it has seized upon a neglected factor. There has been handed over to it by the community a monopoly of the social life of the majority of American wage-earners.[3] They find in it almost their only recreation, relaxation and freedom from care. The saloon gives them more comforts, companionship, music, amusement, and even better food, than they have

at home or in the lodging house. Thus it furnishes them
a material and sociability uplift. Had it no other and
worse features, the saloon would be an ethical uplift,
also. It supplies this satisfaction not by, but in spite of
alcohol and intoxication, altho the "booze" is the one
indispensable factor in procuring them.

But in taking his recreation in the saloon, the workingman is depriving his family of their equal right and
share in relaxation and escape from the burdens of the
day. Women and children must remain at home or go
upon the streets. It thus encourages selfishness and
leads to the blighting of the home, as well as taking the
money that might procure happiness for all. Spencer,
who regarded personal liberty as a virtue to be preserved
above all others, yet insists upon its being limited by the
necessity of granting to others the same equal rights
and privileges. Saloon sociability is essentially contrary to this principle; it is always selfish. With the
family as a basis, it is a clear case of suffering by the
majority to gratify the questionable pleasures of a
minority.

In quality the sociability found in the saloon is usually
worse than none at all. The average saloon is gross and
vulgar. The air is bad, the conversation profane and
obscene. The moral effects aside from the drinks are
usually unwholesome. In the words of a prominent
liquor paper bent on "elevating the trade," "The average saloon is out of line with public sentiment. . . .
It is a resort for all tough characters, and in the South
for all idle negroes. It is generally on a prominent
street and is usually run by a sport who cares only for
the almighty dollar. From this resort the drunken man

starts reeling to his home; at this resort the local fights are indulged in. It is a stench in the nostrils of society and a disgrace to the wine and spirit trade."[4]

Further than this, "the public saloon and saloon system is a vast organized inciter of human appetite. It is an omnipresent, publicly sanctioned temptation to evil. *It exists not because man, by nature, must drink, but because, by proper incentives, man can be made to drink, and there is money in selling it to him.* The craving of large numbers of people for alcoholic liquors is no more to be charged to the Creator than is the craving of certain people for opium, or of many for tobacco, or the irresistible tendency of others to utter themselves in copius profanity. These, and others like them, are strictly acquired habits, perverted and evil habits, acquired in association with companions of evil."[5]

The saloon furnishes pleasure, both the happiness of association and the effects of the drink itself, to a large number of people who do not seem to go to excess and who do not apparently leave any burden on society—the moderate drinking business man, of the middle classes and the men of means. It is shown[3] that 50 per cent of the entire population of Boston patronize the saloons of that city every day; in Chicago the daily patronage is greater than 50 per cent of its 2.000,000 population. Not all of these are dependent upon the saloon for their social enjoyment. For them, therefore, the restriction that would come from the expulsion of the saloon would not be a serious one; they may well be compelled to yield this one privilege in the interests of the public who must bear the burdens of those who do go to excess. The toxic dangers of alcohol are so great, the social vices coming from the saloon are so insidious, its political influence so corrupting to the state, and the type of citizenship it creates so bad, that the pleasures of even the most moderate drinkers become relatively unimportant and should not be considered in face of the larger needs of the community. "A serious thing it may be to curtail the pleasures of mankind; but is it not far more serious to continue pleasures that can be had only by the continuance of conditions that are certain, ever and everywhere, to entail upon countless thousands woes that are immeasurable? The issue is not the wine-cup of which poets sang, but the saloon whose horrors only a Dante could fittingly describe." [6]

The Attitude of the Church.—The three great organized moral forces of society are the home, the school, and the church. Upon their welfare the ethical standards of the state depend. Government recognizes the ethical need when it protects these institutions from the encroachment of the saloon whose teachings run directly counter to their type of instruction.

The church is, or ought to be, pre-eminently the leader in the righting of social, as well as individual, wrongs. In it is found "the highest form of moral organization known to man. In it the best impulses and teachings of the home, and the noblest and purest unfoldings of the school, find their sweetest and ripest fruitage, their development nearest the divine." [7]

The chief aim of the church is to make men better, both individually and collectively. Its methods, are, and must continue to be, "moral suasion," not force, or law. It would defeat itself if it undertook to compel men to be good. But it must hold up the standard of right for the individual and for organized society and government incessantly, or it misses the object for which it exists. It is one of the most hopeful signs of early success in the anti-liquor movement that the Federal Council of the Churches of Christ in America has adopted, in its new social program, a strong plank "for the protection of the individual and society, from the social, economic, and moral waste of the liquor traffic." [8]

In its work the church is in direct conflict with the saloon. Between it, aiming to build up the morality of the community, and the liquor trade as it actually exists in most places, there is nothing in common but inherent antagonism. Only the briefest possible outline of the attitude of the church can be given here.

(1) The teachings of the Bible as the foundation of the Christian religion are essentially against personal intemperance, the offering of temptation to use strong drink, and the reaping of private or public profit from the sale of intoxicants.

(2) In accordance with its fundamental principles and its own experience, the church in America has come, practically, to the conclusion that total abstinence for the individual is the only right and safe method of con- duct. It recognizes the higher freedom of the individual to be governed according to an educated conscience, yet, because of the dangers which lie in the alcohol habit when once acquired, and the personal responsibility for example toward others, it believes that this is the right course of personal conduct for Christians.

(3) Almost every Protestant church believes in posi- tive exclusion of liquor dealers from membership and most of them will not receive contributions from the trade. In the Catholic church there is a growing demand that Catholics everywhere "choose some more honorable way of making a living." [9]

(4) In regard to the traffic, Protestant churches, with the exception of the Episcopal and a few of the smaller denominations, declare for complete prohibition. The Episcopal favors a very high license policy, with the hope of reducing the evils of the traffic in accordance with its emphasis of personal moderation rather than total abstinence. The Catholic church makes no official declaration as to the means of control, but the number of ministers favoring severe restriction or taking aggressive part in local and state prohibition movements, is constantly increasing. This is especially significant as the experience of the church is more largely among the classes who have inherited drinking customs than is the work of the Protestant churches. Cardinal Manning has said: ''I know of no antagonist to the Holy Spirit more direct, more subtle, more stealthy, more ubiquitous than intoxicating drink.''[10] Experience is teaching everywhere the same lesson—that the trade must be removed if the church is to do its best work.

(5) That "it can never be legalized without sin" is a settled principle among the leading evangelical churches. Official declarations emphasize this more and more strongly and urge upon members the necessity of living up to it in practice. They specify the renting of property for saloon purposes, signing of petitions for license, voting for license or for license policies, for men favoring them, or for political organizations that support the traffic or the license policy.

(6) Recognizing the political source of the liquor power, several prominent church organizations have made declarations as to what constitutes good moral conduct on the part of Christians politically. They recognize that it is not the function of the church to dictate

how a man shall vote, but they indicate clearly for what political principles, organizations, or types of men he ought not to vote. The action of the Methodist Episcopal church may be taken as reflecting the ethical standard of the largest Protestant church in this respect. It states that ''We record our deliberate judgment that no candidate for any office which in any way may have to do with the liquor traffic has a right to expect, nor ought he to receive, the support of Christian citizens so long as he stands committed to the liquor interests or refuses to put himself in accord with a crystallized public sentiment for the overthrow of the liquor traffic.''[11]

The Saloon Its Chief Competitor.—The more the church appreciates its social mission in the community and undertakes to improve the conditions which are a menace to its work, the more it learns that the saloon is its heaviest competitor for men, especially young men. It has seized upon a function heretofore largely neglected by the church, the providing of the means and place of sociability for wage-earners, young men and new arrivals in the cities. The brewers equip amusement parks at heavy expense, provide the games and excitements as well as the beer, and get an attendance of thousands every evening during the summer. When the church takes up this work, as it is now beginning to do, in its settlements, missions, clubs, men's Bible classes, gymnasiums, Y. M. C. A.'s, etc., the saloon becomes resentful and attempts to discredit the church, defame its ministers, and counteract its labors to win men.

The saloon is as well, if not better equipped for handling large numbers of men, than is the church. Thruout the country there are more than 200,000 places where liquor is sold openly[12] as compared with the 218,000 churches of all denominations. In 1911 the total number of retail dealers was 218,400, and the ministers of all churches, Protestant, Catholic, Jewish, etc., was 170,400.[13]

Frequently the church buildings are grouped together in the better parts of the cities and towns and are hard to reach by those who need their help most. The tendency of the brewers, the backers of the saloon, on the other hand, is to establish a grog shop, when it is not positively excluded by law, in every separate section or community where it can possibly support itself or create a new trade for itself. The saloon goes where the people are; the church seems to expect the masses to accommodate themselves to it. The saloon runs from 16 to 20 hours per day for six, or even seven days a week. The church is open one whole day and an average of two or three nights more each week.

In Boston a few years ago careful investigation[14] showed that the daily patronage of the saloons, counting "repeaters," visitors and people living in the suburbs, was 50 per cent of the total population. They spent on an average ten cents each visit. At the same time the patronage of all such institutions as may properly be regarded as furnishing competition with the saloon, such as reading rooms, coffee-clubs, and lunch rooms not intended exclusively as eating places, was 76,268, also including "repeaters" and people from out-of-town. The average daily attendance at the Y. M. C. A. was 1,061.[15] The proportionate attendance was 1 at the places free from alcohol to 3.3 at the saloons.

In Chicago there are 1,130 churches, chapels and missions of all kinds. There are, as counter attractions, 7,150 saloons. The former are open from one to three nights per week and all day Sunday. The latter run from 15 to 24 hours a day and seven days in the week, some never closing the year around. If the average attendance at the saloons is the same as in Boston, that is 50 per cent of the total population, and there is no reason to think it lower, there are 1,000,000 visits made daily to these saloons. The Y. M. C. A. in all its departments shows an average daily attendance of 3,351, including men who live in the suburbs.

It has been carefully estimated[16] that of the 17,000,000 young men in the United States between the ages of fifteen and thirty-five 10,800,000, or 63.5 per cent, never attend church at any time. The remaining 36.5 per cent includes all those who go occasionally, merely for amusement, as well as the members and active workers. "It is safe to say that 95 per cent of the young men do little or nothing in an aggressive way to promote the organized Christian work of the churches."[17]

In marked contrast is the vast number that visit saloons, some regularly, some only occasionally. It is not confined within a single million. Figures are not available, but in saloon towns, and particularly in the larger centers, hundreds may be found in drinking places to one in the churches, the same evening. General Secretary Messer of the Chicago Young Men's Christian Association[18] says that on one Sunday night "a careful count was made of the men in a Madison street saloon (in Chicago) at 7 o'clock. The number was 524, and during the next two hours 480 more men entered. At one of the billiard tables young men six deep on all sides were engaged in open gambling. Private stairways connect this saloon with the vilest theater in the city. There are 3,000 billiard and pool rooms in the city, generally adjacent to or a part of a saloon." Another secretary reports an investigation of fifteen saloons in Peoria, Ill., in which, on a Sunday night, 875 young men were found in one hour and fifteen minutes. How fifteen ministers of that city would have rejoiced to have seen those 875 able fellows scattered thro their audiences!

The fact is too evident to be avoided that the saloon has a stronger hold upon the young men of America than has the combined force of all the churches. Further, it has developed and is developing an environment from which it is more and more difficult to lift men, and which makes them less useful after they are reached. "Environment affects conversion before and after."

The presence of the legalized saloon produces a dangerous reaction upon the church itself. It cannot escape the demoralizing effects of the liquor traffic upon the spiritual condition of its own members. The liquor trade is a part of current social order; church members get mixed up with it in every-day business relations, social connections, and especially in political affairs. The saloon maintains its position largely because of its licensed respectability. The effect is seen in the halting attitude of many congregations toward practical anti-liquor work, in their fear of radicalism, in a sort of chronic horror of the political phases of the question, in decrease in spiritual power and influence, and in the distaste of many strong men outside of the church, for church relations of any kind. The church cannot realize its own proper place of usefulness in the community while the saloon continues to be a legal competing institution.

The Traffic in the Foreign Field.—Scarcely less important than the competition that the saloon offers to the church at home is the way in which the liquor traffic handicaps its missions in the foreign field. Whether our civilization is to be a benefit or a curse to the Filipinos, to Hawaii, and in the mission fields of Africa, where the "child-races" and semi-civilized are found, no less than in the older countries of China, Japan, India and elsewhere, depends upon whether American vices, and chiefly American liquor, are to continue to accompany the flag and the missionary.

Before our type of civilization was carried to these countries half of the world was under total abstinence religions, Hindu, Buddhist and Mohammedan, a clear indication that the desire for intoxicants is not a universal human instinct that must be gratified, but a vice that even these religions condemn as morally wrong.

Those nations that were not held to abstinence by religious influence or laws growing out of the native religions, were mostly temperate in the use of such intoxicants as they had. The Chinese have frequently passed prohibitory laws and so there has been little drunkenness in that country except where the people come into contact with Western commerce. It is to the lasting disgrace of Great Britain that the opium trade was forced upon China at the mouth of the cannon and to the great credit of China that she has practically banished that narcotic curse. In India the English trade has almost a monopoly of the liquor business, but American consuls are laboring hard to give the American brewers a fair opening. A missionary says: "In eight years the increase of the liquor traffic in Bengal was 135 per cent. In the central provinces it was 100 per cent in ten years. In Ceylon the revenue from drink is almost 14 per cent of the total revenue. Mr. Cain, ex-member of the British Parliament, says: 'All moral considerations are swamped in the effort to obtain revenue. The worst and rottenest excise system in the civilized world is that of India.' " [19] While most native races have native drinks more or less intoxicating, according to Dr. Crafts,[20] the Ainos of Japan are the only race of heathen drunkards who were not made such by civilization. Drunkenness is with them, as with ancient worshippers of Bacchus, a religious ecstasy. "Thruout the length and breadth of beautiful Japan, in all large and smaller cities and villages, foreign drinks are easily obtainable, to the great injury of the people." [21]

In Central Africa drink from civilized nations created such havoc that its importation was prohibited within a limited area by concerted action of the powers. Yet it is not strictly enforced and the area is too small. Prince Momolu Massaquoi of Ghendinah, who was educated in America, after taking up his rule over his tribe as king, wrote in 1905: "From actual calculation I find that nearly one-half of the goods imported into my territory is in the form of liquor, and that of the worst and most injurious kind. The native has an idea that everything that white men use and export must necessarily be good and an essential element in civilization. It is therefore common to find a man who is poor and not able to get sufficient liquor on which to get drunk, rubbing a drop on his head or on his mustache in order that people may smell it and call him civilized." [22]

Drunkenness is distinctly a vice of the Christian nations. It is their aggressive trade spirit that has carried liquor in immense quantities among these undeveloped races. Especially in warm climates its ravages are fearful. The natives know no self-restraint; they copy the vices of the great white man more quickly than they do his virtues. The exportation of liquors to these tribes is a crime against humanity. Prof. Starr, of the University of Chicago, the noted anthropologist, said in a lecture, ''An African living in an African hut after an African fashion is likely to be a better man than he would be after the Anglo-Saxon introduced his religion, his surface civilization and his rum.''

The liquor traffic is one of the greatest obstacles to effective missionary effort in all Mohammedan countries. All white men are supposed to be Christians. Moslems say when they see one of their number drunk, ''He has left Mohamet and gone to Jesus.'' In Morocco ''drunkenness is considered a Christian sin.'' ''There is no license system, because the sultan cannot derive a profit from sin.''

The rum tragedy in Manila and the Philippine Islands is the great disgrace in connection with our recent era of expansion. An advance agent of a certain American brewery was in the first ranks of Dewey's force, and shiploads of beer were following close after the fleet. This agent hastily threw off his uniform, and in a few days had many saloons established dealing out beer and the stronger American liquors in true American style. Americans were soon known as drunkards by both Spanish and Filipinos. At first disgust, then slow acceptance, has been the attitude of the better classes, while the less civilized yield more quickly to this type of refining influence.

President Schurman, of Cornell University, who was at the head of the Philippine Commission, said: ''I regret that the Americans let the saloon get a foothold in the islands. It has hurt the Americans more than anything else, and the spectacle of Americans drunk awakens disgust in the Filipinos. We suppressed the cock-fights there, but left the saloon to flourish. One emphasized the Filipino frailty and the other the American vice. I have never seen a Filipino drunkard."[23] The Filipinos are moral and sober. When they see drunken, profane and immoral soldiers representing this country they have little respect for the religion they profess. 'If that is your religion,' they say 'we prefer our own.'"[24]

With such a blighting disgrace ruining so much of the noble sacrificing work of missionaries and teachers, it would seem wise economy to apply the whole force of Christian America, if necessary, to stop the exportation of intoxicating liquors and give the church and our type of civilization a fair chance.

Ethical Phase of License.—License means in theory both restriction and privilege—restriction from certain acts for the legal privilege of doing certain others. It rests upon the assumption that the business is partly good, partly bad; that the evils are contingent, not inherent, and so may be eliminated by careful regulation. It has necessarily a twofold character—sanction and condemnation.

In actual operation, applied to the sale of liquors as it is in states with the exception of those having prohibition, it means little in the way of restriction, but much in the way of endorsement, encouragement and protection. It fails to note that intemperance and the evils attending it are inherent in the alcohol and in the vicious sort of sociability permitted or encouraged in saloons. Its application here is therefore wrong in principle and a mistake in practice.

Further, its permissive feature, the public consent to sell intoxicating liquors, usually injurious to the public, granted for a price paid the government, brings it into conflict with public morality.

It is as wrong to set up a false ideal in society as it is to teach a child vicious habits, to steal, to be impure, to have no regard for the sanctity of life, and it is many times more dangerous to public welfare. "Law and government are the sovereign influences in human society. What they sanction will ever be generally considered innocent, what they condemn is thereby made a crime." The educational effect of law is to train either upward or downward. The license law teaches that the traffic is all right if the fee is paid; it puts the social right or wrong on a money basis.

If the sale of liquor is right and needful for public welfare, the trade should not be required to bear such an unusually heavy burden in public support. As it is, the extraordinarily high fees demanded by the government and willingly paid by the dealers, are in the nature of what is called "graft" in current "high finance" and "high politics." If the beverage sale is a danger to society, as the character of alcohol makes it, government has no right to license it; it may not justly attempt to legalize a wrong. It should be attacked and cleared out. If this cannot be done all at once, consent should not be given, any more than it would be given to a gang of thieves or gamblers, all of whom cannot be captured at one time. Without this legalizing phase of license it would be possible to prosecute saloons one at a time as nuisances.

If the traffic is right, the retail sale should not be burdened with the social opprobrium of a $1,000 license fee; if wrong, the fee cannot make it right. The desire of the dealer to pay only proves that he regards the money as a compensation to the public conscience.

To the individual citizen license implies consent to the acts so authorized. The government becomes responsible for the product of the saloon. In our form of government *the individual citizen, favoring that policy, no matter how remotely, and voting for it, is a party to that policy and its consequences.* There can be no ethical distinction between his act and that of the mayor or licensing board who signs the document that hangs over the bar.

"Society is only a collective individual. In a republican form of government 'we the people' have a moral responsibility for our collective acts, and that responsibility rests upon those who make up 'we the people'—in other words, on the voter. A Christian voter has no right to endorse by his vote an attitude or an action by society which he would not endorse as a private Christian." [25]

Assuming that two-thirds of those who patronize the saloon never become drunkards, that all who drink do it voluntarily, and have knowledge of its possible consequences, the saloon is nevertheless a vice and a drunkard factory. The families of the one-third must suffer. Neither the gratification of the pleasures secured by the two-thirds in the saloon, nor the free will of the drinker in choosing his own course, nor the price paid by the dealer, can justify the social consequences.

Harmony of Government with Moral Welfare.—The drinking of alcoholic liquors is not in itself wrong; it depends upon the consequences. If a man drinks in such a way that little injury is done his health, if he can stand the cost financially, and if his acts do not injure others or his indulgence entail lowered vitality upon his children, it must be acknowledged that there is nothing personally wrong in his use of liquor as a beverage, and that government has no occasion to interfere. To restrict him from without is to limit his pleasure, a loss to himself and to the community.

But science shows that in anything more than the most moderate doses, so small as to make its beverage use insignificant, alcohol is for most people a poison. This makes it, to the great majority of people an inherent danger, and so it becomes a moral wrong to society to permit its unrestricted sale for such purposes. The social ethics cannot be determined by the individual effects, but by the great average of consequences. These are of such far-reaching danger that the rights of the moderate self-controlled drinker should not be permitted to stand in the way of the infinitely more important consideration—the lasting good of the whole.

The protection of public morals is another primary duty of government. It, too, is among those unwritten duties of all government called "police powers," for preserving the very integrity of the government itself. It is not the function of society, organized as a whole, to "make men good by law;" but it is as much its duty to protect moral ideals and religious aspirations as it is to see that men do not steal each other's dollars, or maintain a public nuisance that endangers health, or deprive each other of life or limb. The spiritual need is one of the fundamental requirements of society. In its acquisition social regulation is as necessary to prevent undue private aggrandizement as it is to protect a man in the proper accumulation of material wealth.

The state cannot directly make anyone happy, or good, or wise. But the character of public institutions it permits, or to which it gives special endorsement by licensing, makes a great deal of difference to him in his endeavors to escape misery and advance in ethical ideals. The saloon is a source of vice, misery and crime. It is the duty of government to remove this sort of environment.

The state may not make men good by law, but it certainly should not permit men to be made bad in accordance with law.

Institutions tending toward moral uplift are protected fully by law. Churches and church property do not pay taxes because of the public moral service they render. Legitimate business willingly bears the additional burden placed upon it. On the other hand, immoral institutions and sources, such as lotteries and gambling apparatus, are not taxed for the very opposite reason—they are evils from which the moral business man is paying to be defended. Why should the liquor traffic be permitted to have privileges contrary to its inherent nature just because it is willing to pay for them?

The most persistent claim, ethically, for the saloon is that it furnishes amusement and recreation for a large class of workingmen who cannot afford anything better. Legal prohibition is necessary to deal with this phase of the problem satisfactorily. It does not aim to take the sociability features away from the saloon, as do certain other regulative measures, but to remove alcohol and vice from sociability so that thru the money now spent for drink, normal recreation and amusement may be possible.

References and Authorities.

The Social Ethics of the Saloon.

Fehlandt, *A Century of Drink Reform*, 279-292, 300-303.
Barker, *The Saloon Problem and Social Reform*, 37, 41-42, 185-188.
Calkins, *Substitutes for the Saloon*, 2-8, 14-16.
Committee of Fifty, *The Liquor Problem; Summary*, 146-150.
''The Ethics of Prohibition,'' *Internatl. Jr. of Ethics*, IX, 350.
Turner, ''The City of Chicago,'' *McClure's*, Apr., 1907.
[1] Dr. A. W. Small, Univ. of Chicago, lectures on *Ethics of Sociology*.
[2] Mill, *Utilitarianism*.
[3] Committee of Fifty, 147.
[4] *Bonfort's Wine and Spirit Circular*, See Barker, 187.
[5] Fehlandt, 302.
[6] Wheeler, *Prohibition*, 91.

The Attitude of the Church.

Barker, *The Saloon Problem and Social Reform*, 48, 73-85.
Calkins, *Substitutes for the Saloon*, 125-134.
Woolley and Johnson, *Temperance Progress*, 447-465.
American Prohibition Year Book (1911), 46-55.
[7] Hopkins, 166.
[8] Report of 2nd Quadrennial Council, Chicago, 1912.
[9] Third Plenary Council, Baltimore, 1884.
[10] Quoted, *Am. Prohibition Year Book* (1911), 47.
[11] *Discipline* (1912), 509.

The Saloon Its Chief Competitor.

Barker, *The Saloon Problem and Social Reform*, 48.
Cressey, *The Church and Young Men*, 1-7.
Calkins, *Substitutes for the Saloon*, 10-15, 133-146.
Fehlandt, *A Century of Drink Reform*, 300-303.
Peabody, ''Substitutes for the Saloon,'' *Forum*, 21, 595.
Oates, *The Religious Condition of Young Men*.
[12] *American Prohibition Year Book* (1911) from Internal Revenue Reports.
[13] Daily News Almanac (1913), Compilation of Religious Statistics by Dr. H. K. Carroll.
[14] Peabody, 595.

[15] Y. M. C. A. Handbooks.

[16] Cressey.

[17] Oates, *The Religious Condition of Young Men.*

[18] Paper, ''Social Forces in Action,'' J. Wilbur Messer, Gen. Sec., Chicago Y. M. C. A.

The Traffic in the Foreign Field.

Crafts, *Intoxicating Drinks and Drugs in All Lands* (1911).

Dennis, *Christian Missions and Social Progress*, vol. 1, 76-84.

Barker, *The Saloon Problem and Social Reform*, 48-49.

Woolley and Johnson, *Temperance Progress*, 433-445.

Momolu Massaquoi, ''Africa's Appeal to Christendom,'' *Century*, April, 1905.

[19] *American Prohibition Year Book* (1907), 14.

[20] Crafts, 19.

[21] Ibid, 137.

[22] See ref. above.

[23] *The Independent*, Dec., 1899.

[24] Crafts, 201.

Ethical Phase of License.

Barker, *The Saloon Problem and Social Reform*, 67-70.

Fehlandt, *A Century of Drink Reform*, 193-207.

Fraser, ''The Ethics of Prohibition,'' *Internatl. Jr. of Ethics*, IX, 350.

[25] Spencer, *The License Question*, 127.

Harmony of Government with Moral Welfare.

Hopkins, *Wealth and Waste*, 164-179.

Fraser, ''Ethics of Prohibition,'' *Internatl. Jr. of Ethics*, IX, 350.

Fehlandt, *A Century of Drink Reform*, 302-305.

And they fling him, hour by hour,
   Limbs of men to give him power;
Brains of men to give him cunning;
   And for dainties to devour,
Children's souls, the little worth;
   Hearts of women cheaply bought.
He takes them and he breaks them,
   But he gives them scanty thought.
        —WILLIAM VAUGHAN MOODY, *The Brute.*

CHAPTER X

THE LIQUOR CONFLICT WITH SOCIAL INSTITUTIONS

The Family Drink Bill.—"Among our working people," says Prof. Schmoller, of Berlin, one of the most important of recent economists, "the conditions of domestic life, of education, of property, of progress or degradation, are all dependent upon the proportion of income that flows down the father's throat. The whole condition of our lower and middle classes—one might without exaggeration say the future of our nation— depends upon this question." [1]

This is Germany, where beer-drinking is at its best; where moderation is supposed to prevail, where excess is seldom found and where beer is as pure and perfect as science and the supervision of government inspectors that inspect can make it. These are the people so frequently pointed out as suffering little or not at all from liquors. But the facts show that the economic consequences alone of the universal drink custom, especially on the family, are frightful and constitute a menace to the welfare of the race and nation. With low wages and heavy taxes the purchase of four, ten or even twenty glasses of beer per day is a fixed and regular drain; it may not produce the degree of drunkenness found in England and some other countries, but it limits the food supply and makes the drinker dull and slow-going.

The liquor craving at best is an abnormal economic

demand. When fully acquired it is a most persistent and growing item of expense in the family budget. Its gratification takes precedence to that of any legitimate desire or need on the part of wife, children or aged parents. How it conditions domestic happiness is best shown by a study of its relation to each of the three fundamental necessities of life—food, clothing, and shelter.

Among the great mass of people dependent upon their daily earnings, laboring men in factory or office or on the farm, as well as among the poorer classes, the standard of family living will rise as the drink bill is cut off, or fall as an increasing ratio is spent for this purpose. The first heavy burden always falls upon the home—a poorer house or more crowded rooms must be procured. Next in order follows food reduction; cheaper in quality and less in quantity. Last of all, and only when the strictest economy is exacted in order to furnish more money for beer, will most people save to any great extent in clothing. As a symbol of respectability this will be clung to most frantically by the family of the drunkard being drawn down in the social scale by the liquor burden.

It is on the rent that the most heartless saving takes place. The narrowed quarters, crowded rooms, filthy surroundings and broken spirits of the home where a large share of the income is spent for drink must be borne chiefly by the innocent members. The man himself may seek selfishly the companionship of the street corner saloon; the wife and children must endure without relief day or night the unhealthful rooms which his indulgence makes necessary.

The per capita cost of drink is $18.00 each year. Counting the average family at five members, the yearly family drink bill is about $90.00 for temperate and intemperate families alike.[2] Shut the saloon and the average family will have nearly $8 per month additional with which to provide for itself adequate, comfortable and decent living. This would settle the housing problem and wipe out the slums of our great cities at one stroke.

The second great slice made in the family necessities on account of the money spent for liquor is in food. The compulsory education department of the Chicago school board reports[3] that 5,000 school children are sent to school breakfastless, and that of 10,070 cases examined, 55 per cent are sufferers from malnutrition. Neglect, drunkenness of one or both parents, and sickness, were found to be the great causes in most cases. Hundreds of mothers were found who went to bed hungry in order that the children might have something to eat next morning. Often fathers were beneficiaries of the free lunch counters in saloons while the rest of the family went half starved.

It is said that "two temperance people can be supported on the land needed to support the coarse tastes of one regular frequenter of the saloon."[4]

It has been estimated that the food destroyed in the manufacture of intoxicants each year—the rye, corn, barley and other grains—is equivalent to nearly six billion loaves of bread.[5] This would give every man, woman and child of our 95,000,000 population 63 loaves or apportion 315 to every family. There is thus destroyed, without adequate economic return, sufficient foodstuff to give every one in the nation a loaf of bread daily for two months, or more than enough to feed the entire "submerged tenth" a year.

On the third chief item of family necessity, dress, the consequences of the drink bill are not quite so marked, altho equally severe. Clothes are the social and cultural indication of the wearer. They give "standing" as nothing else does. Physical suffering, lack of food, cold, and disease will be borne in silence; anything will be sacrificed before this tag of respectability is let go.

The ragged and shabby appearance of the drunkard's family are only too well told by the heart-rending stories of the old-time temperance agitator. They cannot be overdrawn. They reveal the extreme of the truth They mark the limit of suffering and sacrifice demanded to gratify the drink appetite. The smart, but stylish and cheap, Sunday dress, so often worn by the daughters of the very poor, is but the meanest contrast with the garment which it must replace instantly on reaching home. Wife and children are again the greatest as well as the innocent sufferers because of the money lost on drink.

The Suffering Unit.—In the earlier days the use of alcoholic liquors in the home by the older members of the family and sometimes by children was almost universal, as it is in European countries at the present time. During recent years home drinking has been very much reduced.

During the last fifty years the development of the modern stand-up saloon has had much to do with taking intoxicants out of the home. But the social consequences have varied in the opposite direction. Fewer members of the family drink, but the saloon has made drinking excessive; it has removed restraints; the bar has developed the unlimited evils of the treating habit;

the saloon has become a lounging place for men in competition with the home, while drinking by women in public very recently has grown rapidly. The social and political vices connected with the liquor problem mostly find their center in the saloon. In brief, *the habit has become individualistic; the consequences social. The evils resulting are more than ever shifted to the family as a whole.* All grades of society despise the hard drinker; it is the innocent members, not the sense-blighted inebriate, that feel this social ostracism. The heavy drinker cannot injure himself more severely now than he could a century ago when almost everybody took something; but the wife and children suffer morally, in social standing, and in lack of support, from a drink bill three times as great. He may lose his place in a paying employment more quickly; they degenerate into poverty even more rapidly.

On the whole, for the drinking classes, the saloon is out-substituting the home. Many who now have no place in which to have a good time once had home life, the real kind; many have belonged to wholesome and unquestionable clubs—social, literary and semi-religious, or wholly so. These supplied fully the "club" demands of modern society.

The saloon has preempted this ground for economic purposes. It has added to legitimate attractions those which society is never bound to respect—the encouragement of unlimited personal liberty, evil habits, and the gratification of a craving for morbid sociability. It has made impossible organizations for better athletic, social, or political ends.

To consider therefore only or chiefly the individual drinker, man or woman, is not only inadequate, but also very misleading. The question is not a personal one. *The family is the affected, suffering unit.* It is the proper basis from which to measure the consequences of drink. The individual gets all the good, if there is any —the pleasures of taste, stimulation and sociability; the other members bear the load of suffering. The family is nature's primary social unit, and upon it falls the heaviest burdens that come from drink.

Drink Among Women. — During the period that liquor drinking was being centralized into saloons there was a marked decrease in the number of women drinkers and in the amount consumed by them. Following this were the temperance and total abstinence advances, each of which was more sweeping among female than among male drinkers. Now it has long been considered disreputable for women to frequent or drink in saloons.

Recently there has been a decided reversal in the current of progress. Indulgence in intoxicants among women is again on the increase. Growing independence industrially is removing conventional and social restraint. Enlarged opportunity for self-support, work in factories, stores and offices, has brought a much-needed economic independence to an army of women wage earners but it has been accompanied by two vicious consequences: First, the new industrial equality afforded working girls has suggested powerfully a demand on their part for equal freedom to drink in public places, smoke cigarettes, and for a bold life in general, hitherto confined by custom to men. Second, the low wages paid in many department stores and factories has brought pressure on the employees to eke out an additional income by immoral means, the break-down almost always being by the route of the liquor-serving restaurant.

Among women not dependent upon their own earnings there is a similar demand for equality, a fatally lowered equality tho it is. The saloon and the club take men away at nights; women are demanding and taking similar freedom, especially among some of the so-called upper classes.

There is a decided growth in the drink habit among young and middle-aged women in society functions, at restaurants, soda fountains, and other polite subterfuges and substitutes, to say nothing of the increased patronage of the saloon itself. Some high grade soda fountains and refreshment parlors, making this their main business, are nothing but women's saloons, where would-be refined women and girls may take their wine concoctions and cock-tails, combined with other drinks or "straight," without suffering social odium. Some of these places carry regular retail liquor dealers' licenses. Most saloons in the larger cities have the "family entrance," the side door to wine rooms, private sitting rooms, etc. Beer wagons do an immense trade to residences and flats. Having it right at hand by the bottle or case, the woman inclined to use beer and afforded an excuse by the short-sighted advice of a physician, often drinks to excess when alone and lonesome during the quiet hours of the day. In twenty years in Great Britain there has been an increase of 43 per cent in the number of deaths of males due to liquor; of females, in the same time, 104 per cent,[6] indicating that excessive drinking among women has grown almost three times as rapidly as it has among men, a fearful menace to the future of the British peoples where drinking is much more unrestrained and general than it is in America.

"Luxury drinking" is very common among the society and leisure classes. Lacking a healthful occupation and aim in life, they turn to alcohol for a spur to exertion in the pursuit of further pleasure, or to escape depression. The women of the "upper 400" are almost invariably inebriated to a greater or less degree. Opposite motives drive the poorer and laboring classes to the false relief afforded by intoxicants; over-fatigue, sickness, the awful grind of daily dullness and drudgery, and the craving for excitement, produce "misery drinking," a means to temporary relief from the burdens of poverty and sickness that would be excusable, if its consequences were not so frightful.

Such drinking, whether among rich or poor, is an unmitigated peril to the home, and ultimately, to the nation and the race. The woman of wealth, sipping her champagne in a high-class restaurant-saloon, or in the privacy of her mansion, is as much a monstrosity and blight to social welfare as is the poor wreck, soaked with cheap beer, who starves her children while she rolls on the floor of her filthy tenement.

From the homes of drinking parents, especially of drinking mothers, come most of the criminals and defectives.

(1) The children are predisposed to a nervous instability which leads directly to drink and repeated alcoholism; or it takes different directions, resulting in idiocy, insanity, morbid depression, warped moral judgment and lack of control, crime, homicide or suicide.

(2) Children are underfed during infancy and older childhood, those having the misfortune to escape an early grave growing up undeveloped in mind and body. If such become criminals they are scarcely responsible;

it was the alcohol used by their parents that mutilated their moral character for life.

(3) The home training where mothers drink is less than nothing—there is no escape from the overwhelming example of an inebriate mother.

The Family and National Welfare.—Its relation to the welfare of society as a whole is the final test of the worth or danger of a social institution or custom. The family is nature's first and lasting unit of social organization. On its permanence and purity depend the welfare of the individual himself no less than the continued existence of the state.

From the standpoint of the home and the family, the drink habit, the drink bill and the saloon have no redeeming features. The attractions of the saloon, drawing so inevitably from the home, make them direct competitors. With the family regarded as a righteous institution, the final outcome of ages of experiment, it must follow that to reclaim successfully those suffering from intemperance, the saloon must be replaced by its true substitute, the home. Thousands of drink ruined homes proclaim the additional need of organized force, law and government, in the suppression of the interpolated institution, while all sorts of philanthropic organizations are at work to improve the conditions surrounding needy homes. If, as the drink bill rises that of rent falls, so in the reverse order, rent rises as the cost of drink is reduced. The quality of home life varies inversely as the amount of liquor used. It may not be possible to prove scientifically just which is cause, intemperance or poverty. But, in any event the drink bill is the least excusable and most unnecessary of all waste, and in this sense it is cause. It makes no difference, practically, whether the excessive use of liquor followed or preceded the fall into poverty.

Thousands of women, burdened with the care of large families, are compelled to neglect the most important duties that can fall to them, and seek employment in factories and shops on account of the head of the family having become worse than useless through his slavery to alcohol. Two especially serious consequences follow, both of which serve as complicating causes in two other great public questions. First, neglect in early home training is one of the chief sources of the law-defying spirit among growing boys and girls, and later of fully developed crime. Second, these women lower wages in the labor market, not only for themselves and for other women who enter industrial lines, because they prefer independence, but what is worse, for men who are earning for a whole family. The evil consequences thus fall not only upon the drunkard's wife, driven by abject necessity to desert the home where she is so much needed, but also upon the women of other laboring men's households, where all are temperate, but where the husband's earnings are reduced by this unnatural competitive factor.

Two kinds of inheritance that constitute a serious menace to the race, follow the use of intoxicants by any considerable class of people: (1) Social,—the example of drinking parents, the lack of, or wrong sort of moral training, the psychic effects of drink surroundings, the poverty, disgrace, shame-facedness on small and growing children, are a cause of general inefficiency and crime compared with which even the evil accompaniments of the saloon are very small. (2) The transmission of warped and dwarfed intelligence, accompanying defects in nerve structure, and resulting in epilepsy, impulsiveness and criminal conduct; these all tend toward the formation of racial characteristics. On the scale that liquor, especially beer, is now used among large classes, it means a far-reaching menace to the future of the race.

As Horace Mann said: "The intemperate man, who has no resource but his labor, experiments upon his children to find the minimum of possible subsistence." The cost is too great. Society cannot pay it without mortgaging the future of the race. The family of the wealthy inebriate tends to exterminate itself; that of the poor drunkard become a public burden. Even among those earning fair incomes, as Dr. E. R. L. Gould has said, "The family budget of the average wage-earner is not so flexible that liberal expenditures may be made for drink with impunity. So delicately adjusted is the balance that *the status of a new generation is largely determined by the quantity of liquor the fathers consume.*[7]

"The worst feature of the domestic phase is that the passion for drink ruins affection, breaks family ties and makes men callous to the anguish of wife, children and friends. The frequency of divorce is one of the danger signals. . . . According to the deliberate testimony of the judges who legally severed the matrimonial bonds in the courts, more than two-thirds of the divorces are occasioned by the use of intoxicants. The alarming laxity of family obligations, unless checked, is certain to be followed by ruin and disaster to society."[8]

The regulation of the sale of alcoholic liquors is not a personal problem. It is not to release the slave to appetite, nor to restrict the moderate drinker in the interest of an abstract or ethical good, but to protect the innocent and helpless, and to prevent physical and mental break down in future generations that the matter becomes one for public management. It is often the steady, moderate drinker, who perhaps is seldom noticeably drunk, that entails upon his children the most lasting burden in defective nerve structure. There can be no such personal liberty to injure future generations. No attitude on the part of law will give the family, tempted by the blandishments of alcohol and the saloon, a fair show except prohibition. The government should be on the side of the home, revenue or no revenue.

The City Problem.—The disproportionate growth of large cities is one of the most startling social phenomena of the age. Within a half dozen years, at the present rate, more than one-half of the people of the United States will live in urban communities—places above 2,500 in population. On this basis the census of 1910 classed as rural 49,348,000 or 53.7 per cent; as urban, 46,600,000, or 46.3 per cent. From 1900 to 1910 the rural population increased 11 per cent; the urban 34.8 per cent, more than three times as rapidly.

During the last fifty years there has been a wonderful shift of population from steady-going country life, to the social swirl, business excitement, and political corruption of the great cities. American institutions have been created and guided down to the present, by the higher ideals, deeper religious conviction, the strong young men, and the heavy voting majority of the country; these forces have largely set up the standards of the nation. But the cities are now coming to their own. They will no longer accept limitations from the country, but are taking into their hands the affairs of both state and nation. What the city is the nation will be. Here the people are to live; here the greatest social conflicts are now going on.

The occasions and temptations to drink or to indulge to excess are multiplied in the city. They are more open and easy of access. The nervous haste and excitement lead to a craving for something to prod the flagging nerves. The dangers resulting are greater, too, since there is less opportunity to throw off the alcoholic poison by outdoor life in the open air, or to escape the multiplied forms of suggestion to drink.

Some years ago the far-sighted and friendly critic of American institutions, James Bryce, said that the one conspicuous failure in this country is the government of great cities. Wendell Phillips' prophecy that the time would come when rum, entrenched in our great cities, would strain American liberty and ideals as slavery never did, is already being fulfilled.

The blight of mis-government and of "graft" in public office, the making of a "business" out of various forms of personal and social vice, the exploiting of such vices on a large scale, are intimately connected with the excessive development of the saloon and its part in city politics. Groups of politicians have gained control of the vote-developing features of the saloon, and, in conjunction with the organized city liquor traffic, are able to handle mayors, aldermen, police officials, and usually the people as well. Being so organized, this combination is ready to provide the force of venal voters and officials needed when private corporations enter upon some scheme to get franchises or other great public value at the expense of the people.

It is the cities that resist longest the advances of anti-liquor sentiment and legislation, and constitute the strongholds of the commercial and political liquor power. The traffic is now largely centered and protected in the fifty largest cities of twenty license states. From these points of vantage it not only controls these cities themselves, but it also bombards every smaller city and village, every town, county and country community, and every state from which liquor selling has been outlawed, and in which live 40,000,000 people, seeking to break down or discredit prohibition laws. The political control of these fifty largest cities is almost totally in the hands of politicians who cater to the liquor vote. To the men nominated and elected at the bid of these bosses falls the execution, or defiance, of the liquor laws passed by the legislature of the state. The result is, too often, that they are totally ignored.

The problems of the city are the coming problems of the nation. The liquor problem of the city is the real one of the nation. Here, backed up by distorted ideas of personal liberty, the traffic furnishes the necessary force of venal voters and money required to keep itself in power, defends itself against the higher moral sentiment of the country, and awaits the certain predominance of the city in the politics of the nation to give it a more relentless grip on public affairs than it has ever yet held.

With this certain growth of the political power accompanied by the relative waning of the rural vote, upon which we have depended to save the city from itself and the state from the city, *the overthrow of the political power of the liquor institution within the cities becomes the strategic issue in American reform politics.*

The Saloon and Housing Problem.—A characteristic social problem in large cities is how to provide healthful housing for the poorest classes. It is one of the vital problems of city life. Sociologists have spent a great deal of time investigating, and philanthropists have given money to erect model tenements, yet it is only partially solved. The first need, of course, is better wages. Another, no less important, is often overlooked —the proper use of the wages earned.

It is too often the money spent for intoxicating drinks that makes it necessary in the first place to rent the poorest of quarters and crowd them with roomers to help pay the rent. Wide studies have shown that it is the home, the house, and house furnishings that suffer most for the lack of the money spent at the saloon. Dr. E. R. L. Gould says that ''The economies which are necessary to indulge the appetite for spirits are almost invariably practiced upon the home accommodations.'' [9] This is particularly unfortunate, for it is the innocent members of the family, the wife and small children, who are compelled to remain in these squalid roosts— they cannot be called homes—all day, that suffer most.

It has been found by those who have undertaken large plans of tenement-house reform that it is almost impossible to improve the families in which one or more members drink. They cannot make use of better houses even after they have been provided; they cannot save even the slight amount asked to pay the rent of improved buildings. All that margin, and much more, goes for beer. Then they cannot live with neighbors under improved conditions; they are disorderly and interfere with the peace of others poorer than themselves. Merely securing them good homes, or paying higher wages so they may procure better ones for themselves, is not sufficient while the drink habit remains. The supply must be broken off.

Some few years ago there was effected in Edinburgh a remarkable series of housing improvements among the very poor. One of the chief promoters gives the following testimony as to how the saloon practically ruined the results of their costly labors: "Edinburgh presents an illustration of the extent to which sanitary agencies are connected with the drink evil. . . . Upwards of half a million pounds was expended in rooting out the haunts of wretchedness and vice, while another half-million was expended on improved dwellings and other sanitary reforms. That the result of this great experiment has been largely counteracted by drink is only too apparent. In twelve years the number of drunken cases increased 27 per cent, while the whole population increased 16 per cent." [10] In this region there were 200 men living in low-grade lodging houses; they received fair to good wages, but, spending one-half of it, on an average, on drink, they were unable to have any sort of homes of their own. They simply preferred the drink. To spend public money in contributing to the household comforts of this class would be to do them a positive injury. They possess ample power to improve their own position. [10] This great housing reform was rendered nugatory to the poorer classes by the constant presence and pressure of the saloon.

Assimilation of the Immigrant.—America is "the melting pot" of the nations. To this country are coming each year three-fourths of a million men and women, leaving behind them their old life, and earnestly seeking a better opportunity. The immigrants since 1835, together with their descendants, now constitute far more than half the entire population. They are the America of today. Jacob Riis says of New York, where the "melting" has not yet gone very far: "One may find for the asking an Italian, German, French, African, Spanish, Bohemian, Russian, Scandinavian, Jewish, and Chinese colony. The one thing you will ask for in vain in the chief city of America is a distinctively American community." [11]

No one factor more seriously retards the fusing, the healthful "making of Americans" out of this conglomerate force of eager, aspiring, though largely uneducated, foreign material drawn to this country each year, than does the liquor saloon. Most of the immigrants of the present time have long been accustomed to the use of beer and wine in the old country, but here they are brought at once into very different conditions. The old drinking customs, comparatively innocent, are exploited and developed by the economic and political forces back of the American type of liquor traffic, into an excess not possible in the old country.

The conditions met here are responsible for an aggravated form of intemperance. The surroundings in which most immigrants must live, "the mining patch," or congested city tenements, the high tension, rushing, nervous life, the "speeding up" in the factories, the rapid pace all around that these peasants from the country districts have never known, the excitements of labor disputes and politics, the larger wage, the continuous obtrusive presence of the saloon, the friendliness of the saloon-keeper, usually an earlier arrival of his own people, who welcomes him, supplies his social needs, the vices and fights and politics of the saloon—all combine to make the old drinking customs, good or bad as they may have been relatively, impossible here. A few with educational help break away and become very temperate or abstinent; the larger number are blighted by drink and the saloon as they would not have been in the old country.

The following are some of the ways by which the saloon and its associated interests introduce to the newly arrived future citizens much of the worst, instead of the best, in our present-day civilization:

(1) Not wholly to its discredit, though prompted by commercial and political motives, it supplies his social needs. This function is usually neglected by better agencies.

In a strange land, with a strange language and yet stranger customs, "The saloon has become his social center. Here he has his birthday parties, his christenings, his marriages. The saloon is his employment agency, his social club, his reading room, his savings bank, his steamship agency, his political headquarters. Indeed, nothing is too 'common' for this center of influence. He trusts the owner of the saloon—this countryman of his—who seems so interested in all that concerns him. The saloon-keeper has no pet theories concerning the foreigner, and he knows much about his real needs." [12]

(2) There is a thoroly organized and systematic exploitation of the more ignorant non-English-speaking vote in the great nation-controlling cities. The saloon, or group of saloons in a ward, or that get their beer from a certain brewery, are invariably a part of some political combination. The boss is one of their own race, accountable to the more powerful ward boss for the votes of his fellow-countrymen.

The saloon is the means by which the "superior" race purchases the political power of the "inferior." What can "citizenship" and "the sacred right of the ballot" mean to men who vote for the first time under such influences?

(3) To gain new support, the liquor traffic at times encourages united opposition, among foreign-born citizens, to certain long-existing American institutions.

It is the foreign-born citizens that are misled as to the meaning of liberty and organized into "personal liberty" leagues; these movements, in various cities and states, have practically no object other than defiance of the laws regulating the sale of liquors. It is the foreign-born citizen who insists on having the Sunday saloon in defiance of the older American custom of closing on that day. The Sunday of quiet, rest, and religious worship, unlike the European Sunday, is one of the oldest and most sacred of American ideals. In Chicago, a few years ago, the "United Societies," a federation of foreign and semi-foreign clubs and societies, claiming 120,000 members, defeated a strong citizen movement to enforce the Sunday-closing law. They conducted a gigantic Sunday parade and assembled in the armory for speeches in Polish, German, Italian, and Bohemian, demanding the sale of liquor on that day. They explicitly condemned the State's Attorney for endeavoring to enforce the law, and commended the Mayor for his refusal to do so.[13]

(4) The immigrant's ideas of liberty are distorted in the same way. It is to be expected that, escaping from Russian oppression, the Russian Pole or Jew should at times have a tendency to dislike all government. The saloon stimulates this spirit. It is a standing example

of law defiance near at hand. In its back rooms the violent anarchists meet and plan their propaganda. Here, also, is usually found the rendezvous for criminals —native and foreign.

(5) The saloon assists in keeping alive old-world customs and drinking habits unsuitable to the more nervous, rushing life and climate of this country. The moderate drinking of continental Europe seems not to be possible here.

It is when beer flows freely, in the mining towns of Pennsylvania, that brawls and fights, based on racial antagonisms, are most frequent. Inherited religious and racial feuds, imported from eastern Europe, break out afresh. The Ruthenians are having a feast. It strikes a group of Polish lads that this will be a good time to look in on them and have some fun; the result, a race row. When sober these people are commonly very peaceable, but when maddened by drink, anything serves as a weapon—chairs, lamps, and knives. There are few inebriates, as compared with the heavy drinkers among the Irish, English, or even Americans. But the quarrels and rows of the average Slav saloon are little different from those of the Negro saloon, and the spirit back of them is practically the same.

"The Slavs and Lithuanians are fond of drink and spend their money freely on it. Some spend more money on beer than they do on food. The evidences of drink in the homes are apparent on all sides, and not only do national customs and national tastes and usages make for drunkenness, but the undeniable fact that *the liquor interests are the only American interests which effectively reach the great mass of the non-English-speaking immigrants.*" [14]

(6) But the greatest danger is not to the foreigner himself—it falls upon his children. It is the first native-born generation that suffers most. Alcoholism, the social and political evils of the saloon, and crime, are all more marked in this half-assimilated class than among either natives or foreigners. The parents, born under a foreign flag, are yet under the restraint of the home training, customs, ideals, and religion of the old country. Not so their children. Bright and quick to learn when they have a chance, if raised under vicious surroundings, as so many are, they learn to despise their industrious parents, as slow and "foreign." These idle sons and daughters are often as much a disgrace to their parents as to the older Americans who look down upon and discredit all immigrants because of the actions of these who are not really immigrants.

Native-born children of foreign parentage have a crime tendency at least twice as great as do foreigners themselves.[15] This amazing criminality is almost entirely a product of the saloon environment coupled with bad housing.[16] Referring to the policy of the brewers of Chicago thoroughly to saturate the tenement and working districts with beer, a popular writer of first-hand investigations shows the connection when he says:

"A population of hundreds of thousands of rough and unrestrained male laborers, plied with all possible energy and ingenuity with alcoholic liquor, can be counted on, with the certainty of a chemical experiment, for one reaction—violent and fatal crime. There would be crime of this kind from such a population under any circumstances; but the facilities of Chicago double and treble it."[17]

A thrifty German farmer, living for years near a

small town in northern Illinois, always took his customary beer home each week. But he noted that his sons, growing up and going to town, got their drinks there instead of following the old customs, and the hired men on the farms came back from town several times a week unable to work. The question of voting out the saloons came up. He saw no danger in his own drinking, but, for the boys and the hired men, he threw his money and his influence into the no-saloon fight, gladly, tho it took away his beer of a lifetime. This spirit is far-reaching among the immigrants who have a fair chance to build their new ideals here, free from the deceptive influences of constant saloon associations.

It has been said by unthinking anti-liquor leaders that the excessive increase in the consumption of alcoholic liquors the past fifty years has been due to the immigrant; also, by liquor agitators, that the foreign-born laborer, so much needed in many industries, can not and will not work without his beer. Neither statement is quite fair to the foreigner. The per capita consumption of liquor has increased more than 300 per cent since 1860, but the ratio of foreign-born, in this country, to native-born, has remained stationary.[18] That the old-world customs are retained and drinking is more excessive is due, not so much to the customs, for language and other customs are quickly surrendered, but to the vicious and unhealthy conditions into which he is thrust. Unworthy men of his own race, who have been here some time, who have learned the language, the commercial tricks, the vices, and, most of all, the saloon politics—these become his leaders, his "friends," his exploiters. To the new arrival they *are America*. These men have learned their methods here.

Among the foreign-born are many who would banish the saloon as quickly as the most radical temperance people of earlier native descent. A German-American magazine resentfully denies that "the beer barrel is the German Kaiser in America," and that personal liberty to drink beer is the ideal of Germans in America. In the Birmingham (Ala.) prohibition election, the city was carried largely by the vote of the mills and factories. And it is not a typical Southern city; its population is largely born and recruited from the foreign elements of our American population. Where the saloon interests have not enlisted the active allegiance of the foreign-born peoples on their behalf, and do not hold them in political affiliation, whether drinkers or non-drinkers, they gradually become as willing to banish the saloon as any other class. They are not unwilling to deprive themselves of the privilege of drink for the welfare of the new America of which they are becoming loyal citizens.

Various races and nationalities are living together in America—10,000,000 Negroes, a few remaining Indians, some Chinese and Japanese on the Pacific Coast, the present living, or descendants of, 30,000,000 immigrants who have come from Europe during the past 100 years, the children of a few old families that go back more than 100 years, and nearly a million new and less educated arrivals from southeastern Europe each year. In all probability, they will continue to live together. Therefore, remove the conditions that cause friction or enable one class to use another as a political tool. The liquor trade is one of these; its destruction is a part of the Americanizing program. If it remains, Americans will be foreignized instead of foreigners Americanized.

The Negro and Drink.—Deep indulgence in alcoholic liquors is pre-eminently the white man's vice. Wherever and whenever the colored man, Negro, or Indian, or Oriental, has learned its extensive use, it has been at the teaching of the superior race. On the part of the Negro, the prompting impulse has been imitation—to be like that great superior white race. Released from slavery, under which there was little or no drinking, liquor men began to take advantage of his ignorance and of his longing to have every privilege enjoyed by white men, and proceeded to create a new market, limited, however, by the poverty of the would-be purchaser, and to peddle out cheap liquors to the ex-slaves.

On account of the limited degree to which the colored people have taken to drink, neither in the South nor in the Northern cities, to which they have been coming in increasing numbers in recent years, have they suffered so directly from drunkenness as have the drinking classes among the whites. The Negro is not an inebriate in the sense that the drunken American, Irishman, Englishman, or German is, with hundreds of years of heavy drinking back of him. The country Negro of the South finds it difficult to get liquor on account of the rapidly extending prohibitory laws. In the towns, where saloons yet remain, most of them have so little money that they can pay for drink only at long periods. Comparatively few are habitual drunkards. As a people they have not inherited convivial social customs. Investigation by the Committee of Fifty, chiefly among those in the North, shows that, with the Negro, 14 per cent of poverty is due, directly and indirectly, to drink, while with the white man, 28.6 per cent comes from the same source.[19] It takes time to stamp drunkenness on a race, and the colored man in America has had only one generation, since he has been free to have a choice, in which to learn the vices of civilization. In this one respect his native shiftlessness and his poverty have combined with legislation and restraint by the better part of the white race to keep the Negro sober. This has prevented the utter debauch and destruction that would have followed such wide use of intoxicants as is practiced by the nationalities mixed up with the North.

But the use of liquor by Negroes, relatively smaller in amount tho it may be, is and has been an ugly factor in the friction and quarrels between the races in the South, and has constituted one of the most powerful arguments for the anti-liquor side in prohibition campaigns. It has caused race friction, which might otherwise have been overcome by peaceable methods, to break out into quarrels, revolting crime, riot, and lynchings. Intoxicants act more quickly and more acutely on the brain, emotions, and passions of the colored man, making him insolent, exaggerating his self-conceit, and leading to disturbances where real or imaginary grievances already exist. Further, alcohol stirs up his worst passions and removes the little feeling of restraint so far learned by the lower grades of Negroes. Naturally easy-going and amiable, he becomes impudent and abusive. He is not long tolerated in the saloon, almost always kept by white men, and when on the street continues his hilarity and improper conduct.[22]

Recent students of the crime-producing effects of alcohol reach the conclusion that "quite small doses are often responsible for the commission of reckless, self-pleasing actions and for the inordinate sway of the passions, which are no longer kept in full control by the higher powers of the mind, because these are more or less in abeyance as the result of the paralyzing effects of the drug.'' [23]

If this is true of the Anglo-Saxon, with more than a thousand years of civilization behind him, what may be expected of the Negro, only a hundred years away from the African jungle, in whom passions, emotions, and natural impulses are exceptionally strong from ages of unregulated control. The inhibiting powers have been but slowly developed since freedom, and it is just these faculties that alcohol first attacks, as the scientists show.

Just what place liquor occupies as a stimulant of the special crimes that stir race hatred to the lynching point has not been determined by actual investigation. But there is no uncertainty as to the attitude of the best educated Southern people—those who know the colored man best—on the matter. They are determined to keep liquor from the Negro at all costs. Hon. Seaborn Wright, of Georgia, leader of the prohibition movement in that state, expresses the conviction of the Southern white man when he says that ''the development, the safety—aye, the very life—of the Negro race in the South hang upon his absolute separation from intoxicating liquors. Four-fifths of his crimes against our women come from this infernal source; it is behind nine-tenths of the race conflicts in the South.'' [24] On the other hand, the testimony of the best educated Negroes is that ''the Negro brute is a product of the white man's gambling hells, low dives, and saloons.''

''The laws of the slave-holding states made it a crime to furnish liquor to a slave. . . . When the war ended, the saloon was a closed door to the Negro. In five years, tens of thousands of 'doggeries' and saloons, in every city and village and crossroads, were stretching their paralyzing arms to this semi-savage child-race, destroying all that was best in the Negro mind and heart and body. . . . I tell you, before God, that my people, as masters, were never enemies of this helpless race, as the brewers and distillers, in partnership with the national government, have been since the Negro in the sixties stepped out of the old slave quarters into the open doors of the American saloon.'' [24]

Liquor a Factor in Race Conflicts.—The use of alcoholic intoxicants has a specially ominous place in the quarrels and disturbances that arise where two races, so different as the white and black, are compelled to live together in the same community, in anything like equal numbers. It is not that alcohol hurts the colored man more—the personal injury is actually less—but that it serves as the match to touch off the deeper-lying prejudices into brawls, crime, and riot.

Several factors in which the saloon and liquor are largely responsible are found in connection with nearly all lynchings and riots based on race differences, North or South. First, is a preceding period of lax law enforcement, and a feeling on the part of the people that appeals to justice will be ineffectual or too slow. There is no other institution in America that is so uniformly a law-breaker as the liquor traffic. There is none that so universally succeeds in preventing justice, or that encourages by precept and practice the law-defying spirit that disgraces American government in the eyes of Europeans.

Another factor is the use of liquor by the criminal that has incited the vengeance of the mob, and by the leaders of the mob. Liquor is a predisposing cause for crime among men of any class with little self-restraint; the tongue is loosened, fingers are ready for a quarrel, and impulse and passion are left free to control action. It is the horrible details of such impulsive crimes that stir to vengeance rather than punishment.

Lynchings frequently occur in communities where there are no saloons, but in most cases it is found that the Negro guilty of murder or outrage has been using whisky illegally sold, or was of the floating type that came into a peaceful country, no-saloon community, from the low-down grog shop of the cities. In the North, where race lynchings are beginning to assume the same characteristics as in the South, the liquor conditions are intensified. The mob is almost always the output of the saloons, the loafers and young men and boys from sixteen to twenty-two years of age. It is this type of men that makes the bulk of all mobs. The orderly, peaceable mob, composed of "the best citizens," that "goes quietly about its business," is a newspaper hyperbole.

In a discussion of "The Tragedy at Atlanta," John Temple Graves says that the crimes that stir most often to lynching are, in many if not most cases, due to the consumption of whisky, morphine, etc., by the reckless classes of Negroes—that whisky plus hot weather is the immediate exciting cause, though not finally the ultimate one, of race riots and lynchings.[25]

Stirred by reports of attacks by Negroes on a half-dozen white women in one day, a mob led by saloon hangers-on accumulated and for several days held the city in its grasp. One hundred persons, mostly Negroes, were injured or killed, stores were looted, property destroyed, homes of respectable colored people entered, innocent Negroes shot along with the guilty, and the laws, with city officials indifferent or tolerant, were defied. The Negro brutes and the mob leaders were both the product of Atlanta's saloons. Had it not been for these "low whites" and floating "niggers," the period of high tension on the deeper problem would have passed without disgrace.

Then came the reaction in Atlanta—the serious determination to remove the occasion for such outbreaks. The race question could not be settled at once; the weather could not be changed; but the saloon and its indulgences, its vile talk and fellow-encouragement among the vicious of both races, the saloon and alcohol with excuse neither in nature nor in industrial mistakes of the past that massed the races together—the saloon must go.

This movement was not an attempt to remove from the blacks what the white people wished to retain for themselves. They recognized its dangers to both races. It was an assertion of the truth that what injures one class in a community must be a blight and menace to all. The saloons were closed two weeks. "During that period perfect order was maintained, the recorder's court docket was reduced one-half, and the merchants, especially in the humbler portions of the city, experienced phenomenal trade."[26] Then the people began to ask, "Why not a year?" "Forever?" The liquor traffic fostered and encouraged the depraved and criminal Negro and the vengeful and irresponsible white. Of both Georgia was tired.

Educated Negroes themselves recognize only too well the dangers of liquor in such conflicts—dangers out of all proportion to the amount the colored people use of it, if compared with the foreign-born nationalities of the North.   Booker T. Washington says: "The prohibition movement is based upon a deep-seated desire to get rid of whisky in the interests of both races because of its hurtful economic results.   The prohibition sentiment is as strong in counties where there are practically no colored people as in the Black Belt counties."   "In Birmingham, the Negroes formed an organization and cast nearly all the registered colored vote for prohibition." [27]

Race friction, and with it the lawless law of lynch, is spreading North along with the immigration of the "floating Negro" into Northern cities, where the conditions for outbreak are already too fertile.   Typical Northern race riots were those of the two Springfields— Ohio in 1904 and Illinois in 1908.   In the former,[28] there had been a long period of lax enforcement of law, a murder every sixteen days in the county, and few executions; there was little or no enforcement against vice and the saloon in the city; the authorities catered to these elements; the Negroes had 1,500 votes that were regularly bought and sold by the parties alternately as needed.   There were 145 saloons in Springfield, one to every 283 of the population, nine kept by Negroes. A specially vile colored levee was run by a political boss, and repeated efforts to have it cleared up were thwarted by the party leaders, who needed the 60 or 70 votes that this petty plutocrat handed them in return for protection.   The soil for riot was rich and deep.   A drunken Negro shot a policeman.   A mob of men and boys, mostly between the ages of 16 and 20, recruited from the back rooms of the saloons, battered down the strongest jail in Ohio.   Moral rot had seized the officers of the law, the sheriff, deputies, mayor, police, and the militia company stationed there. They had not been accustomed to enforce law; their habit had been to excuse, to make exceptions, to let off easily in dealing with the law-breaking liquor element, and others who paid for exemptions. The Springfield (Ill.) riot was a repetition of the same fundamental elements.

The South is getting rid of the saloon partly to reduce the opportunities for race friction. Lynchings there have been decreasing the past few years. Race disturbances in the North, on the other hand, are just beginning, and with a fury, when they do occur, no less than that shown by the most lynch-hardened sections of Mississippi or Georgia. Ten million blacks and eighty million whites can live together and work out the solution of their differences, if sober. But an inferior race cannot remain peaceable and hope to advance at the same time if the crime-suggesting and passion-stimulating saloon is left open freely to all.

References and Authorities

The Family Drink Bill.
Gould, *Social Condition of Labor.*
Peabody, ''The Drink Question in Germany,'' *Nation,* 54, 167.
Smith, ''Liquor and Labor,'' *Catholic World,* 47, 539.
Rowntree and Sherwell, *The Temperance Problem and Social Reform,* 7-44.
1 Peabody, 167.
2 See ch. V. this volume.
3 Chicago Record Herald, Oct. 2, 1908.
4 Patton, ''Economic Basis for Prohibition,'' *Annals American Academy,* II, 66.
5 *American Prohibition Year Book* (1912), 42.
The Suffering Unit.
Barker, *Saloon Problem and Social Reform,* 42-43.
Stelzle, *The Workingman and Social Problems,* 45-50.

Smith, ''Liquor and Labor,'' *Catholic World*, 47, 539.
Peabody, ''Substitutes for the Saloon,'' *Forum*, 21, 595.
Fernald, *The Economics of Prohibition*, 378-387.

Drink Among Women.
Kelynack, *The Drink Problem*, 161-188, 232-234.
Barker, *The Saloon Problem and Social Reform*, 42-46.
Horsley and Sturge, *Alcohol and the Human Body*, 311-337.
Fernald, *The Economics of Prohibition*, 383-387.
Miller, ''Alcohol and Degeneration,'' *Independent*, 58, 261.
6 Rowntree and Sherwell, *The Temperance Problem and Social Reform*, 90.

The Family and National Welfare.
Barker, *The Saloon Problem and Social Reform*, 42-47.
Kelynack, *The Drink Problem*, 232-235.
7 Gould, *Social Conditions of Labor.*
8 Barker, 43.

The City Problem.
Stelzle, *American Social and Religious Conditions* (1912), ch. I.
Strong, *The Challenge of the City*, 16-68.
Wilcox, *The American City*, 1-27.
Dole, *The Spirit of Democracy*, 216-232.
Loomis, *Modern Cities*, 27-53.
Wheeler, *Prohibition*, 78-81.

The Saloon and the Housing Problem.
Rowntree and Sherwell, *The Temperance Problem and Social Reform*, 40-44.
Strong, *The Challenge of the City*, 93-106.
9 *The Social Conditions of Labor.*
10 ''Environment and Drink,'' *No. Am. Review*, 161, 460.

Assimilation of the Immigrant.
Hall, *Immigration*, 172-188.
Roberts, *The New Immigration* (1912), 96, 109-123, 262, 305-306, 347.
Grose, *Aliens or Americans?* 233-350.
Strong, *The Challenge of the City*, 131-164.
Stelzle, *American Social and Religious Conditions*, 103-120.
Koren, *Economic Aspects of the Liquor Problem*, 135-147.
Wheeler, *Prohibition*, 81-87.

Turner, ''The City of Chicago,'' *McClure's,* Apr., 1907.
11 *How the Other Half Lives,* ch. 18.
12 Stelzle, 111.
13 See Chicago daily papers, Feb. 10, 1908.
14 Roberts, ''The New Pittsburgh,'' *Charities,* Jan. 2, 1909.
15 Hall, 149.
16 Roberts, 237.
17 Turner, see above.
18 Stelzle, 103.

The Negro and Drink.

Du Bois, *The Philadelphia Negro,* 277-286.
Koren, *Economic Aspects of the Liquor Problem,* 160-185.
Waring, ''Some Causes of Criminality Among Colored People,''
    Charities, 15, 45.
Graves, ''Georgia Pioneers the Prohibition Crusade,'' *Cosmo-*
    politan, 45, 83.
Washington, ''Prohibition and the Negro,'' *Outlook,* 88, 587;
    ''A Town Owned by Negroes,'' *World's Work,* 14, 9125.
Iglehart, ''The Nations Anti-Drink Crusade,'' *Review of Re-*
    views, 37, 468
19 Koren, 180.
22 Ibid, 169.
23 Horsley and Sturge, *Alcohol and the Human Body,* 87.
24 Address at Baltimore on ''The Race Problem and the Liquor
    Traffic,'' *American Issue,* May 9, 1908.

As a Factor in Race Conflicts.

Graves, ''The Tragedy at Atlanta,'' *World Today,* 11, 1170.
Corrigan, ''The Prohibition Wave in the South,'' *Review of*
    Reviews, Sept., 1907.
Baker, ''What is Lynching?'' *McClures;* In the South, Vol. 24,
    299; In the North, Vol. 24, 422.
Washington, ''Drink and the Negro,'' *Outlook,* March 14, 1908.
Waring, ''Some Causes of Criminality Among Colored People,''
    Charities, 15, 45.
Graves, ''Georgia Pioneers the Prohibition Crusade,'' *Cosmo-*
    politan, 45, 83.
25 *World Today,* 11, 1170.
26 Corrigan, see ref. above.
27 ''Drink and the Negro.''
28 Baker: see ref. above.

*Give me a sober population, not wasting
their earnings in strong drink, and I shall know
where to obtain the revenues.*

—WILLIAM E. GLADSTONE.

*The excise is fattened with the rich result
Of all this riot. And ten thousand casks,
Forever dribbling out their base contents,
Touched by the Midas finger of the State,
Bleed gold for ministers to sport away.
Drink and be mad, then; 'tis your country bids!
Gloriously drunk—obey the important call!
Her cause demands the assistance of your
    throats;
Ye all can swallow, and she asks no more.*

—COWPER.

CHAPTER XI

The consequences of the liquor institution in governmental affairs is more far-reaching than appears upon the surface. It is felt most keenly in politics, by which the policies of government are determined, and in its tendency to produce that anti-social spirit—crime—which it is the purpose of government to prevent.

Liquor in Government and Politics.—The liquor traffic has become a powerful factor in American politics. It helps to create the policies, legislation, and administration by which actual government becomes what it is.

The force of the traffic in public affairs is out of all proportion to its size and importance in a commercial sense. The drink custom is exploited politically as is no other custom; the saloon, as a social institution, is "in politics" with a political force of its own, unique and of vast extent. The power of the liquor traffic is exerted, of course, primarily for its own financial advancement. In this it is similar to that of any other closely centered business of a trust character that is seeking every advantage that special influence in governmental policies may give it.

But there are certain distinctive factors about the liquor trust that make its political activity vastly different from that of other aggressions by "big business." They may be stated as follows:

(a) The whole liquor institution, especially the traffic in intoxicants, is in an uncertain and doubtful position before the bar of public opinion. There is much public disapproval of the article that it supplies. The "sugar trust," the "oil trust," the "leather trust," the big steel corporations and railroad monopolists give to society a service which makes for health, material enjoyment, and higher standards of living. The whisky trust and the brewery combines persistently intensify the demand for their product, which injures health, earning capacity, and social welfare, and causes crime.

(b) This disapproval is being partly offset by the present policies of government, which ask and receive from this traffic the payment of immense revenues and license fees, vastly larger in size and different in character from revenues received from other industries.

(c) There is a distinctive voting constituency created, organized, manipulated, and held by the saloon. This is ever ready to do the bidding of the liquor traffic in political affairs.

Previous to the establishment of the internal revenue system, in 1862, there were no such public problems as those now meant by the term "liquor power." The trade was conducted on a small scale; it was not organized or even united, and had no political influence. Since that date, owing partly to the general consolidation of business in all lines, but largely to this special taxing policy, the traffic has become thoroly united and has entered politics to promote its own interests.

This national policy, working in co-operation with the license policies of the states, has been an important factor in three specific changes: the concentration of the business into fewer hands; its organization for protection and development; and its promotion by political influence.

The first result was a radical change in the methods of the liquor industry. The grocery store vending liquor either had to abandon it or go into it as a business; the modern saloon with all its social evils, and its alcohol-selling specialty, was fully developed; the old-time tavern ceased to exist. The many small stills were replaced by a fewer number, but with immensely increased capacity. Larger investments of capital required larger sales, making necessary the extension of the trade.

The consolidation of the liquor traffic has been very extensive. In the twenty years from 1870 to 1890 the number of malt liquor-producing establishments decreased from 1,792 to 1,509, while the capital invested increased from $49,000,000 to over $450,000,000. The same tendency has been manifest among distilleries, until now the whisky trust is one of the very greatest in the country. The retail trade has been steadily passing into the same hands, until now from one-half to two-thirds of the saloons are owned or controlled by the breweries. By means of the brewer's capital many a saloon is started in a new residence or growing community which at first would not support a saloon; slowly but surely the associations and habit are established, a new constituency formed, and the venture becomes a very profitable investment.

The Internal Revenue Act of 1862 led to the first united action of the liquor interests against legislative encroachment. The state prohibition campaigns of the ten years previous had found the trade so scattered and disorganized that no great opposition could be shown.

Consequently, fifteen states passed such laws and the prohibition wave promised to become, steadily but surely, national. Laws were passed on the simple expression of public sentiment, indicating that the majority of the people were for prohibition. The trade was neither respected nor feared.

Within three months after the passage of the act, the United States Brewers' Association was formed, and two years later it sent its first deputation to Washington—the beginning of the liquor lobby at the national capitol.

(1) The Revenue System, a Defense.—The purpose of the federal taxes and internal revenue on liquors is the raising of money. Primarily, it is not desired either to strengthen or weaken that trade. That the traffic is thereby given an argument against restrictive legislation, is a secondary, perhaps an unintended, though very vital, political consequence.

In placing upon this traffic the burden—or privilege—of supplying one-third of the entire national income, the nation reaps social and political results more important than fiscal. They are admirably classified by Fehlandt[1] as follows:

(a) Permission. The receiving of money by government does not necessarily imply indorsement of the means by which that money was made. It depends upon the manner of collection. Fines are imposed as a punishment. They are made as heavy as possible, no receipt is given, and they carry with them the certainty of positive disapproval.

The internal revenue on liquors is entirely different. It is a real tax. It is made only as heavy as the traffic will readily bear, or even less; in fact, as Howe shows, the tax of $1.00 per barrel upon beer might be doubled without decreasing the production of lowering the quality.² It is collected at fixed periods and in 'fixed amounts; receipts are given as for any tax. When paid, the men engaged in the trade are immune from further interference, and enjoy the fullest confidence and permission of the government.

(b) Taxation implies protection. That is what all taxes are paid for primarily. "In levying and receiving a tax the government makes a pledge of service," the service of protection from molestation, and of rights to exist and prosper. When a dealer has paid his federal tax, his local or state license fee, and hung up receipts, no power on earth may interfere with him.

"Though a man's brain be set on fire by the liquor he [the dealer] sells, and he in turn goes home to fire his house or his neighbor's house, or kill his friend in a brawl, or his wife or children, tho the cause may be clearly traced to the liquor he drank, yet the man who gave him liquor not only escapes punishment, but is protected in his right to sell more." This is just; the dealer is receiving the protection for which he paid.

(c) Partnership. Certain facts suggest a relation so close between the government and the liquor traffic that it may not inaptly be termed a partnership. Of its total annual income, the national government receives one-third from this one source. In the production of distilled spirits, "the distiller is little more than the agent of the government." He invests his capital and assumes the risks. His still must be constructed according to approved plans, his machinery must pass inspection and be of an approved pattern, ere he can begin operations. Even the keys of the cistern-rooms, fermenting vats, and warehouses are in the hands of the government, and the distiller is denied access to the place of manufacture save upon permission, or to the warehouse after the spirits have been placed in bond."[3] A government official watches every move in manufacture and reports to Washington. The system is so perfect that it is well-nigh impossible for Uncle Sam to fail to receive his full share in revenue.

Irrespective of the letter of the law, for all political and social purposes, the government is practically a jealous and responsible partner in the liquor trade. The liquor interests are not slow to see the advantage this gives. They boldly and freely announce the relationship; they use it as an advertising scheme and as a publicity resource. Uncle Sam is constantly made to guarantee the strength and purity of certain brands of liquor; their being "bottled in bond" is proof against fraud, and no refusal to acknowledge the partnership is ever made by either party.

(2) **License Gives Protection and Influence.**—In the past the license policy has been used as a sincere attempt to regulate the sale of intoxicating liquors and remove or limit some of the evils. At first it was not known that it would, or intended that it should, be a means of giving additional political influence. Instead of continuing as a temperance measure, however, the system has become a prolific source of the corrupt political power of the saloon and of the larger traffic back of the saloon.

This is a natural consequence of two important factors in the situation:

(a) The questionable position of the traffic before the bar of public opinion.

(b) Its insecure status in constitutional law.

For over half a century the people as a whole have been seriously divided as to whether the liquor traffic is a good institution, or a very bad one; whether it should be banished entirely, or recognized as a necessary industry. The church has been fighting it relentlessly; science has been adding fact to fact to show that even the moderate use of its product is a serious menace to health, morals, and the future of the race; and business requirements have been closing down more and more against drinking by employees. All of this is today accompanied by an intense struggle in many states to banish the sale entirely.

From the constitutional view-point the trade has an even more unsafe position. The right of entering any one of a thousand useful trades is one of those reserved to every American citizen. He may labor with hands or brain; he may sell the product of his labor. But the highest courts have persistently refused to place the selling of alcoholic liquors among such trades. Twelve times the United States Supreme Court has declared that "There is no inherent right in a citizen to sell intoxicating liquors." Twenty-five state supreme courts have echoed this decision.[4] It is evident that it is not a part of "personal liberty" to enter this trade, or to hold property in liquors, or an "inalienable" right to keep a saloon. "By the general concurrence of opinion of every civilized and Christian community, there are few sources of crime and misery to society equal to the dramshop."[5] It is fully established that the trade, therefore, may be burdened with any amount of taxation, or limited to any extent, and it can have no just cause of complaint. *Its very existence is one of sufferance.*

Discredited in public esteem, charged justly with being the source of unlimited corruption and social danger, and having a very uncertain recourse in the final supreme law of the land, it is no wonder that, as the liquor men themselves complain, it is the object of persistent attack, legal and illegal, of "graft" by politicians, and of constant opposition by its legitimate foes.

Under such conditions, the trade gets all the legality it has from the license system. From this it gets its position of apparent equal legal standing, but of greater political influence, than that of naturally legitimate trades. In practical operation it is afforded the same protection as that given other occupations. Many are beginning to believe, as one writer says, that "if such enactments were all repealed, immorality," in which he includes the retailing of liquors, "would still be unlawful (in constitutional law) and could be suppressed on common-law principles, as well as on the ground of public necessity." [6]

Thus the traffic is made, in all but prohibition states, a legal institution by the licensing or special tax laws of those states. These give a definite standing which otherwise it would not have. Its dependence on the license statutes and ordinances keeps the whole traffic continually in the very vortex of politics.

(3) Vote Corrupting Consequence. — The revenue-license policies seriously blight citizenship ideals. For fifty years the federal financiers have paid one-fourth or more of national government expense from the revenues of this one traffic alone. For thirty years states and cities have depended on license money to help pay local expenses. Officials and citizens alike in large numbers are unwilling to kill the goose that lays the golden egg. Active political policy has come to stand for the continuance of this source of revenue. The voter in the booth too often remembers that his taxes are yet unpaid.

This system has clouded the issue between the saloon and the people. It has made a clear-cut decision practically impossible. The question of "saloon or no saloon," of liquor traffic or prohibition, has not yet been met, even in smaller districts, and fought out on its merits, separate from the matter of taxation, an entirely different governmental problem.

This policy, to the liquor dealer, it is safe to say, has been one of self-preservation; otherwise, he would not submit to such severe taxation. He dare not risk the issue on the social value of his product to the public.

Knowingly or unknowingly, our government has adopted a policy for keeping the eyes of the would-be-moral but taxpaying citizen eternally blinded to the real merits of the question.

One of three assumptions must be true: (a) The liquor "business" is a normal, legitimate business, supplying an article of wide human need to society. In this event, the extra heavy revenue policies are inexcusably unjust because of the disproportionate burden for public support placed upon this pursuit. (b) It is normal and legitimate in itself, but has such attendant dangers to health, morality, and safety that the heavy tax is intended as a remedy. If so, it has proved to be a stupendous failure. (c) This industry has such usual and persistent evil results to society that it is not like other pursuits, but is such a traffic as decisive action by sentiment and law might bring to an end. In this even the $230,000,000 annually paid the United States, and the smaller amounts paid to state, city, and county governments, constitute an attempt to collect cash payment for the loss it inflicts—a huge case of social and political bribery.

That the traffic is so able and willing to pay that it constantly seeks close connection with public officials, politics, parties, and policies increases the suspicion that the last assumption is the true one. Further, it offsets much of the public sentiment that would otherwise be against the traffic.

In brief, large numbers of people learn to favor and support the liquor traffic and the saloon, not because they care for liquor, but because "it pays the taxes." They overlook, for the time being, the "consequential cost of the saloon" that government in large part must bear.

The Saloon Vote.—Liquor seems to be a necessary factor in current corrupt politics. Alcohol makes men, morally and financially, willing to sell their votes. The saloon has gathered up and used for its own advantage much of this vote. It has also discovered the exchange value of such a vote in political commerce. The saloon is seeking to evade law and to escape punishment for continued violations of law; this vote is of unlimited service in obtaining "protection."

But the saloon vote has become far too valuable to remain wholly in the hands of the saloon-keeper. The political "machines" and "bosses" long ago discovered that it could serve more than one purposes. Frankly accepting the saloonists' program of escape from obedience to law, they have made the saloon a part of all great political combinations that seek to make "business" out of vice, law evasion, robbery of the public, "graft" on the public treasury, or the stealing of franchises.

The saloon can create and handle votes; the "grafting" trades that seek to get "something for nothing" need the votes. The corrupt politician has his hands on both and makes it his profession to bring them together. In this sense the saloon does not "run politics" now as it did years ago, when it first went in for self-preservation. It has been exploited politically, as, in turn, it has exploited the "down and out" for votes, so that politics as a business runs the saloon. Its *vote is a necessary adjunct to the professional exploitation of the public funds and the public morals.* The saloon and its keeper and bartender are little more than tools of the big brewer, the corrupt politicians that fraternize with the brewer, and the "rulers" of dangerous interests.

There are approximately 200,000 saloons in the United States. If each of these controls an average of ten votes, including both those personally interested in the trade and those so debauched by liquor that they can always be depended upon, a low estimate, this will give the liquor traffic of the nation a manageable saloon vote of 2,000,000. This is not a large share of the whole, but with the vast majority of better voters giving attention only to other issues, or automatically voting "inherited politics," or fearing to "lose their vote" or "scratch a ticket," and noting again that the liquor vote can readily be shifted in part or wholly as needed, one reason can be seen why in most elections the liquor traffic has been able to win far more than its proportionate share of candidates and measures.

Any group of 2,000,000 voters, drugged by alcohol and living in the political atmosphere of the saloon, and controlled in behalf of all sorts of questionable interests, is a serious menace to the welfare of the nation. This inherently vicious vote is, perhaps, a worse factor in politics than even the strong national organizations of the liquor dealers themselves. "The influence of *the saloon,* rather than the influence of the saloon-keeper, is the cause of grave concern. It is true the liquor dealers, thro the organizations—local, state, and national —which they have formed, and the immense capital which they have accumulated, have developed political power dangerous to contemplate. But the chief source of that power is not, after all, in their organizations, nor in their capital, nor in their personal ability; but it lies in the saloons which they control, and thro which they operate to such tremendous advantage. *Whatever purchasable vote there may be is almost sure to be within the reach of the saloon-keeper.*"[1]

Political Alliances of the Traffic.—There is a strong tendency in the politics of the liquor traffic to pool its force with that of various questionable, immoral, or illegal interests, and with legal lines of business which are seeking to gain an unjust advantage in governmental affairs.

It is to be expected that, with anti-liquor sentiment as strong as it is, it will form close alliances with related trades, such as glassmakers, bottlers, coopers, and the manufacturers of brewery machinery and bar fixtures. But it has not stopped with such commercially "allied trades." Its political affiliation with the more dangerous "trades" is yet more important because not so open and aboveboard.

The most conspicuous of these alliances, with which the liquor traffic finds so much in common, have been carefully classified as follows:

(1) "Those with legally precarious interests, such as gambling, vice, etc., which have a common purpose in opposing enforcement of law.

(2) "Those with political machines which want the liquor vote.

(3) "Those with predatory interests which want special favors from legislative bodies, or seek to block hostile legislation, and are glad to join with the liquor power and the machines to elect the kind of officials that they can control." [8]

The legally precarious interests are those that, generally recognized as vicious, are either already illegal or are in danger of being made so at any time. As Dr. Colvin shows, "there seems to be a deep-down, natural alliance between these and the liquor traffic. They have in common the exploitation of human weakness. Alcohol contributes both to those other vices and to the 'business' in such tendencies, because it affects the brain and lessens self-control." [8] Social vice and gambling are frequently made profitable side-lines to the sale of beer and distilled spirits.

It is certain that "in these legally uncertain 'trades' the profits are very large"; that "they can therefore well afford to spend heavily for political purposes"; that, jointly with the liquor traffic, they are seeking "to escape the penalties of the law"; that this fact is itself "a powerful unifying incentive." This is "all too clearly evidenced by the corruption in all our large

cities, by the prominent part taken in city councils, and
by their control and graft in police forces."

"In license cities the liquor men are continually vio-
lating the restrictive laws, such as Sunday closing, selling to minors, and after hours. This continuous violation of law is one point that identifies liquor closely
with other exploitative interests. Also, in common
with them there is a constant fear of further regulation,
or restriction, or prohibition; it is therefore vitally
important that they keep in politics constantly to prevent further restriction." [8]

The well-known connection between the liquor traffic
and the political machine has already been discussed.
The saloon vote is for use by the political organization
that gives most advantages in return; or it is divided
between several machines or parties when it is desired
to keep any of them from taking an anti-liquor attitude.
The saloon vote can be handled "in bunches," so that
it is unnecessary for politicians to reach each voter sep-
arately. "Its supply is elastic—more money, more
votes, if desired. . . . These is no class of voters so
boss-able as those debauched by liquor. Consequently,
machines are glad to avail themselves of liquor support
and are afraid to alienate it." [8]   That is, to the average
candidate, seeking merely to be elected, the saloon vote is
preferable to an equal number of more intelligent votes,
for it is less bother to reach and convince them. A little
money, an implied promise or two, and the machine
does the rest. Typical conditions of alliance between
liquor, vice, and the political machine were brought out
in a grand jury investigation in Danville, Ill., in 1911:

"Danville, with her 28,000 people, has forty churches
and ninety licensed saloons; but nearly 200 dens of

vice, including a large number of blind pigs, police-protected, liquor-selling dives, and gambling hells, winked at by the powers that be, provide the means utilized by the dominant political machine to keep itself in power. By means of this organized system of protected vice and drink, a horde of venal voters, conservatively estimated to be from 20 to 25 per cent of the citizenship of the district, and men of every variety and trade, profession and intelligence, are kept available for every emergency by the trusted saloon-lieutenants of 'the men higher up.' '' [9]

"Co-operating with the party machines," [8] Colvin further shows, "the liquor traffic in many cases has effected a 'triple alliance' with the predatory interests, such as the trusts, franchise-grabbing corporations, etc. The machines want office, the liquor traffic wants power, and the predatory interests want special privileges, immunity from prosecution, or the maintenance of *status quo*. . . . The kind of men that the liquor traffic seeks to elect for its own purposes are those, as a rule, that can be bought by the trusts. So we have an alliance that results both in the corruption of voters and the election of corruptible officials."

A brewery legislature or saloon city council, with rare exceptions, is "easy picking" by a public-utility corporation that wishes to get special privileges. The liquor traffic is a chief factor in the steady stream of "graft" stories that comes from legislative halls.

A Cause of Crime.—In spirit crime is a rebellion against social order and welfare. There are three chief ways in which the drink habit and the drink traffic produce or encourage this anti-social spirit: (a) The action of the alcohol upon the brain of the user; (b) the ex-

ample and associations of the saloon; (c) the tendency
of the traffic persistently to ally itself with illegal, questionable, and immoral trades and political enterprises.
All these create about it a peculiar crime-yielding atmosphere. Drink may be a lesser cause of poverty, one of
many complicated causes of ill health, and a factor in
social degeneracy; but, most of all in quantity, is it a
disturbing element in social morality and good order.
It makes it harder for men to live together in peace.

Continued use of liquor dulls the mental powers,
especially the judgment; it overthrows conscience, and
lets the animal passions—revenge, lust, anger, hate—
run with lessened control. The first state is intoxication
itself expressed in recklessness, disregard for others,
disorder, and disturbances. Slowly but surely these
lower mental characteristics become a part of the character, while ideals and other spiritual qualities lose
their place. Beyond this individual effect of intemperance there are the associations accompanying many
saloons, and the contempt for law expressed by the
liquor seller toward the legal restrictions governing his
trade.

The facts of every-day experience justify the large
charge made against drink as a cause of crime. The
arrests for drunkenness and minor misdemeanors resulting from drink, disturbances, improprieties, rows, petty
fights, vagrancy, etc., constitute one of the very largest
of all lists of crime. It is distinctly larger in communities that have saloons than in cities, counties, and states
from which the sale has been banished. The trying and
punishing of "drunks," "disorderlies," and similar
offenders is the chief business of the police courts.

For years judges have declared that from 40 per cent

to 95 per cent of the cases that are called before them are there on account of drink. The authorities in prisons, reformatories, and penitentiaries, where the severest crimes are punished, declare that intemperance has been responsible for from 60 per cent to 80 per cent.

Dr. W. C. Sullivan says: "In the cases of 200 male offenders convicted of murder or of grave homicidal attempts, the number of cases in which the criminals were of alcoholic habits amounted to 158, and in 120 of these, or 60 per cent of the whole series, the criminal act was directly due to alcoholism." [10] In a larger group of 500 cases of less serious character, he found that 82 per cent were attributable to alcohol.

The Massachusetts Bureau of Labor, under the direction of Carroll D. Wright, made an investigation in Suffolk county, which includes Boston, that gives us some very definite facts. The total number of sentences passed during the year for which the investigation was carried on was 16,897; of these 12,289, or 72 per cent, were clearly due to drink or rum offenses. This includes both those chargeable to drunkenness and to illegal sales, by far the larger number being for drunkenness. In addition, 2,097 other crimes were committed by men under the influence of liquor and in which it was a contributing cause, so that the total summary charges up to liquor 14,368, or 84 per cent of all the crimes of Boston for that year.

Whether mere drunkenness is considered a crime or not, no one will doubt the seriousness of drink as a source of crime when we take our facts from state prisons and reformatories. Men are not sent to penitentiaries for being drunk or for mere disorderly conduct. Here are found those who commit the more serious grades of offenses against society. The part that liquor had in causing this sort of crime is the heaviest count against it.

The investigation conducted by the Committee of Fifty among a large number of state prisons and reformatories is one of the most conservative and widest that has ever been made. There is certainly no reason to believe that their conclusions have been overdrawn. Their final conclusion is that 49.95 per cent of crime is due to liquor.[11] This does not include minor crimes, a much larger per cent of which is always due to drink.

The final conclusions of the Massachusetts Bureau of Labor place the amount, exclusive of drunkenness, at 50.88 per cent.

As a general conclusion, it may be said that the social burden is as follows:

(1) One-half, 50 per cent, of all severe crime, worthy of prison punishment, is declared by our most conservative investigators to be due to drink. Other authorities make it from 60 to 75 per cent.

(2) By far the largest amount of arrests for minor crimes, disturbing the peace, assaults, etc., are due to drink. The amount is anywhere from one-half to three-fourths, varying with conditions.

(3) To these must be added offenses against the liquor laws: violations of the hours of sale; sale to minors, etc.; laws made to regulate the business and diminish its evil influences. These are all crimes induced by the traffic itself. The total of this is immense.

(4) The social consequences of drink—degenerate social conditions, ill health, poverty, inherited tendency toward moral obtuseness and crime—all these have a direct relation to additional crime.

Kinds of Crime Resulting From Drink.—While alcoholic intemperance is one of the most prolific of all the sources of crime and crime-producing conditions, it should be noted that it gives rise chiefly to certain classes of crime. The counterfeiter and the swindler must be men of moderation and cannot succeed if they deaden their nerves with intoxicants. Offenses against the federal government are seldom due in any important part to drink. The crimes in which liquor is at the bottom are those which are most corrupting and demoralizing to society. As classified in law, they are chiefly offenses against safety, order, and morals.

(1) Drunkenness and intoxication. As noted above, this is the largest single cause for arrest in our cities. Drunkenness openly is an offense against public decency and morals. It is not so much because the man is drunk as it is for the protection of the public morals that he is arrested and punished. He is disgusting in the eyes of the public; he disturbs the peace; he is just on the verge of injuring himself or someone else; crime is imminent in carousal. His example is a public menace. Young boys and others are tempted to imitate his spirit of bravado; their respect for public order is lowered and, either with the use of liquors or without, they are, in turn, in danger of following the suggestive force of this example.

(2) Offenses against property. A large part of severe crime has as an aim the appropriation of the property of someone else. Liquor destroys personal respect for others; much more does it lead to disrespect for the material property of others. The violence of the drunken man leads to destruction; his growing needs

and his lowered moral ideals, to stealing, burglary, and robbery.

(3) Personal assaults are peculiarly apt to follow drink. Fights and knock-downs in quarrels; intentional and unintentional attacks of violence upon unoffending citizens; cruelty to wife and children; attacks prompted by sex passion, and by passion and drink combined. The total amount is very large; it varies directly with the amount of liquors sold and used.

(4) Wholesale crime or mob violence is partly due to liquor. No matter what the direct cause of rioting may be, it is the usual thing to find that the leaders have come from saloon associations. Here they fire passions with heated talk and deaden judgment with alcohol. The right to strike, the only means employees have at present in a final test of strength with organized capital, becomes a public danger when intoxicated men stir up the passions of the strikers and get them drunk. It has become the custom whenever there is danger of riot to close the saloons, so clearly are they the source of the violence which sometimes accompanies a strike. In mobs of passion, such as lynchings, drink plays an equally important part. The lawlessness of the saloon creates a spirit of disregard for law; it has been the source of the corrupt forces that lead in this sort of crowd crime.

As a curious but significant indication of the public danger caused by drunken men, and thru them by the saloon, are the following figures of policemen injured in London. There was in 1902 a total of 2.970 policemen injured while on duty; of these 1,655 were assaulted by drunken prisoners, 68 were attacked by dogs, 40 were injured while regulating traffic, 20 at fires and eight in dispersing disorderly crowds. "This proves that a drunken man is worse than a runaway horse, a mad dog, an excited crowd, or a raging fire."

It is these very kinds of crime that government is organized to prevent. Public order, safety and morals must be preserved if nothing else is done, or government fails of its chief purpose.

Crime an Unavoidable Consequence.—It has been established beyond doubt that there is a causal relationship between the use of intoxicating liquors and crime. It is important to note how this connection is established, and whether it is inherent, or contingent and curable. There are many who drink who are at the same time perfectly law abiding citizens, that the underlying connection is often overlooked. What is this connection and is it a necessary one?

The first answer is that of the concrete facts themselves. Police court records, judges, and prison officials and other observers agree that liquor is one of the chief excuses given for crime. It is noted that crime varies in a similar ratio with the average amount of liquor consumed in a community. When there are restrictions limiting its use crime diminishes. Says ex-Governor Martin, of Kansas, who was strongly opposed to prohibition before he saw it in working operation in his own state: "The abolition of the saloon has not only promoted the personal happiness and general prosperity of our citizens, but it has enormously diminished crime."

The effects of alcohol upon the brain and nerve centers make crime inevitable. Alcohol retards thinking processes and quickens impulsive acts; the sober man thinks, then acts; the intoxicated man acts before his slow-thinking brain has time to consider. His brain does not work right. A motion, a quick response; he does his thinking next morning in a cell. The *moral equilibrium is destroyed. It matters little whether we fire up the locomotive beyond control or pitch off the engineer.*

It is the alcohol and its effects which people desire when they drink. Intoxication itself is a temporary suspension of mental and moral control; insanity, as the original meaning of the word indicates. It places both physical and mental powers at the mercy of any evil impulse or passion or sudden temptation. It enables a man to carry out deeds which in a saner moment he would not dare undertake; he drinks to overcome conscience and give him "nerve" enough to accomplish his purposes.

The effect of the parental drinking upon the family, its social standing, relative poverty, etc., all help to fix the conditions under which children must grow up. Often they are trained from the earliest to be familiar with evil and crime and never know anything better. The hereditary effects of alcohol are more to incline children to crime, and mental deficiency which may lead to crime, than they are toward making them drunkards. These are unavoidable consequences of the continued use of liquors.

The associations of drink and of the saloon have a crime-educating effect. Saloons are not by any means all "schools of crime." In fact, comparatively few of them are voluntarily so. Many would not willingly harbor criminals, and yet the associations, found in most saloons ultimately lead to this. On the other hand, there are saloons in every city which are indeed the very hotbeds of crime; places where those planning invasion upon society come together to make plans. Here young men learn to hate society and honest labor and take their first lessons in living without work.

One class of crime having a sort of affinity for saloon association is that of a political nature; corruption, bribery, purchasing of voters, etc., find here a congenial companionship. Drink serves as a medium to all transactions. The saloon is the rallying point for corrupt forces in politics. A crime against the government, the people as a whole, is none the less a crime than if it were directed against a single individual or his property or life. It is, indeed, more dangerous to the future welfare of society. A few citizens may be murdered and society will fill their places with others; but *the crime of political corruption defiles the means by which social welfare is preserved.*

The tendency of the liquor trade is to react upon the men engaged in it, creating a spirit of lawlessness. Under present conditions it is practically impossible for a saloon-keeper to be honest and law-abiding even if he wants to.

The trade is itself notoriously a law-breaker. Its inherent tendencies, moral and economic, are to violate all legal restrictions. Its chief economic support is a vicious appetite, that for alcohol. Thus dependent upon what is abnormal in mankind for its existence, it cannot be that its influence upon the men engaged in it should be other than demoralizing. In most of our cities the midnight and Sunday closing and similar restrictive features are openly disregarded, except when a temporary reign of ''righteous indignation'' is stimulating the police to unwonted efforts. Illegal sales and ''blind tigers'' are found in license cities in even larger numbers than they are in prohibition districts and states. There were more "joints" in high license Lincoln, Neb., in 1901, with its 40 open saloons and about the same population, than there were in Topeka, Kan., with its prohibition and no legal saloons.

The only class of laws which are really obeyed are those which relate to revenue and license payments. These are met promptly. In return the traffic demands and expects a sort of general amnesty from society for its violation of all other governmental regulations.

The actual experiences of a clean-cut German-American who undertook to run a saloon in New York City on honorable business methods shows how impossible it was for him to succeed without actively encouraging intemperance, and social and political vice. He says:[12]

"I lost patronage because I refused to allow my saloon to become a hang-out for criminals, and a place of assignation.

"I lost a big source of revenue because I refused to encourage hard drinking among my patrons.

"I lost all possibility of a margin of profit by refusing to pay politicians a monthly bribe to break the law."

This honest saloon-keeper found out that to be the "proprietor" of a barroom was to be the "Man Friday" of the beermaker; that the brewer held a mortgage on his fixtures, "so much larger than the value of the property it covered," that it was practically certain that it would never be paid off; that the brewer made something like "350 per cent gross profit on the beer at the price he sold it"; that it is a common trick in the business for saloon-keepers to fill up original bottles of

high-priced liquors with the cheapest grades of fire-
water, and "sell these for any brand of liquor that is
called for"; that "to me the drinking habits of my
patrons appeared frightful"; that "intemperance, intoxication pursued to the point of senselessness—and
this not once in a while, but frequently or daily—was
common"; that "my unmarried patrons spent about 75
per cent of their earnings in drink"; that "even the
married men, I believe, spent an average of at least
25 per cent of their wages in this way, and many of
them more"; and finally that "in my numberless con-
versations before and behind the bar, I found that
'honesty' was laughed at and derided."

References and Authorities.

Liquor in Politics and Government.

Fehlandt, *A Century of Drink Reform*, 139-218.

Howe, *Taxation in the United States Under the Internal Revenue System*, 205-208, 257-261.

Artman, *The Legalized Outlaw.*

Lilly, *The Saloon Before the Courts.*

Ritter, *Moral Law and Civil Law.*

[1] *A Century of Drink Reform*, 139-171.

[2] Taxation in the U. S.

[3] Fehlandt, 152.

[4] Artman, 87.

[5] Crowley v. Christensen, 137 U. S. 86.

[6] Ritter, 258.

The Saloon Vote.

Bryce, *American Commonwealth*, II, chs. 43-44.

Rowntree and Sherwell, *The Temperance Problem, and Social Reform*, 114-115.

Wheeler, *Prohibition*, 76-81.

Turner, "The City of Chicago," *McClure's*, April, 1907.

[7] Wheeler, 76.

Political Alliances of the Traffic.

Barker, *The Saloon Problem and Social Reform*, 21-35.

Turner, ''The City of Chicago,'' *McClure's*, April, 1907.

American Prohibition Year Book (1911), 141-152.

Anti-Saloon League Year Book (1912), 121-123.

Williams, *Alcohol*, 59-63.

''Experiences and Observations of a New York Saloonkeeper,'' *McClure's*, Jan., 1909.

Turner, ''Tammany's Control of New York,'' *McClure's*, June, 1909.

8 Colvin, ''The Alliances of the Traffic,'' *Intercollegiate States-man*, Feb., 1913.

9 *Prohibition Year Book* (1911), 149.

A Cause of Crime.

Cutten, *Psychology of Alcoholism*, 202-205.

Lombroso, *Crime, Its Causes and Remedies* (1912), 96.

Horsley and Sturge, *Alcohol and the Human Body*, 92-94.

Koren, *Economic Aspects of the Liquor Problem*, 133-159.

Roberts, *The New Immigration* (1912), 233-247.

Barker, *The Saloon Problem and Social Reform*, 55-61.

10 *Alcoholism*, 162-164.

11 Koren.

Kinds of Crime Resulting.

Kelynack, *The Drink Problem*, 189-198.

Roberts, *The New Immigration*, 236-239.

Horsley and Sturge, *Alcohol and the Human Body*, 87-90.

Koren, *Economic Aspects of the Liquor Problem*, 138-141.

Baker, ''What Is a Lynching?'' *McClure's*, Jan. and Feb., 1905.

An Unavoidable Consequence.

Cutten, *The Psychology of Alcoholism*, 198-203.

Horsley and Sturge, *Alcohol and the Human Body*, 87-94.

Barker, *The Saloon Problem and Social Reform*, 56-66.

Kelynack, *The Drink Problem*, 190-191.

Wheeler, *Prohibition*, 76-77.

Hopkins, *Wealth and Waste*, 160-163, 196-206.

12 ''The Experiences and Observations of a saloonkeeper,'' *Mc-Clure's*, Jan., 1909.

CHAPTER XII

The end of the government is the welfare of mankind.

—LOCKE.

Whenever a community attempts to deal with the saloon question, instead of having to deal with one of its own citizens, it finds itself in a struggle with great corporations which operate over a large area, and have a pecuniary interest in cultivating the appetite for drink; instead of settling the question by consulting its own voters, it must engage in a war with foreign power.

—WILLIAM J. BRYAN.

CHAPTER XII

THE SOCIAL DEMANDS FOR COMPLETE ELIMINATION

In the past the attention both of reformers and of more scientific students of the liquor problem has been centered largely on the individual user, or seller, or voter. The defenders of the saloon, too, have made their fight on the ground of the right and privilege of each individual to enjoy or suffer for himself.

The problem today is far from being merely personal, whatever it may have been in the past. Its big, blighting, dangerous facts are now chiefly social. The enjoyment of the glass, of continuing an old custom, of the making of a living by this particular trade, are of the individual; but most of the dangerous consequences, the suffering and future risk, go to society, the family, the community, the nation, and the race. The mental and physical weakness, the inefficiency for the struggles of life among the children of drinking men, now known to be due to even the moderate daily use of alcohol, can in no sense be regarded as a matter of "personal liberty." The injury to health and economic efficiency, the crime caused, the corruption of politics, the dictating hand of "the liquor interests" in public affairs, the social influences of the saloon in the community, its mis-education of new peoples coming to this country— these are the all-important phases today. The scientific view is substantiating practical experience and the ideals of human brotherhood that "no man can live unto himself." The personal claim is misleading, because it puts emphasis on minor parts.

The Social Welfare Basis.—It is their effects upon the community as a whole, upon the health, happiness and morality of large masses of people, and upon the permanency of the nation, that condemn the drink habit and traffic. It is not so much that harm comes to the individual user, as that others must bear so large a burden of undeserved consequences, that calls for action on the part of organized society.

It may not be inherently wrong to drink a glass of liquor or to manufacture in response to a pre-existing call for intoxicants, for occasional use. But the consequences of the drink habit and the saloon, the impossibility of preserving such moderation that no evil will result, and the active creation of a new demand, produce a deep-seated wrong that strikes at the foundations of community and national life.

It is an absurdity and a contradiction of the purposes of government that an institution which is a danger to public welfare should receive the sanction of law— the only method by which the whole of society speaks authoritatively.

To provide for the public health, safety, and morals, is the very first duty of the police powers of the government. With all these the liquor traffic conflicts; it is thus marked as an anti-social institution to be exterminated:

(1) The general use of alcoholic liquors is a serious danger to public health, the necessary physical basis for all individual, as well as social welfare. Mankind has used intoxicants for thousands of years; he has grown

so accustomed to their action that the most far-reaching evils were not discovered until modern science took hold of the liquor problem. Alcohol is directly and indirectly a cause of disease, physical and mental, to an extent heretofore claimed only by the most extreme of its enemies. Its worst consequences are its insidious deterioration of the classes persistently using it, the inherited tendencies to obtuseness, idiocy, and innumerable varieties of nervous weakness and general lowered physical vitality, the weakened power to resist disease, the tendency toward vice, and crime—these lay up a fearful burden for future generations. The recent massing of large populations in great cities, away from outdoor exercise and fresh air, greatly increases these effects.

(2) Economically the liquor traffic consumes wealth but produces nothing. It is not a mere luxury. It injures labor, the vital factor in all production, it employs a few men where the capital invested ought to employ many men; it decreases the length of life; it throws upon society a consequential burden of poverty, imbecility, inefficiency, lunacy, crime and its punishment, and general incapacity, that is so immense as to be almost beyond calculation.

(3) The saloon is not merely a place of retail trade; it is a great public educational institution. It influences the thoughts, morals, politics, social customs and conversation of its patrons—gives a bent to their character—such as the grocery and shoe store never do. By suggestion, example and its emphasis of a distorted meaning of personal liberty, it teaches indulgence of the lower passions, instead of their restraint, and creates the alcoholic craving as a new one. By defying restric-

tive regulations it breaks down respect for law. It teaches the three-fourths of a million foreign immigrants annually coming to America that the ballot is a commodity to be sold to the highest bidder, and trains up a host of voting citizens opposed to many of the fundamental principles of liberty and justice.

(4) The saloon furnishes a place of sociability and relaxation of some considerable value to the poor man who can get nothing better. This is one count in its favor. But even this is more than counteracted by its competition with the home and the fact that the enjoyment must be limited, selfishly, to one member of the family while the wife and children, equally needy, suffer all the more on account of it. The alcohol should be eliminated and the club features left to develop in a normal way.

(5) It is only on its sociability side that the saloon gets any ethical support. Aside from this return that it makes to the class who can least afford its burdens, "the public saloon and saloon system is a vast organized inciter of human appetite. It is an omnipresent, publicly sanctioned temptation to evil. It exists, not because man, by nature, must drink, but because, by proper incentives, man can be made to drink, and there is money in selling it to him."[1] For this reason it is unreservedly condemned by the church as immoral, and should be declared unconstitutional and an outlaw by the government. The placing of liquor selling under the license policy gives it social standing, permission, and authority, and makes each citizen responsible for the character and consequences of the saloon. There can be no distinction, on moral grounds, between the acts of the men, officials and parties that endorse this

policy, and those of the dealer who proposes to make a livelihood out of the vice of intemperance. The voter is free ethically only when he has protested by act against the principle in which he does not believe.

The moderate, self-contained drinker cannot demand that the public sale of that which injures many of his fellows shall continue on the ground that the consequences of his own drinking fall upon himself alone. The right thing for him is to give it up willingly; if he refuses, the public welfare demands that he shall be compelled to do so.

In the wide-extending so-called moderate use of alcoholic and similar narcotic drugs by the younger adults of the nation, both men and women, lies the certainty of serious physical and mental deterioration—a threat so dangerous that no other public question can surpass it in immediate importance.

The tense, stimulated, nervous, modern life, that "gets the results" industrially in a day that formerly took a year makes laborer, office man, and manager alike more quickly susceptible to the action of alcohol. It is more dangerous; its results more certain; the dependence upon it for supposed stimulation, when once established, is more confident,—and delusive.

Its presence in the nerve centers of the civilization of today is like sand in the finest watch of today, as compared with sand in the "old clock on the stairs" of the times when the drinking customs now in vogue were first established. *The liquor institution is seriously out of date—the unburied dead-hand of the past ages dragging down the manhood and hindering the evolution of the present.*

Commercializing the Narcotic Habit. — During the past few years under new public health conceptions the war on contagion and acute disease has lengthened the average life and greatly increased happiness. The germs of fevers, plagues, and "the great white death" have been attacked; the carriers of infection, the fly, mosquito, rat, waste matter, rubbish, are being relentlessly destroyed.

The public attitude toward another source of almost unlimited danger to health, safety, morals, and happiness—the narcotic cell poisons—of which alcohol is chief, is vastly different. This attitude must be changed until it classes alcohol with the mosquito, the rat, and waste matter, so far as daily use is concerned; and with arsenic, cocaine, and other deadly drugs so far as exceptional use is concerned.

Men enjoy the effects of alcohol—intoxication; they also enjoy the effects of morphine, cocaine, opium. Old customs approve the use of alcoholic liquors; but the habits and traditions of ages are being shattered in a day, under rapid changes of present-day life; the language of a million people is transformed in half a generation on arrival in this country from Europe, while frequently a group of immigrants, landing in a clean community, get away entirely from the drinking customs of the fatherland. No—it is not so much love of drink and social customs that are at the root of our excessive intemperance, as it is *the commercial and political influence of the liquor traffic, and ignorance of the newer scientific facts,* that *keep alive and encourage false ideas about drink and the saloon.*

Among the big, outstanding factors the most inexcusable is the excessive commercializing of this vice of intemperance, and the hand of the traffic in politics. The gratifying of narcotic habits is always a profitable "business." The pressure of high profits in the trade and its high-tension political affiliations, coupled with the persistency of the drink demand when once created, yield *a continuous inexhaustible supply* of drink, cheap and always near at hand. That the mass of young men, growing up under such conditions, should drink is unavoidable; that older men should tend toward greater indulgence is psychologically necessary. The *accessibility* is one of the large causes of increasing, or heavy, drinking. The battery of saloons opposite every entrance to a great factory, catching the attention of men morning, noon, and night, has a far deeper result than merely to furnish a drink or two to a thirsty working man.

"Let us recognize once for all," says Homer Folks, "that liquors are not made to be drunk, but to be sold; that the most difficult factor in the problem of intemperance is not the man who wants to drink, but the man who wants to sell drinks." [2] The social settlement, friendly society, and charity organization; the church, club, playground, and "substitute for the saloon," as matters now are, must compete unjustly with the highly developed "business" in alcoholic dissipation.

Commercialism has exploited the drink habit in America as opium has been exploited in eastern lands. In China opium indulgence has been far-reaching, backed by inherited customs, social usage, intense physical and psychic cravings, and commerce. But, the commercial and political forces are outside of China—their location is in India or Great Britain, so that the question can better be seen in its parts. China, for a period of years, has steadily been reducing the sale and use of opium, banishing it by law. The Chinese people are giving up the drug. The one resisting force against this marvelous freeing of the Chinese millions from the opium blight was and is, not the "craving," tense as that may be, but the "opium monopoly" with its corrupting hand in the politics of Great Britain. Revenue to the government, profits to the opium trader, are the great forces that have so long retarded this humane advance by a "heathen" nation.

With alcohol in America the commercial and political elements are even more prominent. Educational methods, doubtless, would now be far along toward doing away with most of the alcoholic blight, had it not been for the political blunder that has made national and local governments dependent upon liquor revenue and legalized license. In all sorts of anti-liquor campaigns, those to educate sentiment, to learn the facts, to let the public know, pro and con, thru the newspapers, in movements to find the social value of the saloon, in local option, and all sorts of prohibition campaigns, there is little actual fighting done by the man who really wants *to keep using;* it is done by those who want *to continue selling.*

Dr. Henry Smith Williams, summing up the latest results of scientific investigation, shows that one ounce of absolute alcohol is sufficient to produce "a distinctly deleterious effect on the average individual." Taking the amount of liquors consumed in the United States reduced to terms of absolute alcohol, he makes the startling deduction that this will "supply each and every adult—women as well as men, with no allowance for teetotalers of either sex—with this ounce dose of alco-

hol on each week-day of the year, and with a slightly
larger dose on every Sunday. It would suffice, in other
words, to *keep every adult in America permanently
alcoholized to a scientifically measurable extent.*[3] If
this small amount reduces efficiency and health, what
must be the total of the burden borne by the 20,000,-
000 who are the real consumers of alcohol?

This is certainly the narcotizing of a nation, under
cover of an age-old custom and of the delusion that
alcohol is a stimulant. In origin co-ordinate with slavery, polygamy, duelling, and gambling, the alcohol habit
has been given a new lease of life in this twentieth
century by obtaining vast commercial and political
power.

Relation of Solution to Sources.—The influence of
alcohol in society is co-extensive with almost the whole
of human history. But in all the ages the human system and human society have not become immune to its
destructive effects. On the contrary, these consequences seem to have grown worse in proportion to use,
with density of population, commercial progress, and
the rapid-pace living of present-day civilization. As
new forces have been brought to deal with intemperance,
such as science and industrial restraint, other factors,
such as political and commercial greed, have added to
the intensity and difficulty of the problem.

There has been an almost infinite number of theories
and methods proposed for the settlement of this age-
old modern question. Some have gained wide acceptance and left lasting results for the better tho far
from scientifically correct. Others have greatly retarded progress. To all, old and new, should be applied the practical test: Does it reach the sources, one

or more? Or does it merely deal with symptoms? How does it work in practice?

The four chief sources of the ugly complicated liquor problem, as has been shown,[4] are: first, the desire for excitement or stimulation together with the created physical craving for alcohol; second, the opportunity to make money in the gratification of this demand by means of an artificial agent—alcohol; third, social custom and sociability; and, fourth, political approval.

It is interesting to note how far some of the most important reform ideas and methods so far tried have really reached the sources of this social disease:

(1) Educational Movements by scientific, practical, church, and other reform societies, are all aimed definitely at the psycho-physical source, the desire for alcohol, and influence indirectly the social.

By strengthening will and showing the consequences of indulgence they tend strongly to prevent the formation of the habit, or to keep the young from knowing, by personal experience, what the psychic attractions of alcohol are. They create sentiment against the saloon by pointing out its dangers. Education is of more importance than "substitutes" as a means of counteracting the social attractions and the false idea that the saloon is "the poor man's club." It is the only method that effectively meets the influence of inherited or imported drinking customs. It is immensely practical and must continue to be the main dependence in all sort of anti-liquor reform.

But such methods are not sufficient in themselves. They do not touch directly all of the sources. In spite of the great pledge-signing campaigns they do not greatly help the drinking man, after the habit has been well formed. Too many that take the pledge slip back again if they are left to face the saloon day by day. These methods are practically useless in dealing with the economic source. "Moral suasion" has succeeded in getting a few men to quit selling, but their places are quickly taken by others. While the opportunity for profits is so great there will be men found to go after those profits. These methods only indirectly touch the political source; they are effective in so far as they stimulate the voter to resort to political and legal activity, or create a moral antagonism to the license and revenue systems that bring the traffic and government so close together.

The early "moral suasion" efforts illustrate the evolutionary steps by which advance in the reform so far has been made. At first the plea of the societies was for moderation in the use merely of distilled liquors; then malt liquors and wines were included; then, after further experience had shown that this did not reach the source, total abstinence from the former and finally total abstinence from all intoxicating liquors, irrespective of the amount of alcohol they contain, was the required standard. Each step grew out of the discovered inefficiency of the preceding stage.

As a consequence of educational methods on a wide scale, there has developed a deep hatred of the drink habit and drink traffic among a large number who never use it at all, and a strong desire to see its evils removed in another large class who would be willing to give up the occasional use to save the community from the corruptions which come from the saloon.

(2) **The Regulation or Control Methods**. The demand that organized force, government, should supple-

ment educational methods arose when temperance societies found that alone they could not cope with the
open temptation and commercial strength of the saloon.
The first extensive response was the attempt to regulate
the sale with a view to reducing opportunity for excess
and removing the more obtrusive evils.

The license and regulation methods do not reach effectively any one of the four fundamental sources. They
are planned on the theory that the evils are incidental
to the habit and trade and may be removed by careful
restriction. They eliminate a few of the ''low-down
dives'' but increase the attractiveness of the high-grade
places, thereby encouraging, rather than diminishing,
the formation of the habit among more respectable
young men. All the means necessary to afford full
gratification of the appetite are permitted. License,
especially high license, centralizes the trade into the
hands of a few, discriminates against the poorer saloon-
keeper on a financial, not on a temperance or regulative
basis, and acts as a monopolistic force, putting the control of the sale more and more into the hands of the
brewers. The large fee compels resort to every possible
means to increase trade, thereby accentuating the economic incentive. The games, free lunch, and other attractions added to the high license saloon make it more
than ever a substitute for healthful social centers. The
license policy as such is the very backbone of the political influence of the whole liquor traffic and the occasion
for ''the saloon vote.''

State monopoly merely transfers the economic desire
for profits to the government and voter. It seems to
stimulate the physical source by emphasizing ''pure
liquors'' with the false suggestion that such are less

harmful. It reduces the social attractiveness of the saloon, but complicates, instead of eliminating, the political sources. The dispensary, while a state institution in South Carolina, became one of the finest examples of corrupt political machinery in the country. Its influence was the chief factor in keeping liquor in the state for years after popular sentiment had asked emphatically for prohibition.

(3) The Social and Industrial Group. The providing of "substitutes" or counter attractions for the saloon is one of the more recent proposals as a definite temperance measure. It assumes that the saloon has gained a place for itself in social custom; that "it ministers to a forgotten need" in our civilization by providing a common meeting place and center for sociability; that, while bad in its results, there must be something to take its place before the demand for it can be met effectively.

The plan seeks to provide healthful amusement and recreation places so that men will not go to saloons for this purpose, and to encourage the payment of larger wages and the bettering of home conditions so that there can be no legitimate excuse for doing so. As a purposeful method of reducing intemperance it has a vital place in any worth-while program of reform. It represents an effort to accompany the negative and destructive methods of reform with constructive efforts; in principle it is, therefore, perfectly sound.

This method goes straight to the social source. It also strikes, more or less directly at the psycho-physical by opening opportunities for men to work off their desire for stimulation and excitement in healthful ways. But it cannot supply those mental states peculiar to alcoholic intoxication. For these, and these alone, many men, rich, poor, and middle class alike, seek the saloon and alcohol. It leaves the economic and political sources absolutely untouched.

Heavy restrictions against the use of intoxicants by business houses, railroads, manufacturing plants, and other big industrial establishments, purely for business reasons—the retaining of a more steady, clear-minded, and all around efficient force of employees—is one of the new methods acting in a decided way for the settlement of the national problem. In some concerns the rules are so stringent that they give to this new force in the temperance movement the term "industrial prohibition." Its application is extending so rapidly that it may be depended upon as one of the strongest factors in the struggles of the future.

(4) The Prohibition Group includes those measures which seek legal banishment. They aim directly at the psycho-physical source. By cutting off the supply they prevent the gratification of the desire for intoxicants and its formation where it is not yet found. By whatever cause the abnormal craving for intoxication may exist, whether on account of previous alcoholic experience, poorly prepared food, over work, nervous tension, lack of healthful recreation or inherited tendencies, education and prohibition are the only remedies which interfere seriously with this tremendous source of the liquor evil.

The prohibition methods strike more directly at the economic source than do those of any other group. They take away at once, in proportion as they are enforced, the very capacity of making a profit out of the traffic. They tend to turn this force, so relentlessly hostile to temperance, into other commercial lines in proportion to the decisiveness of the banishment and size of the territorial unit in which it has taken place. The hope of gain, of course, will drive a few men to try to continue an illegal trade, but this exists in equal proportion under license. State prohibition has the advantage in reaching the manufacturer as well as the retailer, making it more difficult for the would-be illegal seller to obtain his wares. But both are hindered by the operation of the economic force outside their own spheres —the centralization of the trade into large cities, from which shipment can be made direct to individuals in "dry" territory. Local methods, especially those carrying facilities for early reversal, leave hope alive in the heart of the ex-saloon-keeper, encourage him to illicit business, and keep him from entering at once some other trade. But local units conform more nearly to variations in public sentiment, and thereby tend to produce more rigid enforcement.

The political source, the most inexcusable and unnecessary of all the four, is seriously hit when prohibition is put into operation. Local prohibition removes merely the license influence in the small community without reference to the policy of the state. It cannot be expected that it will go far toward affecting the larger national political power of the traffic. The state method, going several steps further, strikes a more telling blow by removing the license policy of the state and doing away with the political influence of the fees from the saloons. But the state has to fight the national liquor organizations, the policies of the federal government which insists on taking revenue from the locally-outlawed dealers, and the larger political influences back of these policies.

Of the various methods for obtaining prohibition, state legislation, state amendment, local banishment, partisan, non-partisan, omni-partisan, or an opportunist combination of several or more of these, the partisan method is the one which has made the most direct attack upon the big political source of the liquor problem. Others have weakened it in particular states, but no other movement has so seriously sought to lead public sentiment up to a front attack on this one of the four sources.

As to the social source only are the prohibition methods deficient. They regard it negatively—that with the money saved from the saloon most drinking men could supply themselves with more recreation and social enjoyment than can possibly be procured at the saloon. To reach this source effectively, however, neither substitution nor prohibition alone is adequate. The two supplement each other and should work co-ordinately.

It will be noted that no one method or group of methods reaches completely all the four sources; also, that no other method reaches so many of the sources as does legal prohibition. Most emphasis will, therefore, be placed upon legal banishment. But along with the immense general education necessary to obtain prohibition should go aggressive work by all efforts that reach effectively any one or more of the four fundamental sources.

(5) **A Wider Program** than any yet proposed, including general education as to the scientific facts about alcohol, with special attention to the drinking classes, the providing of better wages, home, life, and recreational opportunities, the encouragement of ''substitutes'' for the saloon, industrial restriction against drinking

employees, temperance pledge signing, local, state, and national prohibition, removal of the revenue-license system, and the obtaining of united political support to insure anti-liquor administration after legislation, is what a study of the actual sources of the whole liquor problem demands.

The Necessity for Complete Overthrow.—Prohibition, without doubt, is a severe measure. If the evils arising from the saloon were such that they could be cured without resort to such drastic remedy, the principle of liberty in American democracy would demand that it should be done. Legal prohibition, applied to manufacture, sale and transportation, implies the removal of all opportunities for obtaining liquor other than by private home making for personal use. As a matter of policy even the strongest advocates of prohibition seldom favor making the act of drinking, itself, illegal. They propose simply to remove the open and powerful temptations toward creating or increasing the habit, being convinced that, since the desire for alcohol is abnormal, it will consequently die out and alcoholics will then not be missed.

Some of the unfortunate results doubtless can be removed by regulative and restrictive laws, by limiting the sale to certain districts and removing it altogether from resident sections of cities. Temperance societies may do their noble work of rescue and prevention; counter attractions may be established in mining, factory, and shop neighborhoods, and better home life encouraged, thereby overcoming some of the influences of the saloon. But these measures are very incomplete in themselves; *the great characteristic dangers are inherent in the liquor*

*and the trade themselves, and can be reached effectively
only by complete prohibition.*

Ethyl alcohol is the essential agent in all liquors used
as popular drinks. It is the one necessary ingredient
always present in some proportion, large or small. It
is the intoxicating element that gives the effect desired
when drinks of any kind are taken for their own sake.
In certain liquors other poisons are present, and in high-
grade wines there are several by-products of distillation
that injure even more quickly than alcohol, but generally speaking, the purest liquors are the worst.

The character of the trade seems to partake of the
inherently bad qualities of the article it sells to the public. All efforts to elevate the saloon, to disentangle it
from social and political vice, and to prevent its encouragement of excess, have signally failed. Judging by a
hundred years' experience, the evils of the saloon are not
contingent and cannot be separated from it. Where
exceptions occur they are due to the unusually self-
controlled character of the community or nationality
where such retail sale is found. The saloon is the chief
source of morbid and degenerate sociability. Low morals
and ideals prevail; alcoholic drinks are a necessary
accompaniment of the social vice; anarchy and crime
find here their home. "The bar, rather than the bar-
keeper, is the source of degeneracy, and if every saloon-
keeper emigrated or died to-morrow, and the saloons
continued, there would be but a slight or temporary
change for the better."[5]

Its public educational effects are absolutely unavoidable as long as the trade continues. No other institution
so persistently violates law and, by its example, so per-

sistently corrupts public respect for law. In this it is blighting, at its foundation, the necessary means to social welfare and national safety. The absolute immorality of granting legal life, permission, and authority to any business that yields such consequences is certain; it educates downward public ideals and the moral tone of the nation. This danger cannot be measured, but is far more menacing than the annual drink bill of $1,700,000,-000, or the heavy loss of life due to drink.

As supplemental to other reform efforts, the banishment of drink is imperative. Private and organized movements for the rescue of the drunkard, to provide better housing and sanitation for the poor of the city slums, toward cleaning up municipal politics, against gambling and other similar evils, need to have the destruction of the liquor trade accompany or precede their advance in order to insure real success. City missions, coffee-houses, rescue homes, clubs for the poor, settlements, and a thousand other agencies are now burdened by the fact that a peculiar co-operation exists between their competing enemy, the saloon, and the city authorities, and that it is given a privileged protection, on account of the fees and "graft" that representatives of the law and the city treasury get out of it.

The liquor trade can not be a benefit to public welfare in one community and a danger in another: the above facts show this clearly. Any local form of government is inadequate. A policy at least as wide as the state should prevail, because the sources of the trouble itself are not only state, but nation wide.

Official investigation in Great Britain, following the South African war, inspired by the fact that it took 300,000 veteran British troops, supposed to be the best soldiers in the world, to defeat 25,000 abstaining Dutch farmers, found that the most serious causes of the inefficiency of the English were the wide use of chemically prepared foods and the increasing use of stimulating liquors by the classes from which the troops were recruited.[6] In so doing it recognized the most serious danger to the trade and military supremacy of the nation.

In America, where the per capita consumption is somewhat less than in Great Britain, but where tenser, nervous life and higher requirements make alcoholic deadening more disastrous to the individual and the community, national prohibition is a measure of social hygiene more and more imperative from year to year. Complete enforcement need not be expected all at once. The habits and customs of centuries do not change suddenly. But the public social act, the sale, and, above all, the approval of government, must be stopped. That it can be done has been conclusively demonstrated. Politics is the present stronghold, the final resort, of the liquor trade. Science has routed its food and stimulation claims; industry is enforcing total abstinence in many lines; and even its legal standing is found to rest more on the public psychological effect of the license granted than in constitutional law. The most necessary move, whether it comes first or accompanies local and state overthrow of saloons, community by community, is to deal a death-blow to the political source and strength of the traffic.

From this, personal temperance and a stronger, cleaner type of national manhood will follow, logically, as the natural output of cleaner moral and industrial environment. But "it would not do to stigmatize such laws as attempts to reform the moral conduct of others; or to make men honest and virtuous 'by a system of coercive legislation.' The reform may follow, or it may even have been the object of those enacting the law; but it follows not as a coerced reformation, but as a natural result of the changed condition which the law has created.'' [7]

References and Authorities.

The Social Basis.

International Journal of Ethics, IX, 350-359.
Kelynack, *The Drink Problem*, 229-239, 122-151.
Fehlandt, *A Century of Drink Reform*, 299-305.
Horsley and Sturge, *Alcohol and the Human Body*, 243-277.
[1] Fehlandt, 302.

Commercializing the Narcotic Habit.

Williams, *Alcohol*, 101-108, 150-151.
Baker, ''The City of Chicago,'' *McClure's*, April, 1907.
[2]Homer Folks, Secy. State Charities Aid Assn. of N. Y., *Review of Reviews*, May, 1911.
[3] Williams, 107-108.
[4] See ch. II.

Necessity for Complete Overthrow.

Fehlandt, *A Century of Drink Reform*, 139-171, 299-305.
Horsley and Sturge, *Alcohol and the Human Body*, 16-19.
Artman, *The Legalized Outlaw*, 165-169.
[5] Wheeler, *Prohibition*, 76.
[6] Kelynack, *The Drink Problem*, 230.
[7] Wheeler, 27.

INDEX

APPENDIX

Questions and Suggestions for Study Classes

For a short course, eight weeks or meetings, study chapters II., III., IV., V., VI., VIII., XI., XII. Omit entirely or read rapidly chapters I., VII., IX., X. It is much better, however, to master the entire book, taking a chapter to a lesson.

These questions are intended to suggest to teacher and student the most important points in each chapter. It is expected that they will stimulate further study and thought—sometimes raise questions that the text does not directly answer. Some of them are especially fitted for free discussion.

The leader is not expected to use all of the questions. Select those best adapted to your own needs.

Others with local bearing may and should be added whenever possible. Keep in mind the practical question, Do the facts here given apply to our own immediate experience with the liquor question?

Encourage freedom of discussion and freedom to present all sorts of opinions.

Of course the use of the essays, debates, talks, etc., suggested for the various lessons is optional, but it is urged that as many of these be given as is feasible. They will greatly brighten the class work.

CHAPTER I

LIQUOR A SOCIAL INHERITANCE

*AIM: To get an understanding of the development of the liquor
problem.*

Was intemperance greater or less a hundred years ago, when
the temperance movement began, than it is to-day? Was the
liquor problem simpler or more complex then? Why?

Compare the proportion of persons that used drink a century
ago with the proportion to-day. Compare the per-capita use of
liquor in 1840 with that of to-day. Did people use more beer and
malt liquors? more distilled spirits? How about the amount of
alcohol?

Describe the six stages thru which the liquor problem has grown
complex and difficult.

When did alcoholic indulgence begin? When did men first discover its dangers?

On what occasions did primitive peoples want alcohol, and
what for?

What races have discovered intoxicating drinks of their own?

Describe the use of intoxicants on social occasions (a) in
England before the founding of the colonies, (b) in the early
days of the United States.

What was the origin of the saloon? Has it always been a
place of sociability? What double part does it play?

Is it correct to say ''the unamerican saloon''? Give reasons.

What part do the social customs of the past play in the liquor
problem of to-day?

Subjects for Essays: 1. Drinking among the Greeks and
Romans.   2. Intemperance in Bible Times and Bible Lands.
3. Intemperance in the Days of the Puritans and Pilgrims.

Question for Debate: Resolved: That thruout history temperance has grown with civilization.

CHAPTER II

SOURCES OF THE LIQUOR INSTITUTION

AIM: *To realize the human forces and motives that create the liquor habit and traffic.*

What facts and forces in human nature may be considered as "sources" of the liquor problem?

Why do men drink? Do they have a natural desire or need for alcohol that must be met?

Why do men sell alcoholic drinks?

For what variety of reasons does liquor appeal so strongly to so many persons?

In what ways is the liquor problem to-day different from the question of fifty years ago?

What are two common meanings of the term, "liquor problem"?

Fewer people drink now than formerly; how is it that the total consumption does not decrease?

Why has not the temperance activity of one hundred years reduced the consumption? Does the economic law of supply and demand work (normally) in the case of alcohol?

Has the shift to "light beers" reduced intoxication? Why? Can beer be called a "temperance drink"?

How does the personal desire for alcoholic drinks usually get its start?

Should drinking be left to individual choice as are matters of food? Why?

What must determine the attitude of society toward the liquor traffic?

Subjects for Essays: 1. Problems Involved in the Liquor Problem. 2. The Bigness of the Liquor Problem. 3. The Foundation of the Saloon.

Question for Debate: Resolved: That the temperance reform is making progress.

CHAPTER III

THE PSYCHO-PHYSICAL ASPECTS

AIM: *To realize the deceptive illusions on which the desire for drink is based.*

Why is alcohol attractive to so many persons?

What is the character of the happiness that intoxication furnishes?

Does man inherit an appetite for alcohol?

What is the essential ingredient of all intoxicating liquors?

How far would the liquor problem be settled if only pure liquors were made and sold?

Is alcohol a stimulant or a depressant?

Why have men so long believed that liquor stimulates? Compare it with opium and other narcotics.

What is man's chief motive in taking narcotics, including alcohol?

How little must a man drink in order to be "a moderate drinker"?

When is a man drunk?

Compare the mental state of the man "intoxicated" temporarily by the first few drinks with the mind of the permanently deranged or insane.

What percentage of insanity is due to intoxication?

Subjects for Essays: 1. Alcohol and Good Fellowship. 2. "I Can Take It or Let It Alone." 3. Self-deceived Drinkers.

Question for Debate: Resolved: That "total abstinence" is a better name for the anti-liquor movement than "temperance."

Talk by a Physician or a Specialist in Mental Diseases: Alcohol and Insanity.

CHAPTER IV

ALCOHOL AND HEALTH

AIM: *To estimate the physical and mental consequences to society of alcoholic indulgence on a wide scale.*

Name some of the ways in which alcohol interferes with health.

What is the action of alcohol on living matter? With what other well-known toxins should it be classed?

How many deaths, annually, are due to alcohol?

What diseases does alcohol cause, wholly or in part, by its presence in the body?

How does alcohol open the way for the invasion of disease germs?

Does a man who uses drink get sick more readily than the non-drinker? Does he recover more slowly?

How does the alcohol problem compare with the tuberculosis problem?

How does alcohol, in causing poverty, over-work, and immorality, affect public health?

Is "beer a food"?

What are hospitals and physicians doing about alcohol as a medicine?

Does drinking by parents influence the physical and mental capacity of their children? What scientific investigations go to show that it causes degeneracy?

Which puts the heavier burden on the community, the steady, moderate drinker or the excessive alcoholic?

Subjects for Essays: 1. Alcohol the Curse of Hand Workers. 2. Alcohol the Curse of Brain Workers. 3. Alcohol as a Medicine.

Question for Debate: Resolved: That alcoholism is a more terrible disease than tuberculosis.

Talk by a Physician: Temperance Hospitals, and What They Prove.

Talk by an Insurance Man: Special Rates for Total-Abstinence Men.

Exhibit and Discussion of Scientific Temperance Charts.

CHAPTER V

THE PUBLIC COST OF LIQUOR

AIM: *To estimate and realize the cost of the drink traffic and its burden on the nation.*

What is America's national drink bill? How has it been changing during the past twenty-five years?

Has the number who use liquor been increasing or decreasing in recent years? How do you explain this?

Into what four parts is the drink bill divided?

How much of the payment for liquor goes to the farmer? What would be the effect on his market if the traffic ceased?

What would be the effect on labor now employed by the traffic if the money spent for liquor should be spent for other manufactured articles?

Does the capital invested in liquor employ its due share of labor, or pay its due proportion in wages?

What factors make the profits to the liquor-dealer unusually large?

How large a share of the payment for liquor does the government get? Could the nation do without this revenue? Would this loss of revenue have any off-set?

What class of persons pays the liquor tax? On what class does it fall heaviest?

Is there a loss of efficiency from two or three glasses of beer per day?

What four great classes of loss are caused by drink?

What part does drink play in making criminals, dependents, and defectives?

Subjects for Essays: 1. Can We Afford to License Saloons? 2. What the Nation Spends for Liquor and for the Necessities of Life. 3. The Cost of Liquor-Produced Crime.

Question for Debate: Resolved: That poverty causes drink rather than drink causes poverty.

Talk by a Public Official (preferably one dealing with public finances): The Saloon a Losing Proposition.

CHAPTER VI

INDUSTRIAL WELFARE AND THE LIQUOR TRAFFIC

AIM: To gain an appreciation of the fact that the greatest economic burden caused by liquor is not the money lost at the saloon, but the reduction in the producing capacity of the nation.

Do breweries, distilleries, and saloons produce wealth, destroy wealth, or merely change the form of wealth?

Does liquor make a nation more capable of producing wealth?

Name five ways in which liquor affects the earning power of a people.

Why is the saloon able to compete successfully against the clothing-store and grocery for the drinker's last dollar?

Do non-drinkers suffer or prosper when others drink?

"If you let liquor alone it will let you alone"—is this possible in an economic sense?

What is the heaviest burden that drink lays upon the working man, in your estimation?

Why is the steady use of beer daily a heavier burden to the working-man than an occasional heavy debauch?

How does drink affect wages?

In the struggle between capital and labor which side gets most aid from the saloon? On which side does it claim to be? On which side IS it?

What is the attitude of organized labor toward the saloon? What is the attitude of the labor-unions in your town or city?

Which is more radical, "industrial prohibition" or "legal prohibition"?

Name some of the reasons why big industries are becoming more strict about employing drinking men.

What part does drink play in keeping the ranks of the more poorly paid kinds of labor over-crowded?

What should government do with a traffic which wastes wealth and capital and injures labor?

Subjects for Essays: 1. Why Every Worker Should Leave Liquor Alone. 2. How to Make Working Men Appreciate the

Consequences of Drink.   3. Work in Which Drinkers Are Especially Dangerous to the Public.

Question for Debate: Resolved: That public welfare requires that employers, as well as employees, should be total abstainers.

Talk by a Working Man (if possible, a labor-union man): Drink the Enemy of the Worker.

Talk by an Employer: Why I Will Not Employ a Drinking Man.

CHAPTER VII

RELATION OF ᵀIQUOR TO EDUCATION

AIM: To make clear the educational activity of the liquor traffic, its competition with the schools, and its influence on public schools.

What does Jack London mean when he says, ''I—and millions like me—was lured and drawn and driven to the poison shops''? (See pp. 151 and 154.)

In what ways is the saloon a competitor with the school?

How is school attendance affected by saloons in a town? Compare in this respect a ''wet'' town with a ''dry'' town that you know.

What happened in the high schools of Kansas City, Kan., when the saloons were driven out?

Which was affected most, the topers or the future supply of topers?

Do children of drinkers learn more rapidly, or less rapidly, than children of abstainers? Why? How about crime among the children of drinkers?

How does the saloon corrupt the ideals of freedom which immigrants have when they arrive in this country?

What is the ''personal liberty'' urged by saloon men? What is the real meaning of the cry?

Subjects for Essays: 1. What Saloons Teach. 2. Saloons Are the Foes of the Immigrants. 3. How Intemperance Curses Childhood.

Question for Debate: Resolved: That the saloon is the worst enemy of the public school.

Talk by a Teacher: The False Education Given by Saloons.

CHAPTER VIII

THE SOCIABILITY PHASE OF THE LIQUOR PROBLEM

AIM: To understand the appeal that alcohol makes to man's social nature.

Does a drink of liquor make a man more sociable? Does it make him enjoy the company of others? In what way?

How much liquor would be used if men always had to drink it alone?

How far is the saloon "a social center"? What classes of persons find their social life in it?

Is the saloon "the poor man's club"? What sort of social life does he get there?

In actual experience do coffee clubs, reading-rooms, and other "substitutes" compete successfully with the saloon if left to face it alone?

How far would the removal of treating and of social drinking settle the drink problem?

What kinds of counter attractions are needed as substitutes for the saloon?

What saloon attractions does substitution not reach?

Subjects for Essays: 1. The Custom of Treating and Its Results. 2. "The Poor Man's Club." 3. Is a Reformed Saloon Possible?

Question for Debate: Resolved: That it is the duty of the churches to furnish substitutes for the saloons.

Talk by a Business Man: Drinking as an Adjunct to Business.

Talk by a Social Worker: Attractions of the Saloon.

CHAPTER IX

THE ETHICAL PHASE

AIM: To study the effect of alcohol and the saloon on moral ideals and the church.

Is it right or wrong to drink? By what standard are we to judge?

Make two brief lists showing: (1) the chief pleasures furnished by alcohol and the saloon; (2) the chief miseries caused by them. How do they compare in number? In quality?

On what ground does the saloon come nearest to getting ethical support?

What is the temperance program of the Federal Council of Churches in America? the attitude of Protestant Churches? of the Catholic Church?

What about voting for candidates sympathetic to liquor?

Compare the saloon as competitor with the church in our cities: (1) as to number of young men that each gets; (2) as to the number of hours each is open.

What is the attitude of your local church? What is it doing?

How does liquor affect foreign-mission work?

Is it ethically right for the govern..ent to license the sale of liquor? If not, who and what are responsible for the policy and its consequences?

Subjects for Essays: 1. How the Saloon Affects Character. 2. Rum and Missionaries in the Same Ship. 3. Law and Conscience.

Question for Debate: Resolved: That it is sinful to legalize the saloon.

Talk by a Pastor: Why and How the Churches Should Fight the Saloon.

CHAPTER X

THE LIQUOR CONFLICT WITH SOCIAL INSTITUTIONS

AIM: To appreciate how seriously liquor complicates all our
social problems and delays all forms of social betterment.

Where does the first heavy burden of the drink bill fall?

What is its effect on the home? on food? on clothing?

How does this heartless saving on decent quarters affect standing, health, and ambition?

Which is the greatest sufferer, the individual, the family, or the community?

In what ways does the saloon conflict with home ideals? Does it encourage the drift away from home?

Is drinking among women on the increase?

Why should not women drink as well as men in these days of woman's growing independence and freedom?

In proposing reform which should be taken most into account, the drinker and his desires, or his family?

How does liquor make the rapid growth of large cities dangerous?

What is the effect of the saloon on efforts to provide better houses for the poor?

Do immigrants drink more or less after arriving here? What facts account for this?

How does the saloon serve as the "friend" of immigrants?

Is the foreigner responsible for the 300% increase in the consumption of liquor since 1860?

Why does liquor play so important a part in race conflicts?

Subjects for Essays: 1. How the Money Spent for Drink Should Be Used. 2. The Drunkard's Family. 3. The Saloon-Keeper an Enemy of Society.

Question for Debate: Resolved: That no social reform is so important as the abolition of the saloon.

Talk by Some Worker among the Poor: How Strong Drink Degrades.

CHAPTER XI

THE LIQUOR TRAFFIC IN POLITICS AND GOVERNMENT

AIM: To learn in what ways liquor gets its power in government and politics.

How is the liquor traffic different from other kinds of ''big business''?

Is political corruption a crime? Is it more or less dangerous to a community than theft or arson?

Why is the liquor traffic in politics?

What was the original purpose of the revenue system?

How does license mean permission? protection? partnership? punishment?

What is the constitutional position of the saloon?

Can the government in fairness heavily harass a traffic while accepting a large share of its profits?

How does the saloon control votes? Is political corruption a serious crime?

What is the effect of corruption in politics? What is its effect on public morals?

What do such interests as gambling, vice, the liquor traffic, etc., have in common that tends to unite them for political purposes?

In what way does liquor cause crime?

What kinds of crime come most naturally from drinking?

How large a part of all crime may be ascribed to the liquor traffic?

Subjects for Essays: 1. Crimes Caused by Drinking (a study of a week's newspapers). 2. What Is ''the Saloon Power''? 3. How to Win ''the Saloon Vote.''

Question for Debate: Resolved: That it is poor public policy to license saloons.

Talk by a Politician (preferably an office-holder): The Saloon in Politics.

Talk by a Police-Court Judge (or a lawyer): The Saloon and Crime.

CHAPTER XII

SOCIAL DEMANDS FOR COMPLETE ELIMINATION

AIM: To discover, in summing up, what forces demand the abolition of the saloon, what forces resist this prohibition, and along what lines the anti-liquor campaign may best be conducted.

Where does the big danger of the liquor problem lie, in its injury to individuals, or its consequences on society?

Compare the personal consequences of drink with its social results.

What is misleading in the argument that, if a man drinks too much and hurts himself it is nobody's business but his own?

Is it logical to conclude that the safety and welfare of society inevitably call for complete elimination of the saloon? Why?

Is it possible to settle the liquor problem without the hard hand of legal prohibition? Why not?

What sources of the liquor habit and traffic do government regulation and license reach? What do they fail to reach?

What sources of the liquor habit and traffic are affected by "substitutes for the saloon"? Which do they fail to reach?

What sources of the liquor habit and traffic do prohibition methods reach? Which do they not reach?

What must a well-rounded program of reform, seeking to reach all sources and forces, include?

Subjects for Essays: 1. The Call for Abstinence. 2. The Need of Better Provisions for Recreation. 3. The Argument for Legal Prohibition. 4. Next Steps in the Anti-liquor Program.

Question for Debate: Resolved: That legal prohibition of the liquor traffic, while fundamental in the temperance reform, is alone insufficient.

Closing Talk, Temperance Worker: What *you* can do.

www.ingramcontent.com/pod-product-compliance
Lightning Source LLC
LaVergne TN
LVHW011344080426
835511LV00005B/119